Here is wha

The ... alloons Devotionals

"I love Yellow Balloons. I have often searched for some consistent tidbit of God in my daily routine…when I found your daily devotional I decided to see what it was about. I was amazed to find so much food for thought. So many devotionals are feel good inspirations, while yours give me something to ponder and work on. In my little world there have been many let downs and broken promises. Yellow Balloons is really helping me discover a different perspective for viewing them and laying them to rest. I will be eternally grateful for each one's wisdom."

"Thank you for your daily Yellow Balloons devotionals, they have had such a positive impact in my life recently. My father unexpectedly passed away this past year…upon his passing, a friend recommended the Yellow Balloon devotionals. I am so thankful he did, as these devotionals have been such an amazing encouragement to me during this trying time. They have become a consistently uplifting part of my daily routine. I appreciate the words in these devotionals more than I can express, and I hope you know what an impact they have had on my life, as well as the lives of many others!"

"Thank you for the devotionals. they are very meaningful and often you give a new slant on a specific topic, generally accepted myth or life in general. Finding new, truthful perspectives is difficult, any devotional dealing with how to obtain a new point of view whether worldly or spiritual is always beneficial."

"The devotional that love wrote! What a difference the truth and light can make in a believer's life! Thank you for a year of fresh new insight and God's Holy Word!"

"These have encouraged me and I have passed them on to encourage others. Truly we are so blessed and perspective reminds us of that daily. Your words help reinforce our gratitude."

"It is with great pleasure and gratitude that I am writing this recommendation. I had just gone through the roughest two years I have ever encountered. It is through this period I discovered Yellow Balloons. These devotionals have transformed my life in a tremendous way. They have taught me how to see objectively and through the lens of the Scriptures. I chose to be transformed by the knowledge gained and thus made better choices and I am now reaping the good benefits of the actions. Praise be to God!"

"Thank you, Yellow Balloons, for the daily inspirations. I always look forward to reading them in my email as the words minister to me as a believer and follower of Christ."

YELLOW BALLOONS DEVOTIONALS

366 Days of Discovering a True Perspective

Yellow Balloons Devotionals: 366 Days of Discovering a True Perspective

Print ISBN: **978-0-578-97201-5**

First Edition: 2021

Yellow Balloons Devotionals / Tim Dunn

Book Cover Design: Annabel Hutchinson

Printed in the United States of America.

This book is dedicated as a memorial to Moriah, and is a testimony to how our lives can be blessed by choosing a true perspective.

AN INTRODUCTION TO THE DEVOTIONALS

In 2018, Tim Dunn wrote a book, **Yellow Balloons - Power for Living Life Above the Circumstances.** The book opened with the tragic event of losing their 20-month old granddaughter, but was primarily about the immense influence choosing a true perspective has on our wellbeing.

Stewarding well our time on earth hinges on viewing life as a once-in-an-existence opportunity. When we have this perspective, every circumstance brims with potential. Trusting God and being a faithful steward is the path that leads to ultimate fulfillment in life.

As our team considered how to promote Tim's new book, we came up with an idea to write a few devotionals based on the significant themes in the book - including Angels are Watching - What Heaven Can't Do, The 2-Minute Ride of Life, How to be a Faith Superhero, the three different terrains of life - Mountains, Plains, Valleys... just to name a few. We wrote thirty devotionals, marketed them as an entry ramp for the book, and were surprised by the enthusiastic response. This told us there was something more in our daily snippets than an advertising opportunity.

The devotionals themselves proved to be a powerful tool to help people discover a true perspective and successfully navigate the complexities of life. We are grateful to be able to partner with thousands of subscribers.

At the request of one of loyal subscribers, we have selected one year's worth from the best of the best of the Yellow Balloons devotions and put them into print. This is the fruit of that effort.

We are constantly humbled, inspired, and encouraged by the feedback we receive from our subscribers. As we considered how to pick the "best of the best", we looked to our subscriber feedback to answer the question: "What makes our devotionals worth the investment of your time?"

Without a doubt, the word we hear most often to describe our devotionals is "practical". We think there are a few reasons for this. First, choosing a true perspective is a daily activity. It is not a one-time choice. That makes each Yellow Balloons devotional directly applicable to each day. Additionally, our devotionals are concise. We try to say things as quick and direct as we can, while also being engaging. The devotionals hit on a number of themes, each a particular perspective that reminds us of the immense privilege we have to be children of God.

For the print version of our devotionals, we've decided to add a "Point to Ponder" at the end of each day. While the devotionals are brief, we hope their impact compounds. Our points to ponder help you consider what to do differently and/or how to continue to consider the implications for what was presented in that day's devotional.

Another thing we noticed about the description of "practical" is the devotionals appear to help readers overcome obstacles. It invites readers to grapple with how to properly view circumstances, which then lays a firm foundation for taking appropriate actions in those circumstances.

A unique feature of our devotionals is embedded in the structure. Although, most days are based on a verse autonomous from the prior day, we also splice in an occasional series. You will sometimes get 4-7 devotionals in a row focused on a character in the Bible (Abraham, Ruth, Noah, etc.), a Book of the Bible (Ecclesiastes), a chapter or passage (James 1, The Sermon on the Mount), or a specific verse (Romans 1:16-17). These occasional series give people a chance to marinate on a theme for a few days at a time before returning to the traditional structure. We have found this to be an engaging mix of newness and consistency and a feature we hope adds energy.

We pray these daily devotionals usher you toward experiencing the bounty of Kingdom of Heaven. We hope they are encouraging and help uncover opportunities otherwise neglected, forgotten, or unseen. Every day is a unique opportunity to worship God, love others, and pursue our best. It requires a proper perspective to recognize such opportunity. Thank you for allowing us to join you in the difficult journey of discovering truth, applying it in our lives, and worshipping the God who makes it all possible.

If you are interested in receiving the full quiver of our devotionals (over 500 and counting) delivered Mon - Fri to your inbox, go to **yellowballoons.net** to subscribe. There you can also learn more about Tim Dunn and the Yellow Balloons cache of material.

JANUARY 1: THE REFEREE

"For if you live according to the flesh you will die, but if by the Spirit you put to death the deeds of the body, you will live." – Romans 8:13

There is a war going on inside each of us. The flesh and the spirit. Mortal enemies in every sense of the word. Day after day, round after round, they wage battle, fighting for our very souls.

Popular culture sometimes depicts this as an angel on one shoulder and a devil on the other, each whispering in alternate ears.

It feels a lot like a boxing match. Each fighter is seasoned and prepared. Ready to attack and defend. A strategy established, adjustments on the ready. The fight goes back and forth - jostling, confusing, sometimes difficult to watch.

But there is a critical aspect of this epic conflict we often overlook. There is one other character in the ring.

The referee.

The referee decides the winner of each round. Discerns and enforces the rules. What is permissible and what isn't.

We are the referee in the battle between the flesh and the spirit. We have the spirit in us and we have the flesh in us. We cannot get rid of either. They are each a part of who we are. But the core of our identity is standing in the tension and choosing between the two. We referee the winner. We get to decide the victor.

One of the tactics of the flesh is to convince us there is no referee. That our true self is fully flesh and life is about deciding how much to give in to the demanding Spirit, who wants to spoil our fun.

Choosing a true perspective about ourselves is one of the most important choices we make. All of the flesh's victories are by forfeit. If we fight to know the truth and choose the truth, the spirit within us will win.

The choice about who we serve and how we live lies with the referee.

Ponder Today: What maneuvers of the flesh do I, as the referee, have a habit of permitting? What limitations do I put on the potential of the spirit within me?

JANUARY 2: THE ANGEL'S INTRIGUE

"It was revealed to them that they were not serving themselves but you, when they spoke of the things that have now been told you by those who have preached the gospel to you by the Holy Spirit sent from heaven. Even angels long to look into these things."
– 1 Peter 1:12

When we think about angels, we consider them superior beings. They dwell in the realm of the divine, carrying out direct orders from God and watching over us with care.

According to 1 Peter, the angels watch over us with great consideration. They are fascinated by the unique ability of humans. Enraptured by the part we have to play. The angels look on us with intrigue and, perhaps, a certain modicum of jealousy.

What is it that we have that would fascinate the angels?

Faith.

The ability to make our choices. The courage to believe in things unseen, to put our deepest trust in something we cannot fully understand. There is a profound beauty to the mystery of being human. Our unique place in the cosmos is a place of honor.

We love to focus on the weakness of our position. We take for granted the great opportunities in front of us. The unique wonder of humanity.

Faith is the intrigue of angels and humanity's unique opportunity. The mystery of meaning on this earth. The divine drama played out in each human life.

True perspective invites us to see from many angles. It helps us better understand our place in the divine drama. It ushers greater depths of self-awareness, ownership, and thankfulness.

Ponder Today: What will the angels whisper of you today?

JANUARY 3: THE RICHES OF THE KINGDOM

"I counsel you to buy from me gold refined in the fire, so you can become rich; and white clothes to wear, so you can cover your shameful nakedness; and salve to put on your eyes, so you can see." – Revelation 3:18

Humans are motivated by the pursuit of success. We are drawn to concepts like value and worth. In a broken and imperfect world, these pursuits most often manifest in superficial ways. Money. Fame. Yet, we are unsatisfied by the wealth the world has to offer. Unfulfilled by the desires of the flesh.

Our longing remains.

The Lord invites us to purchase from Him all the riches we want. God is not talking about money and possessions for self-serving purposes. He is talking about peace and wisdom so that we might worship Him through stewarding this precious life.

We are searching for the truest of treasures, the heart of meaningful success. Material wealth is only a means to an end. Instinctively, we know there is a greater end than material. We hope money will help serve as a means to that end. But we often get stuck in the means and forget the end altogether.

Through wealth or poverty, the true riches lie in how we steward the life given to us. How we see the world around us. How we treat one another. How we view ourselves. If we ask God, He will grant us all the richness of His Kingdom. He will give us the opportunity to see the world from His perspective, which will transform the way we see all other things.

There is no greater treasure than wisdom. There is no fortune worth more than a true perspective. If we ask, He is there, ready to endow upon us the wealth of the Heavens, the transformational riches of true perspective.

Ponder Today: What is it you truly want out of life?

JANUARY 4: AN ACQUIRED TASTE

"To the Jews who had believed him, Jesus said, 'If you hold to my teaching, you are truly my disciples. Then you will know the truth, and the truth will set you free.'"– John 8:31-32

We like the idea of truth when it benefits us, when it makes us feel good. But sometimes truth is difficult to accept or comprehend. Sometimes it hurts. And when it hurts, we push against it. We avoid or deny or try to explain it away.

Truth is an acquired taste.

It is much easier to deceive ourselves, to dodge the sometimes convicting truths of self-awareness, than to face it with courage and humility. We tend to defend, deflect, and rationalize.

A choice to permit deception is a shackle on our souls. False perspective entraps us. Perpetuating deception eliminates choices. But we have the key to unlock these chains.

Adopting a true perspective centers on a willingness to pursue the truth. To ask ourselves, "what is true?" rather than "what do I want to be true?"

John tells us that truth is fully available through adherence to the teachings of Jesus. The truth sets us free. It unlocks the chains of inaccuracy and falsity. Freedom may not feel like we imagined – it comes with the companionship of responsibility – but it is freedom nonetheless. Beautiful, complicated freedom.

It takes courage and boldness to pursue the truth. And although pursuing truth is difficult, in the end, there is nothing sweeter. Nothing more nourishing or necessary. Nothing more challenging and nothing more freeing.

Ponder Today: When do you have a difficult time accepting truth?

JANUARY 5: THE AIR UP THERE

"Then a cloud appeared and covered them, and a voice came from the cloud: 'This is my Son, whom I love. Listen to him!'" – Mark 9:7

When Jesus brought Peter and John to the mountain of Transfiguration, Peter had the great idea of setting up tents. "Let's stay here a while!" he says. But the voice of God swoops in and beckons Peter to listen and learn.

The mountaintop is valuable for resetting our perspective to what is true and important. For learning. It is not where we are meant to spend our days.

When climbers summit Mount Everest, they are in what is called "The Death Zone". There is not much time to enjoy the view. If you don't start the descent soon, you will die. As beautiful as the view may be, the air up there is just too thin to survive.

A trap of mountaintop experiences is trying to replace the mundane of the plains and the sorrow of the valley with the ecstasy of the extraordinary. This is not a sustainable approach.

Our mountaintops are made for joy. They are made to inspire. Mountaintop experiences prepare us for life on the plains. Shortly after being told "Be quiet and listen", the disciples followed Jesus back down. Rather than building huts on the summit, they rejoined the other disciples and went to work, healing a mute boy.

Peter never forgot the experience. He came down the mountain and then did what we ought to do. He took the inspiration and used it to fuel a substantial and meaningful life.

Ponder Today: When we have a mountaintop experience, we can either use it as a catalyst for our journey or undermine our journey by making the mountain an idol we must return to in order for things to be ok.

JANUARY 6: GOD'S SUCCESS

"But he said to me, 'My grace is sufficient for you, for my power is made perfect in weakness'. Therefore, I will boast all the more gladly about my weaknesses, so that Christ's power may rest on me. That is why, for Christ's sake, I delight in weaknesses, in insults, in hardships, in persecutions, in difficulties. For when I am weak, then I am strong." – 2 Corinthians 12:9-10

The Apostle Paul endured a difficult circumstance. He doesn't tell us the precise problem. He only calls it a "thorn in the flesh."

We all know what it is like to have a thorn that festers. It infects. It aches. It impedes movement.

This problem was a real source of pain and struggle for Paul. So he asked God to remove it. God had worked many miracles through Paul. He knew God could heal him. But God said "no." Paul asked again. Again the answer was "no." Then a third time. But this time, along with the "no" came a message. "My grace is sufficient for you."

Sometimes our greater opportunity is to endure the pain in order to experience grace. And in this case, the grace, or favor, of God was to demonstrate His power through Paul's weakness. Once Paul adopted this perspective, he began to view his thorn as a blessing.

Paul concluded that God had given him this limitation in order to keep him from getting puffed up from all the amazing revelations God had shown him.

Trusting God is a challenge, especially when our circumstances are not what we want them to be. We have a problem and we want to fix the problem. No one likes pain. And it is fine to ask God for help. God did not chastise Paul for asking. But sometimes God has a different definition of success than our comfort. Sometimes God wants to demonstrate something great through our weakness.

God is the God of all. He is the Lord. He is the powerful and capable one; wisdom and truth itself. And when we walk in dependence on Him, even our weaknesses and difficulties are valuable.

Ponder Today: How might your weaknesses be an opportunity to promote God's strength?

JANUARY 7: THE VENDOR

"Delight yourself in the LORD, and he will give you the desires of your heart." – Psalm 37:4

Too often, we treat our relationship with God as if we were ordering something from Amazon. We think we can peruse the options and click on the things that look most appealing to us. I'll take an order of peace - immediate delivery; a couple bags of success; and a consistent supply of getting-things-my-way.

We learned when we were children that God was around and could help us in our need. We don't need Him all the time, but we check in when there is some discomfort, make our request, and tap our feet impatiently as we wait for the prize to come.

We misinterpret verses like this one to mean that God is our Cosmic Vending Machine. There at our beck and call to fulfill our every superficial wish.

The Lord, however, wants more for us. Not less. More. He wants us to feast. He wants us to eat what will truly fulfill us. He wants to give us meaning and purpose, belonging and love.

God wants to give us what we really want. Not the safe and superficial substitutions we imagine. The real thing. Love. Joy. Purpose. He is not interested in the shadowed version of our longings, the perversions we've mistaken for our desires. He is interested in what we truly want, what is truly best for us.

Ponder Today: If God has not given us something, it is either because we do not need it or He has already given it to us in another way?

This following is a 7-day series on the life of Abraham:

JANUARY 8: DAY 1 - PARTIAL OBEDIENCE

"The Lord had said to Abram, 'Go from your country, your people and your father's household to the land I will show you'... So Abram went, as the Lord had told him; and Lot went with him." – Genesis 12:1, 4

We know from Stephen's recap of Israel's history in Acts 7 that God appeared to Abram (whose name was later changed to Abraham) in his hometown of Ur. God told Abram to leave his family and country behind, and relocate to the Promised Land.

And Abram obeys...kind of. He leaves his home in Ur, but does not leave his family. He takes his father with him along with his nephew Lot. But they didn't make it to the land God had in mind. They got about halfway there, then stalled out in Haran.

God didn't blast Abram for not obeying fully. In Haran, God called him to leave his home and his father's household once again. This time, he leaves his father behind. He is closer to full obedience. Abram is not in full obedience of God's command until he and Lot part ways in the Promised Land.

Abram's journey is a lot like ours. We are often in partial obedience. But Abraham's story is incredibly encouraging. Throughout the progression from partial to complete obedience, Abram is blessed by God. He ends up being called God's friend. God nurtures, nudges and encourages Abram. When Abram shows partial obedience, God seems to say "this is a good step, here is one further".

We are like Abram in Haran. We've obeyed partially, God remains steadfast in his calling, and we have the opportunity before us to move forward. In fact, the word "Haran" in Hebrew means "crossroads". Like Abram, God has promised us great blessings for obedience, but we have to first leave places of comfort in order to experience those blessings.

We are always at a fork in the road with our relationship to God, needing to decide - do we trust God with our next step, or is this the step where we say "I know best on this one?" We are Abram at Haran, God's disciple standing at a crossroad with a decision to make.

Ponder Today: In what areas of life are you walking in partial obedience?

JANUARY 9: DAY 2 - MELCHIZEDEK: THE FIRST TITHE

"After Abram returned from defeating Kedorlaomer and the kings allied with him, the king of Sodom came out to meet him in the Valley of Shaveh (that is, the King's Valley). Then Melchizedek king of Salem brought out bread and wine. He was priest of God Most High, and he blessed Abram, saying, 'Blessed be Abram by God Most High, Creator of heaven and earth. And praise be to God Most High, who delivered your enemies into your hand.' Then Abram gave him a tenth of everything. The king of Sodom said to Abram, "Give me the people and keep the goods for yourself."
– Genesis 14:17-21

When Abram and Lot enter the land God promised, their prosperity becomes so great the two cannot practically live in the same area. Lot decides to settle in an area near the city of Sodom. Soon after, Sodom is invaded and Lot is taken into captivity.

Abram mobilizes his servants and rescues Lot, along with the loot the raiders had carried away from Sodom and its four allied cities.

On his way back, as a prosperous and conquering hero, Abram is greeted by two leaders.

The first is one of the most mysterious characters of Scripture: Melchizedek. He is a king as well as a priest. He greets the conquering Abram with a gift of bread and wine. Melchizedek reigns over the city of Salem (which means "peace"), later known as Jerusalem. Melchizedek paints a picture of Jesus Christ, the coming prince of peace and true high priest, who gave humanity a gift of his body as bread and his blood as wine.

Abram gives to this priest of God a tenth of everything he recovered from the raid. Hebrews tells us this was a tithe, the earliest mention in Scripture.

The king of Sodom has a different approach. He starts to bargain to regain the people. Abram answers by declaring that he doesn't plan to keep a single thing for himself because he does not want Sodom to be able to have any claim on him. His integrity and freedom are of much greater importance.

We are often faced with the same choice. Will we use our wealth, opportunities, relationships, and commitments in a way that pleases the Lord? Or will we bow to the empty idol of "More"? Will we "tithe" to God, or cling to our possessions? Will we pay homage to Melchizedek or Sodom?

Ponder Today: If where you send your possessions reveals your allegiance, where does your loyalty lie?

JANUARY 10: DAY 3 - ACCEPTANCE: A ONE-WAY COVENANT

"Abram believed the Lord, and he credited it to him as righteousness. He also said to him, 'I am the Lord, who brought you out of Ur of the Chaldeans to give you this land to take possession of it.' Abram said, 'Sovereign Lord, how can I know that I will gain possession of it?'" – Genesis 15:6-8

Abram trusts God, but doesn't understand how all of this is going to work. He asks God how he can know God will deliver on such an amazing promise. God does not chastise Abram for asking this question. He grants Abram's request by giving him a contract, a covenant that guarantees the outcome. What happens next is an incredible scene.

In the tradition of the time, they exchange a "blood covenant". Animals are slain then sliced in two and set on opposing sides of a path, making an alleyway. Tradition dictated that the two covenant participants walk through the path, between the dead animal halves, representing each person's agreement to the terms. The carcasses flanking them on either side testified to the penalty for breaking the oath: death.

God institutes a blood covenant with Abram, but with a twist. After the carcass-strewn alleyway is prepared, God appears in the form of a torch, and passes through the path of promise - alone.

God's message here is clear: this is all on me! This is not a conditional promise. I am making a covenant granting you this land, requiring nothing further from you.

God's acceptance is just like this. It is hard for us to receive, but sometimes God's promises are unconditional. God accepts us as His child without further condition. It is a matter of grace. His relationship to us as father does not alter based on how we behave. He grants this to us unconditionally, through a blood covenant - the blood of Jesus.

Although the land has been granted unconditionally, their possession and enjoyment of the land is yet in the future. It will require further obedience. It remains to conquer and live faithfully in the land to enjoy the blessing of it. But it is always theirs. This covenant is not a promise of ease. It is a promise of ownership, heredity as God's children.

We can earn approval, but we cannot earn his acceptance - that is freely given. God promised it. He passed through the alley of death on a cross to declare it for us. A one-way covenant granting us a place in His family - forever.

Ponder Today: Why do we find it so hard to receive unearned gifts from others.

JANUARY 11: DAY 4 - TRYING

"So after Abram had been living in Canaan ten years, Sarai his wife took her Egyptian slave Hagar and gave her to her husband to be his wife. He slept with Hagar, and she conceived."
– Genesis 16: 3-4

Up to this point, the Lord has told Abram he will conceive a son, but many years have passed without a child being born. So Abram and his wife Sarai do a very human thing. Since Sarai is old and beyond child-bearing years, they find a way for Abram to conceive a son, consistent with the custom of the day. Sarai offers her Egyptian maid Hagar to be a birth mother. To this point God had only promised that Abram would father a child, not that he would father a child from Sarai. So this fulfills the prophecy/promise of God.

The Bible does not criticize them for taking this action. He blesses Hagar as well as her son Ishmael. But God has something much better in mind. God later reveals that the child of promise will not be Hagar's son, but will come from Sarai.

God gave humans the ability to choose. That is the way we are most like Him. And He encourages us to take action. But sometimes our actions are far inferior to what God has in mind.

Once Sarai had passed child-bearing age, it wasn't unreasonable for them to follow the custom of the day to allow Abram a means to father a son. It might be something like us adopting. But God gives them something much greater. Something beyond human comprehension. A miracle child will be the heir to the promise.

All along the way God is leading, teaching, empowering Abram to make choices, while holding the future completely in his hands. This is another kind of miracle. The miracle of a sovereign and loving God that encourages us to choose, then blesses us beyond what we can imagine just for trying.

Abraham's story should be an incredible encouragement for us. He was an ordinary man who made choices we might not approve of, given hindsight. But Abram wasn't reading a story. He was living a story. And it seems God blessed him just for trying.

As we try to steward our actions and decisions, we can lean on the character of a loving God who desires us to grow and learn, and redeems our choices.

Ponder Today: The key to success is the courage to try.

JANUARY 12: DAY 5 - TWO-WAY COVENANT

"Now when Abram was ninety-nine years old, the Lord appeared to Abram and said to him, "I am God Almighty; Walk before Me, and be blameless. "I will establish My covenant between Me and you, And I will multiply you exceedingly." – Genesis 17:1-2

God makes multiple covenants with Abram. We can think of it as one covenant with multiple parts. Like different articles of the Constitution.

Abram had already been declared righteous in God's sight solely by faith. That statement had no remaining conditions.

This provision in chapter 17 is different. It is mutual. God has a role and Abram has a role. What God does will depend on what Abram does. Abram's part is to live faithfully, righteously. "Blameless." If Abram does this, then God's part is to reward Abram with additional blessings, to multiply him "exceedingly".

God had already promised unconditionally to make Abram's descendants as the stars of heaven. So "multiply exceedingly" must extend beyond mere numbers. And of course it did. God will later grant that Jesus, the deliverer of Israel and eternal king of the earth comes from the seed of Abram. And the Bible declares that Abram is the father of all who believe.

From these various provisions we learn that God's acceptance is unconditionally given. And when He grants a reward or gives a gift, it is irrevocable. We can possess these gifts and still have amazing future rewards connected with our current choices. Rewards continue to accumulate if we continue to walk in obedience.

God calls us to be people who walk in faith now to sow seeds that bless future generations. Like Abram. We can take from Abram that when we exert effort to walk in faith, God blesses it beyond what we can imagine. However, no matter how well we might do, or how many rewards we might accumulate along the way, there is always more to strive for. Some of Abram's greatest tests still lie ahead.

Ponder Today: Few things usher peace into our soul more than understanding the difference between God's acceptance and His approval.

JANUARY 13: DAY 6 - WHAT'S IN A NAME?

"Abram fell facedown, and God said to him, 'As for me, this is my covenant with you: You will be the father of many nations. No longer will you be called Abram; your name will be Abraham, for I have made you a father of many nations." – Genesis 17:3-5

The name Abram means "exalted father" and the name Abraham means "father of nations". At this point, Abram is ninety nine, and has only been a father for thirteen of his ninety nine years. Ironically, he lived childless for eighty six years with the name "exalted father". Now, with a mere one son, God changes his name to "father of nations."

By giving Abram this new name, God is reminding Abraham who he is. Not because it is apparent to observers. But because of God's promise. It might be laughable to onlookers to think of an old man with one son as a father of nations. But based on God's promise, it is a reality.

This establishes an important connection between faith and speech. Speaking what is true helps us believe and live what is true. God is giving Abraham a way to remember His promise repeatedly, daily: every time he hears his own name.

When we believe, we are given a new identity in Christ. We are new creations, with new desires and new gifts. But our old man is still there and doesn't want to be supplanted. Let's speak this new reality: we are receptacles of the Holy Spirit. We are children of the Royal King. We are filled with the resurrected power of Jesus. This is what is true. Let's speak it. It is our new identity, our new name.

Our old nature is still a reality, but it is no longer our master, unless we choose it to be. Speaking what is true helps us shift our perspective of ourselves from what we were (the old man) to what we are (a new creation).

Let's speak our new name, our new identity, and live our new nature. In doing so we will be walking in the footsteps of Abraham.

Ponder Today: Speak often what is unseen but true. Name God's promises, and speak them as often as you speak your name.

JANUARY 14: DAY 7 - WE WILL RETURN

"Abraham said to his young men, "Stay here with the donkey, and I and the lad will go over there; and we will worship and return to you." – Genesis 22: 11-13

This last great story of Abraham appears to mirror the first. When Abraham's story begins, the Lord appears to Abram and commands him to leave his relatives behind and go to the land he will show him. A bit bizarre, to leave home not knowing where you are going. But God asked Abraham to trust, and he did. Here God commands Abraham to leave his home and travel to Mount Moriah to do something even crazier - to sacrifice his son. Again, God asks Abraham to trust.

The Book of Hebrews tells us that since God had promised Isaac would be the child from whom he would become a great nation, Abraham reasoned that God would resurrect Isaac after he was sacrificed. This is confirmed by this verse. When he left the servant to go sacrifice Isaac, Abraham stated with confidence that "we" will return. And they did. Not because of resurrection, but because God provided a ram as a substitute sacrifice.

This last great story is brimming with perspective for us to embrace. No doubt Abraham was grateful and thankful when the ram was substituted. Jesus is our sacrificial lamb, who died in our place. A perspective of profound gratitude is an appropriate foundation for every day.

Abraham's willingness to trust God's resurrection power led to his life's greatest testimony. As believers after Pentecost, we have been filled with God's resurrection power. By walking in that power, we can walk in Abraham's shoes, and display God's power to those around us.

In each instance this requires an initial step to leave a place of comfort, and journey to a place to which God calls us. Like Abraham, our next opportunity to trust is not far away. But also like Abraham, God has given us promises upon which to found our trust.

Ponder Today: Trusting God is not always easy and comfortable. Truth is an acquired taste.

This concludes our 7-day series on the life of Abraham.

JANUARY 15: NAVIGATING TRAGEDY

"Waters flowed over my head; I said, 'I am cut off!' I called on Your name, O Lord, Out of the lowest pit. You have heard my voice, 'Do not hide Your ear from my prayer for relief, From my cry for help'. You drew near when I called on You; You said, 'Do not fear!'" – Lamentations 3:54-57

Tragedy comes upon us like an unsuspected tide. We are walking along the beach, relatively content, feeling safe and in control. And without warning, we find ourselves under water. Drowning.

Tragedies hurt. The pain they inflict needs to be addressed. At some point in our lives, the wave of sorrow will cause us to tumble. But the Lord is available in the pit. He is there to hear us, to comfort us, to cast off our fear.

When tragedy strikes, we face vital choices. We must choose a perspective. Will we make excuses, cast blame, or hold grudges? Will we curse God? Or will we see him as a source of comfort?

We must also choose a response. Although we cannot sidestep or ignore sorrow, we can decide to whom we will call when our circumstances seem too hard to bear. We can decide whether to share our grief or hold it to ourselves.

To avoid is to ignore our grief. Dusting ourselves off and trying to go on as if nothing happened is not the proper response. God is near. We can call out to Him. The Lord hears us in tragedy. He sees our anguish and turns his ear to our cries.

Ponder Today: God's comfort does not eliminate pain, it rests within it.

JANUARY 16: SOUVENIRS

"Then Gideon built an altar there to the Lord and named it 'The Lord is Peace'. To this day it is still in Ophrah of the Abiezrites." – Judges 6:24

The journey of life is a two-minute ride, over more quickly than we anticipate. One syllable in the cosmic story. We are called to make the most of the journey. To steward and enjoy the brief existence we have been given.

When we ride a roller coaster, there is usually a spot where a camera flashes and takes our picture, screaming with hands raised and hair disheveled. People buy the picture to remember the moment. In Scripture, there are many monuments or ceremonies intended to create memories. Gideon built an altar to mark the significance of an important moment. We celebrate Christmas to commemorate and remember God's great gift to humanity.

But there is also a sense in which every choice we make in our lives is a souvenir moment, an altar to the Lord. Every choice we make is a snapshot along the journey. An opportunity to act on belief. A checkpoint of choosing.

Today is a small blip on a short journey. But it carries significant opportunity - the potential to jolt eternity. The brief chance to live a life of faith is much more than a souvenir that will end up in the trash. Opportunities to decide (rooted in faith) will make up the portion of our lives that last. Our decisions have eternal significance.

Ponder Today: Today, you are constructing an altar for the Lord. What will it contain?

JANUARY 17: IF I HAD IT ALL

"His divine power has given us everything we need for a godly life through our knowledge of him who called us by his own glory and goodness." – 2 Peter 1:3

It is all too easy to believe the subtle lies of the flesh. Chasing its empty promises is like chasing a desert mirage. Usually the empty promise is wrapped in the cloak of "If I had more, then I would be happy." The "More Monster" has claimed many victims. More money, more prestige, more of most anything.

We spend time thinking about what we would do with a million dollars (or if we have a million, ten million). How would we steward our fame or political position (or if we have a political position, a more powerful one)? We imagine what we don't have and what we might do if we had it.

Our imaginations get the better of us. We drift into thinking about what we could do with what we don't have, and forego thinking about what to do with what we do have.

All the while, we are living life on the plains. We miss the amazing opportunities to enjoy what we do have because we are imagining the kind of character we might have if we struck it big, if we had more.

More is never the complete answer. More will never usher in the life we deeply desire.

We can adjust our perspective to consider with gratitude what we do have. We can focus on exercising the best stewardship of what we currently possess. And we can enjoy all the goodness God has given us, for God has richly given us all things to enjoy.

Ponder Today: You are not lacking anything you need to live a godly life today.

JANUARY 18: THE POWER TO SERVE

"For you were called to freedom, brothers. Only do not use your freedom as an opportunity for the flesh, but through love serve one another." – Galatians 5:13

Each of us has been granted a unique set of passions and abilities. We can feel it in the recesses of our soul. And we can also sense we are meant to use these gifts for something important. We have a longing for greatness. A capacity to do good. Like the superheroes in the movies, we have talent that's eager and ready for action.

The temptation is to use this power for selfish gain. As Uncle Ben tells Spiderman, "With great power comes great responsibility". The only difference between a superhero and a super villain is in where they direct their powers; to promote self or to serve others.

Throughout the Bible, we see the call on humanity to serve one another. Jesus washes the feet of the disciples. Paul talks about the church as the Body of Christ, imploring us to bear one another's burdens. The message is clear. Our gifts are meant to help others.

The villains in the movies are the ones who use their powers of intellect, skill, and money to build devices and schemes that serve their own lust for power. They attempt to use their abilities to control others. To make others serve them.

Heroes, on the other hand, see that their power is a responsibility. It is an equipping toward serving others, meant for the edification of the community as a whole.

Our unique passion and ability are vehicles of tremendous power. God has granted us the awesome responsibility to choose how to use them.

Ponder Today: Since serving others is the best use of our power, it is not only best for others but is the best way to utilize our abilities for our own best self-interest.

JANUARY 19: MAKING ME ANGRY

"Therefore each of you must put off falsehood and speak truthfully to your neighbor, for we are all members of one body. "In your anger do not sin": Do not let the sun go down while you are still angry, and do not give the devil a foothold." – Ephesians 4:25-27

"He's making me so angry!"

"She made me so mad yesterday."

We've all used this kind of language. These statements signal we have adopted a victim mentality. We shifted the responsibility for our happiness onto others. We have ceded control of our happiness to others. Now, we cannot be okay until something external changes.

In truth, no one can make us angry. People and circumstances do things that trigger a reaction in us. But the choice of how to respond belongs to each of us on our own.

The circumstance does not make us angry. It does not have that control. The circumstance simply provides a prompt. The resulting anger or frustration is a signal that a choice needs to be made. But emotions have no business making choices. Choosing is something we should do based on our purpose and values.

The emotion is an alarm, letting us know our values have been pressed and a choice needs to be made. It's not the person or the circumstance that actually makes us angry. It is the internal value(s) within us that feel threatened. It is a result of what matters to us, what we've experienced, and the purpose we are living toward.

We need a true perspective about our anger. We need to acknowledge our feelings. Then we can make choices based on values rather than emotions. Time is of the essence. It's in our prompt and purposeful action that we can avoid our anger leading to sin.

Ponder Today: What is the difference between an emotional trigger and taking responsibility for our own emotions?

JANUARY 20: AT THE TABLE

"Here I am! I stand at the door and knock. If anyone hears my voice and opens the door, I will come in and eat with that person, and they with me." – Revelation 3:20

The greatest treasure Jesus offers is relationship. The opportunity to mingle with the Creator of the Universe. It begins with hearing his voice and opening the door. For He is always inviting. And His invitation is to share bread together.

When we sit and break bread together, we share in the necessity of life. Hunger reminds us of our dependency on food to survive. Sharing a meal reminds us that we need one another. Intimacy develops around the table. There is something about sharing a meal that leads to personal connection. Fellowship and sharing of lives is inevitable around the dinner table.

This is the true nature of riches in the Kingdom of God. A seat at his table. Listening to His voice. Absorbing His wisdom. Altering our perspective to live in His ways.

Jesus offers us the most valuable thing conceivable. A relationship with God. To sit and share stories. To laugh and cry and be with one another. To hear and receive wisdom and insights - insights that turn into treasure.

There is no greater treasure than Jesus at the table. To glean his perspective. All we need to do is hear his voice. He is calling. He desires to give us the riches of the Kingdom. It begins with opening the door and letting him pass the potatoes.

Ponder Today: Why do we tend to bond over shared meals and time at a shared table?

JANUARY 21: THE ONLY WAY TO HEAL FASTER

"Not only so, but we also glory in our sufferings, because we know that suffering produces perseverance; perseverance, character; and character, hope. And hope does not put us to shame, because God's love has been poured out into our hearts through the Holy Spirit, who has been given to us." – Romans 5:3-5

Pain hurts. It is unpleasant. A digging kind of sorrow. A nagging sort of torture.

As such, we avoid pain at all costs. It is a classic human instinct. We see pain coming and we fight or run. We hide from pain.

When pain inevitably catches up with us and finds its way into our story, we do our best to quiet it. We rub dirt over it, sweep it under the rug, pretend it isn't there. We lie to our friends, our spouses, even our own self. Our instinct tells us to ignore it until it goes away. Our society tells us to get over it quickly, that we aren't okay if we don't feel okay (or pretend to).

But it doesn't quite work, does it? Sorrow is like an alarm clock. It won't go off until you acknowledge it. We cannot explain away our sorrow. Nor can we outrun it. So many of us are acting in unhealthy ways because of years and years, layer upon layer, of unaddressed pain.

As counterintuitive as it sounds, the quickest way to heal is to press into the hurt. Not to make an idol out of it or drive yourself over the cliff, but to name it and address it. Share the truth of your hurt with those who love you most. It will hurt more upfront, but the back-end is a quicker path to healing.

Although pain hurts, sorrow is an opportunity, a path to growth, intimacy, and perseverance. As such, the best way to get over pain is to find the lesson, to feel your way through it honestly. We cannot side-step our hurt by ignoring it. The only way around is through. And in the end, a messy acknowledgment is the quickest route to healing.

Ponder Today: What pain are you trying to avoid?

JANUARY 22: MAKING WEALTH

"In the wilderness He fed you manna which your fathers did not know, that He might humble you and that He might test you, to do good for you in the end. Otherwise, you may say in your heart, 'My power and the strength of my hand made me this wealth.' But you shall remember the Lord your God, for it is He who is giving you power to make wealth, that He may confirm His covenant which He swore to your fathers, as it is this day." – Deuteronomy 8:16-18

When we ask for improved circumstances or material prosperity, we tend to think we are asking to be placed on a finish line. But like Israel when they departed Egypt, the reality is we are asking to be tested. To see if we will humble ourselves and be excellent stewards.

The Biblical perspective about material wealth is that it is a tool, a resource, an opportunity to serve. It is God entrusting us with a responsibility. Money is power to accomplish. God wants us to use that power to act as stewards, and accomplish His will. When we acquire material wealth, it is an opportunity to serve. We are often confused because we do not know what we are asking for.

The world tells us money is desirable to fuel an endless chase to indulge our appetites. We can purchase status to gain the approval of man. Our significance. The irony is that when we adopt the world's perspective and say "I did this", it leads to enslavement. Money becomes our master. Proving and validating ourselves becomes a black hole, one that no amount of money can fill. Which steals away our ability to enjoy and use our money, causing us to hoard or waste it. The prodigal wanted to chase his appetites - his inherited money gave him the power to enslave himself to those appetites.

If, instead, we remember it is the Lord who gave us the power to make wealth and honor Him with our use of money, it actually allows us to enjoy our finances and use it to serve others.

God offers us unlimited spiritual wealth by giving us a path to acquire His wisdom. Only through spiritual wealth can we properly hope to steward physical wealth. We gain this through listening to Him. Through the experience of walking by faith.

Ponder Today: The only way to be content with physical wealth is to perceive it as a tool for something greater than yourself.

JANUARY 23: ADVERSITY

"But he said to her, 'You speak as one of the foolish women speak. Shall we indeed accept good from God and not accept adversity?' In all this Job did not sin with his lips." – Job 2:10

Life is full of adversity. We lose loved ones, get fired from jobs, suffer miscarriages, and experience rejection. The story of Job is famous in part because of the extremity of the main character's adversity. It is this very thing that makes Job so relatable. And it is Job's response that makes the story inspirational.

Adversities are a constant ingredient of life. We would prefer to have only easy situations, perfect settings, and good circumstances. But the fall of man has made it so that this existence, in some way or another, is going to be like Job's.

There are times when it feels like we are brimming with adversity. When we "can't find a win". Life is tough. Being human is not for the faint of heart.

Just as we relate to Job's situation, we have an opportunity to replicate his response.

Job "accepts" adversity as an opportunity to trust God. He did not go looking for adversity. But he acknowledges the reality of it and the choice he has in its midst. And he chose to live righteously.

Nothing about adversity is easy. We cannot completely avoid it. We cannot control it. What we can do is follow the example of Job and not let adversity define us. Not allow it to lead us into sin. We can see it as an opportunity for worship. A chance to trust. An invitation to be an example. A catalyst to know God by faith.

Ponder Today: How might your current adversity be inviting you into worship?

JANUARY 24: LORD, SHOW ME MY CHOICES

"Rise up; this matter is in your hands. We will support you, so take courage and do it." – Ezra 10:4

Even in the most frightening of circumstances, there are still choices available to us. How will I respond to this tragedy? What will I say? What will I do? Circumstances limit our choices but nothing can completely eliminate them.

Perhaps we should start praying that God would show us our choices. Pray He would empower our ability to see Him, to choose a perspective in alignment with His, and own the journey he has entrusted us with.

It is tempting to run from our choices. To feel as though the circumstances are so stacked against us that we no longer have any choices.

God calls us to participate in His Kingdom. Seeing the world, our circumstances, our daily tasks, and our relationships by the light of His Son is an option available to us daily.

We are looking for shortcuts, easy answers, for someone to just do the thing for us. Secretly, we like the idea of having no choices; it lets us off the hook.

Our choices are powerful and they matter in the Kingdom of God. The Lord will bless you with circumstances and manifestations of His Goodness. He will also bless you with choices.

Every day, we are faced with a myriad of decisions. In the midst of triumph and pain and apathy, there are choices to be made. Choices about perspective. Choices about our thoughts and actions.

Ponder Today: Praying for God to intervene in our circumstances is one way to pray. Another is praying God reveals the power and opportunity of the choices we make in response to whatever circumstance we face.

JANUARY 25: A CONSISTENT PERSON

"Therefore, my beloved brothers, be steadfast, immovable, always abounding in the work of the Lord, knowing that in the Lord your labor is not in vain." – 1 Corinthians 15:58

There are few things in life more difficult than consistency. It might be the most sought-after aspect of human identity, the secret key to being oneself. "How do I be who I truly am?" Everywhere. Always.

In an effort to find who we are, we adopt the suggestion of our surroundings. And when our surroundings change, so do we - navigating a sea of influences, reacting to a maze of experiences, and exploring a confusing atmosphere of people and relationships. Consistency is difficult and elusive. We can be blown back and forth by the wind.

Life will throw an array of circumstances our way. Some will be the mountaintop, some the valley, and most the plains. How do we find that part of us that is truly and deeply us? How do we tether our identity into the ground so that our values and our longings determine our identity rather than our circumstances?

The simple answer is that we decide to. In pursuing truth, we bind ourselves to an accurate perspective. A perspective that allows us to see every circumstance for what it is worth, feel every emotion involved, and own the choices we make in response. Perspective is the key to consistency. And truth is the key to perspective.

Ponder Today: If we cannot name our values, we cannot remain consistent in our choices.

JANUARY 26: THE PRESTIGE

"Should you then seek great things for yourself? Do not seek them. For I will bring disaster on all people, declares the Lord, but wherever you go I will let you escape with your life" – Jeremiah 45:5

The Latin word of prestige means "to create an illusion". In other words, to trick someone.

As we endeavor to have people think more highly of us, we create illusions that don't line up with who we actually are.

When we seek "great things" for ourselves, we are trying to create an illusion. We want people to see our stuff. We are hoping for a misdirection. We want others to look at what we have carefully constructed to distract them from the truths we are afraid of within ourselves.

The calculated care and wisdom of the Lord doesn't want us to stand propped up on lies. For our best good, he wants to expose the illusion of superficial prestige so that our full calling might be awakened and enacted.

The "great things" we pursue are often idols. They are prestige. We are trying to climb a mountain to show how high we can go. Old as the Tower of Babel (old as the Fall) is humanity's desire to make themselves great in the eyes of others, rather than be all God made us to be.

God is for us. He has filled us with the power of his Spirit that gives us all we need to pursue the life of a faith superhero. The true manifestation of our good is rooted in the deep relationship of truth and our trust in him.

Ponder Today: The most tragic victim of our deceptions is most often ourselves.

JANUARY 27: WHAT HEAVEN CAN'T DO

"The fundamental fact of existence is that this trust in God, this faith, is the firm foundation under everything that makes life worth living. It's our handle on what we can't see." – Hebrews 11:1

Heaven is full of goodness. But not all good things are in Heaven. Sound strange? It is. But there is one good thing available to us on this Earth that will no longer be an option in Heaven.

Faith.

The unique opportunity of this life is the invitation to experience and exercise faith. It is the one good that is not available in heaven and will no longer be an option once we leave this world.

Faith is not easy. The circumstances of this world make trusting in something we cannot see a very difficult endeavor. It requires a level of humility that is fascinating to the angels. The strange (and sometimes tragic) circumstances of the human experience give us an excuse – we don't understand; we cannot see!

The unique opportunity of humanity is the ability to trust what we cannot comprehend. To put our hope in what cannot be seen or explained definitively. What an incredible challenge! What an inspiring opportunity! To know God in this way. To trust Him beyond all senses.

What will you decide? In the midst of your confusing, frustrating, and strange circumstances, will you step into the only goodness Heaven cannot do? The angels are watching. God is prompting. You have the chance to praise God in an incredibly unique fashion. Perhaps this is the very reason life exists.

Your circumstances are not a punishment or an indictment. They are an opportunity, terrain for the most incredible choice we can make. Faith.

Ponder Today: Faith is not just believing something exists; it is trusting in its goodness.

JANUARY 28: A PERSPECTIVE ON POSSESSION

"For we brought nothing into the world, and we can take nothing out of it." – 1 Timothy 6:7

Our materialistic society advises us to live our lives a bit like Pac-Man, gobbling up everything around us. To be like a child who shouts "Mine!" as soon as they see any toy in the possession of another. But reality is that everything we ever possess is just passing through our hands, on the way to somewhere else.

Recognizing this reality allows us to adopt a stewardship approach to all we own. The question of a steward is not "How can I continue to possess?" This is because the steward recognizes that they are only managing on behalf of someone else. The proper stewardship question is "What is my proper duty?" while this temporarily passes through our hands.

We are stewards for God in this life. God is the true owner of all. We know this by faith. But even observation tells us this is reality. We are only owners for a time. Someone else will eventually possess all we currently possess.

We may be entrusted for a while with land, money, houses, or investments. We have gifts, imagination, emotion, and skills. But in the end, it all belongs to God. The power of this truth unlocks our freedom, our participation, and our truest perspective. We no longer need to cling. We need not worry about loss. We can free our focus to steward well. Peace and truth are found in this fact: The Lord is The Lord of All.

Ponder Today: How can your possessions be tools for the Kingdom of Heaven?

JANUARY 29: THRILL OF THANKS

"... always giving thanks to God the Father for everything, in the name of our Lord Jesus Christ." – Ephesians 5:20-21

There are a variety of roller coasters. Some that loop. Some that go backward. Some are steel and some wooden. Some twist and turn and some just drop straight down.

All of the roller coasters in the world are balancing between fun and fright. We call these "thrill rides". They jolt us around, make us dizzy, twirl our insides all over the place, and mess up our hair. But there is something exciting about the ordeal. There is some joy in the chaos.

Our lives are like a thrill ride. Circumstance, setting, and season twist us around. They plunge us deep and fly us high. Sometimes our insides feel like they have dropped out. Other times we are so dizzy we feel sick. But if we have the correct perspective, the thrill remains through it all.

Life is an incredible journey. It is a gift from God. It is a never-to-be-repeated experience wherein we have the opportunity to walk by faith. And the key to thriving in a world that can be topsy-turvy is thankfulness. If we see our amazing adventure through the eyes of faith, we can actually give thanks "for all things" because we understand the incredible privilege we have to participate in the journey.

The thrill ride of life enriches us in a variety of ways. It challenges and convicts us. It develops character and intimacy through pain and perseverance. It shows us glimpses of glory beyond what we could have imagined. It takes us beyond ourselves while making us deeply aware of ourselves. All of it is an opportunity. All of it is a cause for thankfulness.

Ponder Today: What are you thankful for today?

JANUARY 30: A BINARY CHOICE

"You, my brothers and sisters, were called to be free. But do not use your freedom to indulge the flesh; rather, serve one another humbly in love." – Galatians 5:13

Freedom is the ability to make choices. Slaves don't get to choose. They do as directed by their masters.

When we are made new creations in the power of Jesus, it gives us a new capacity to choose. We are no longer slaves to our flesh. We have the power to chart a godly path. We have the power to choose.

And our choice is binary. We can either choose to indulge the flesh, as before, or we can choose to humbly love others. We can now walk in the Spirit or we can continue to walk in the flesh. There is no third option offered.

This Galatians passage goes on to tell us the consequences of our decision. We reap what we sow. If we indulge the flesh, we will reap relationships characterized by biting and devouring. Turmoil. Division. Bitterness. Separation.

On the other hand, if we sow to the Spirit and serve one another in love, the entire law of God is fulfilled. That means harmony, togetherness, teamwork, and unity.

Jesus set us free from our fleshly taskmaster. But we are still free to go under its power. Paul urges us to recognize our freedom and make the right choice. To choose love rather than strife. And that begins with humbly serving others.

Ponder Today: How free you are is less about the circumstances that limit you and more about how you use the freedom you possess.

JANUARY 31: HUMILITY AND HONOR

"Before a downfall the heart is haughty, but humility comes before honor." – Proverbs 18:12

Humility is a difficult challenge for believers. Haughtiness comes in many forms. It comes in aggressive bragging, inflated (inaccurate) selfishness, and "thinking more highly of ourselves than you ought". But it also takes another form. Haughtiness can come in silencing our self, hoarding the gifts of God, and denying our responsibility.

These latter tendencies are the mask of false-humility. The kind that throws away any sense of self in fear of making too much of the self.

Humility is simply seeing things as they truly are. Honor (and in that sense pride or glory) is not a poison to be avoided. We just need to approach it with accuracy. It needs to be grounded in truth or the whole pursuit will be out of whack.

Too often we neuter our passions, muffle our calling, and silence our character because we are afraid of pride. We want to look humble rather than be humble. Shying from the calling of God in our lives, the part we have to play in the Kingdom, is its own kind of blasphemy – stifling the image of God within us.

Humility is not about eradicating the self. It is about placing the self in proper context. It is about seeking the truth of who we are in light of who God is. Pursuing truth is the noble act of humility.

Ponder Today: It takes courage to listen and courage to speak. More courage still, to balance the two in truth.

FEBRUARY 1: DOES THAT REALLY HURT?

"The LORD is my shepherd, I lack nothing. He makes me lie down in green pastures, he leads me beside quiet waters, he refreshes my soul. He guides me along the right paths for his name's sake. Even though I walk through the darkest valley, I will fear no evil, for you are with me; your rod and your staff, they comfort me." – Psalm 23:1-4

Have you ever seen a small child fall down, tripping over their shoe laces or accidentally bumping their head against the wall? There is, in the aftermath, a moment that seems to be frozen in time. Is the child going to cry? Are they truly injured? A parent will often preempt the response by making a joke or encouraging their kid that he is ok.

Sometimes we cry because of the fear of pain rather than the experience of pain itself.

Once we get a taste for pain, it is easy to become overly fearful of it. We adopt a confirmation bias. Out of our fear of it, we are looking for pain.

This threat permeates our worldview. Everything could hurt. Everything might offend me. We find what we are looking for. And so many of us are looking for pain, peering for it around every corner.

Our perspective often invents offenses. We want to justify our way of thinking, eager to blame others for our hurt, dissatisfaction, or ineptitude. We act as though things hurt when really, we are just trying to massage the circumstances to get our way. Does it really hurt? Or have I learned that tears get me attention?

Obviously, we can push too far in this direction. Acknowledging what truly hurts is vitally important. We have to be able to honestly name sorrow when it strikes. But we must be equally able to see when it is just the threat of pain that scared us into offense or sadness or anger. We should not cover up true pain. Neither should we adopt imagined pain.

If we want to live a life of truth, we need to be able to ask ourselves, "Does this really hurt?" and have the courage to answer.

Ponder Today: Whether real or imagined, slight or severe, you are stronger than your pain.

FEBRUARY 2: SEDUCED BY THE AMAZING

"Call to me and I will answer you and tell you great and unsearchable things you do not know." – Jeremiah 33:3

We are obsessed with the extraordinary. Action Sports. Romantic gestures. Superhero movies. We can't get enough of it. Our lives long for the amazing.

It is easy for us to think that "amazing" and "new" are synonyms. That, for a thing to be incredible, it has to be rare. This leaves us constantly chasing more. The new spiritual high. The miraculous event. In the process, we pass over so much that is truly amazing.

The real beauty is in the everyday, the mundane, the here and now. We get excited when we hear verses like the one above. We lean in expecting Jesus to part the sea or strike down our enemies. The unsearchable riches he whispers are of the "ordinary": peace, hope, love, service. We might back away feeling underwhelmed. But these are the greatest treasures of heaven and earth.

Do not be seduced by a false perspective. You have all you need for life and for godliness. Do not be seduced into waiting for a magic circumstance. What you truly need is a transformed perspective. The miracles are just a tool to show you what is available all the time. Choices. Thankfulness. Awareness. These are the elements of living that are truly divine. Truly Amazing.

Ponder Today: There are incredible things around you that you overlook. You are surrounded by miracles.

FEBRUARY 3: THE WHOLE PICTURE

"Let each of you look not only to his own interests, but also to the interests of others." – Philippians 2:4

When we take a group photograph, our critical eye naturally turns to ourselves. When surveying the result, we are occupied by one question: "do I look good enough in this picture?"

Our perspective gravitates toward self-focus. If we are blinking or our hair is out of place or we are making a weird face, we want the picture retaken. We want to look our best. Evaluating how others look or the overall quality of the photo is usually an afterthought.

Our perspective problem is that we default to believing self-focus is in our self-interest. The Bible offers us a conclusive truth about this: it is not. In fact, self-focus is self-destructive. Our true self-interest lies in taking the best interest of others into account. The world is bigger than any one of us.

Widening our view to include the interest of others helps us develop a true perspective. The passage immediately following this verse tells us that this attitude of service toward others is what Jesus had when he came to earth. His perspective was that doing what His Father asked was in His true self-interest. He gained the rewards and approval from His Father for His faithful service, which made all the service worthwhile.

Jesus told us that the second greatest command is to love others like we love ourselves. Self-interest is presumed. But by seeking the best for others, we make the world bigger than just ourselves. This leads us to discover our purpose. We need the whole picture in order to truly be ourselves. And that begins with shifting our perspective to realize our true self-interest is best served by seeking the best for others.

Ponder Today: What is best for you today includes doing what is best for others.

FEBRUARY 4: REPRIEVE

"'Father, if you are willing, take this cup from me; yet not my will, but yours be done.' An angel from heaven appeared to him and strengthened him." – Luke 22:41-43

In the scene at the garden of Gethsemane, hours before his arrest, Jesus models for us the process of gaining a true perspective.

First, he makes his request known. He shares the honest emotion of his experience. He shares his own perspective.

It is essential for us to be honest. Truth begets truth. If we are honest about the place we are in, we make room for even more truth to permeate our perspective.

The second step to Jesus' model of obedience is listening to God with an openness that is seeking the highest reality. Jesus seeks comfort through reprieve. He is granted comfort through presence.

Jesus' cup was not lifted from him. It often is not lifted for us either. Jesus does not make a demand. He makes a request. And then he opens himself to the will of the Father.

Truth dwells in the will of the Almighty God. He is the home for truth. The arbiter of accuracy. The authority. We cannot discover truth until we come to him and request it.

The reprieve comes in his presence. Truth can be hard; it can lead to challenging circumstances and difficult decisions. But there is nothing in the world so beautiful and necessary as a true perspective. And there is no way to it other than the presence of God.

Ponder Today: Like Jesus, your reprieve comes not through comfort but through His presence.

FEBRUARY 5: DRAGON TREASURE

"For the love of money is a root of all sorts of evil, and some by longing for it have wandered away from the faith and pierced themselves with many griefs." – 1 Timothy 6:10

In The Voyage of the Dawn Treader, C.S. Lewis uses the story of Eustace to demonstrate the power of perspective. Greedy and awful, the boy Eustace lives with a perspective centered on self. He always feels slighted, even as he continues to act in a mean and menacing way.

On a magic island, Eustace comes across a dragon's treasure and believes his lust for riches is now fulfilled. When he puts a bracelet around his bicep and falls asleep, he becomes a dragon. The bracelet becomes so tight on his (now) dragon arm he finds himself in utter agony. The treasure he thought would give him joy instead brings agony.

In a similar way, false perception harms us. It whispers lies, suggesting the intrigue of the grass on the other side without mentioning its dangers. Preying on our fears and our tendency toward dissatisfaction, our perception can take us on quests for treasures that become snares.

Choosing a true perspective allows us to escape the idea that "dragon treasure" will bring us happiness. The false idea that joy comes through changed circumstance.

In his suffering, the dragon-boy is humbled. He helps others, even as he laments his circumstance. In the end, he learns a true perspective, that joy is founded in serving. The secret to the life we long for is not in any external treasure. It lies within, and is unlocked by discovering a true perspective.

Ponder Today: Today's circumstantial wish can become tomorrow's idol. In fact, today's wish could be today's idol.

FEBRUARY 6: IN WHOM

"So that your faith would not rest on the wisdom of men, but on the power of God." – 1 Corinthians 2:5

When we think about faith, we often think about an outcome during an event, circumstance, or season. I believe this or that will happen. I believe things will be ok.

The truest and most important aspect of faith is the object of the faith, in whom we place our trust. When we believe in specific circumstances, we disqualify our perspective from trusting God if the circumstance does not work out like we imagine.

Faith in outcomes is really hope. The foundation of faith is not in outcomes but in power. There is a fine, but distinct, line between believing the Who and the what. There is an immense difference between believing in Him who can do all things and believing a specific thing will be done.

Faith is the choice to trust God. It is obeying without knowing what the outcome will be. Faith unleashes the power of God's Spirit. The true height of human capacity.

Faith means trusting in God even when we do not like or understand what he is doing. This, in fact, is the very thing that makes faith so powerful, so advantageous to us. The outcomes we want, even if we get them, don't always work out how we imagined. Our wisdom is flawed and incomplete, but God's wisdom is true and boundless.

Ponder Today: God Himself, not the circumstances in which he reveals Himself, is the true object of your faith.

FEBRUARY 7: THE TRUE GOSPEL OF PROSPERITY

"I counsel you to buy from Me gold refined in the fire, that you may be rich; and white garments, that you may be clothed, that the shame of your nakedness may not be revealed; and anoint your eyes with eye salve, that you may see. As many as I love, I rebuke and chasten. Therefore be zealous and repent. Behold, I stand at the door and knock. If anyone hears My voice and opens the door, I will come in to him and dine with him, and he with Me." – Revelation 3:18-21

The gospel is filled with admonitions about accumulating the riches of God. God wants us to prosper. But God wants us to prosper in a manner that will never fade.

There is a false prosperity gospel that says "You can be (earthly) rich if you get God to listen to you." The true prosperity gospel is that we can have infinite riches, all the gold we want, by listening to God. This is a lasting treasure, not just mammon.

Since God's rewards are beyond our comprehension, we try to whittle the riches of God down to something we can grasp. Something more intellectually and physically tangible. Something more immediate. In essence, something smaller.

If we hear His voice and open the door, He will enter into an intimate relationship with us. This is the sort of intimacy only shared among close friends and relatives. This intimacy is the source of true riches. All the gold we want, straight from God. Intimate relationship with him is the path to our greatest treasure.

This verse was written by Jesus to those he loves. It can apply to anyone. But it is written to His children. Our Perfect Father does not rebuke and chasten other people's children. He rebukes and chastens His children.

He ends this passage with a promise. If we respond, He will come in and dine with us. He is ready and willing. He's just waiting for an invitation. Listening to Jesus in intimate fellowship is the path to true prosperity. This is truly good news. Infinite riches available to all. It just requires a true perspective about what it means to be rich.

Ponder Today: While you are waiting for God to open the door of circumstance, He is waiting for you to open the door to Him.

FEBRUARY 8: HOW TO BE A SUPERHERO: STEP ONE

"The seed which fell among the thorns, these are the ones who have heard, and as they go on their way they are choked with worries and riches and pleasures of this life, and bring no fruit to maturity. But the seed in the good soil, these are the ones who have heard the word in an honest and good heart, and hold it fast, and bear fruit with perseverance." – Luke 8:4-15

A superhero might be in a hurry to right the injustices of the world, to cleanse the rot of society. But in all the superhero movies, we see that the biggest struggle a superhero faces is curing the injustices within.

Justice and goodness start on the inside.

Before we can truly contend for external justice, we have to win our internal fight, constantly choosing the spirit over the flesh. If we start rushing into external battles either to avoid the internal ones or in a false belief that solving the one will inevitably solve the other, we are on the slippery slope of losing our way.

The first step toward becoming a faith superhero is to seek goodness within ourselves. To be willing to discover and address hidden places, where truth and justice are lacking within our own hearts. Only by listening to the Spirit of God can this be achieved.

The best way to test whether we are making good inner choices is an honest evaluation of our behavior. Good soil produces vibrant plants. If we are sowing to the Spirit by choosing the Spirit, we should be reaping the fruits of the Spirit, such as peace and joy.

We change from the inside out. Yet we observe from the outside in. Our circumstances won't transform our heart. Our heart transcends our circumstances.

Ponder Today: How can you be better today?

FEBRUARY 9: REFINED BY FIRE

"These trials will show that your faith is genuine. It is being tested as fire tests and purifies gold--though your faith is far more precious than mere gold. So when your faith remains strong through many trials, it will bring you much praise and glory and honor on the day when Jesus Christ is revealed to the whole world." – 1 Peter 1:7

Deeply seeded in each of us is an inherent fear of rejection. We can wear it on us like a heavy cloak, feeling its weight on our shoulders.

Rejection hurts. But rejection can be a refining fire. It can challenge our convictions, our attitudes, and our perceptions. It can put us to the test, so to speak. It can dig at the heart of who we truly are.

What part of us will we steadfastly refuse to alter, even if it risks garnering rejection from people around us? Rejection is not nearly as tragic as the stifling of one's true self.

Jesus endured immense shaming, from political as well as religious leaders. The Bible tells us to expect the same kind of treatment from the world. If we embrace this, as Jesus embraced it, we can view rejection as a way to refine our faith into twenty-four-carat gold.

Not everybody is going to love the choices we make. And sometimes people reject us because we are behaving badly, in which case we ought to repent. The challenge is to weed through various rejection, shedding the ugly parts rejection might expose while strengthening the parts of us that need to remain unchanged. Then trouble, no matter its source, becomes an opportunity to grow. To be refined.

And the result we are promised is praise, honor and glory from Jesus when He returns. When that day comes, all the rejection we might have faced from people will seem as nothing compared to praise from our Lord. For now, we are invited to see that time by faith, and choose a perspective that testing of our faith is preparation for that Day.

Ponder Today: Rejection is not an eternal indictment, it is an opportunity to learn and grow.

FEBRUARY 10: THE HEALING PAINS

"And after you have suffered a little while, the God of all grace, who has called you to his eternal glory in Christ, will himself restore, confirm, strengthen, and establish you." – 1 Peter 5:10

The paradox of pain is that the best way to be freed from it is to press into it. When we experience life in the valley, we want to make every effort to shortcut or short-circuit the pain. We slap a coat of paint over it. We dismiss it away with platitudes. Anything to silence the agonizing drone of suffering.

This does not solve our pain. It actually prolongs it. When we treat our pain like a beach ball that we try desperately to stuff underwater, one of these days it is going to pop to the surface in full force.

Pain is not solved by avoidance or denial. It is not actually "solved" at all. Pain is a unique life circumstance that can only be treated with honesty and hope.

Our best strategy is to approach pain with a perspective of truth. To lay our cards on the table, ask the tough questions, and experience it for all it is worth. When we share our pain with others, we are investing in relationships, and allowing God space to work. The One who is our comfort will be with us every step of the way. Pain is an opportunity to experience the valley of life with the Creator of Life.

Ponder Today: Pain is not a problem to be solved; it is a reality to be stewarded.

FEBRUARY 11: IRRITANTS

"Therefore I, the prisoner of the Lord, implore you to walk in a manner worthy of the calling with which you have been called, with all humility and gentleness, with patience, showing tolerance for one another in love." – Ephesians 4:1-2

Often, we are praying for things like patience or boldness. Sometimes what we mean is that we want God to remove the circumstances that trigger the need for patience. Or that we want to be so patient we aren't irritated to begin with, which is kind of impossible.

True love, the love of God, is a choice. We can only practice patience when an irritant is present. We don't "feel" like being patient, we feel like screaming. We have to choose to be patient. The same thing works for boldness. We think boldness is an absence of nerves and that is what we often pray for. But you have to be scared to be bold. Fear is a necessary component of bravery.

God grants our prayers for patience by putting us in situations that require us to be patient. An irritant. The circumstance is the opportunity to make our choice.

The power to choose love comes from Love Himself. God is love. When we choose to love, we unleash his Spirit to flow through us to others. Only through God's help and guidance can we make the proper choices. But making the proper choices requires the opportunity to do so. We are actors in a play and we need a scene.

Transcendence is the power to live above our circumstances. We don't need to avoid them to live fruitful lives; we need to make the most of the opportunities they provide.

Ponder Today: God grants our prayers for patience by putting us in situations that require us to be patient.

The following is a 4-day series on the character of Ruth:

FEBRUARY 12: DAY 1 - A FOUNDATION OF VALUE

"Then [Naomi] said, 'Behold, your sister-in-law has gone back to her people and her gods; return after your sister-in-law.' But Ruth said, 'Do not plead with me to leave you or to turn back from following you; for where you go, I will go, and where you sleep, I will sleep. Your people shall be my people, and your God, my God. Where you die, I will die, and there I will be buried. May the Lord do so to me, and worse, if anything but death separates me from you.' When she saw that she was determined to go with her, she stopped speaking to her about it." – Ruth 1:15-18

Ruth is one of the most incredible characters in all of Scripture. She finds herself in challenging circumstances and takes ownership of her choices. She makes a host of seemingly small decisions that turn out to have big effects, including becoming a mother in the lineage of King David, and ultimately of Jesus Christ. Her first choice is to decide to trust her mother-in-law Naomi and serve Naomi's God and people.

Ruth is from the neighboring country of Moab. She marries a sojourning Hebrew man, the son of Naomi, who then dies. Her bereavement response is to commit to follow her mother-in-law, Naomi, to return to Israel after Naomi has lost both her husband as well as both of her sons. This doesn't make a lot of sense from an outside perspective. Why go to a foreign land with a woman in need of help? Why not go back home and marry a local Moabite who will provide her with security?

Ruth's choice is about trust and commitment. She knows it is on her to decide who to trust. She commits to trust Naomi, Naomi's people, and Naomi's God. Ruth has apparently seen something that is true and right in the character of Naomi. As the story unfolds, we find Ruth fully backing with actions these words of commitment. The people of Israel will say of her that she is better to Naomi than seven sons. And we shall see that it is out of her loyalty and service to Naomi that will flow her greatest blessing.

Commitment to character and values is not easy. It is a tough choice. Ruth chooses to commit to Naomi, her people, and her God, even though there is little visible hope for circumstances to improve.

Ruth looked beyond comfort and committed to character. She went all-in and never looked back. Eventually, she was honored like few others. When we look beyond our circumstances, make wise choices about who to trust, then follow our commitment with our whole heart, we are setting ourselves up for God's greatest blessings in His perfect timing.

Ponder Today: What are you committed to and according to what value have you made those decisions?

FEBRUARY 13: DAY 2 - TAKING ACTION

"And Ruth the Moabitess said to Naomi, 'Please let me go to the field and glean among the ears of grain following one in whose eyes I may find favor.' And she said to her, 'Go, my daughter.'" – Ruth 2:2

If the story of Ruth ended in Chapter 1, we might say "wow, what an incredible and surprising choice she makes" as her and Naomi ride off into the sunset to return to Naomi's native land of Israel. But that is just the beginning.

Ruth doesn't know what lies ahead for her and her mother-in-law. What she doesn't do is sit back and bemoan the difficulties. She does not complain about the situation. She does not complain and she does not blame.

Rather, Ruth asks herself an important question. One we all ought to consider. In essence, she thinks, what can I do?

Ruth exercises self-governance. She is not a victim to her circumstances; she is a person of agency who can influence and act upon her circumstances.

Ruth takes initiative, she works hard. In Israel, those harvesting the crops left the corners and scraps for the poor. Ruth takes the humblest of stations, and goes to the fields to pick up grain as a poor woman. Interestingly, Naomi gives her permission, but does not come along. That does not deter Ruth. Ruth does what she can do.

Ruth does indeed "find favor" with one of the owners of the fields, Boaz. And it changes her life forever. Boaz sees Ruth in the field, helps her, and later acknowledges her reputation as a woman of noble character.

Time spent complaining, blame-shifting, or demanding things from others is time wasted.

Like Ruth, we have one life to steward. One life to make the most of. Nothing and nobody will steward our journey for us. What we do with our opportunities, the choices we make, are ours alone. Ruth made a great choice who to trust - Naomi, a woman of character. Now Ruth demonstrates her own character by taking the initiative to steward her actions. Her small choices of good stewardship turn into great blessings. Our path is the same.

Ponder Today: What does it look like to take initiative in your own life?

FEBRUARY 14: DAY 3 - THE COURAGE OF CHOOSING

"When Boaz had eaten and drunk and his heart was cheerful, he went to lie down at the end of the heap of grain; and she came secretly, and uncovered his feet and lay down." – Ruth 3:7

As the story of Ruth progresses, she continues to show strong character. At Naomi's suggestion, she displays one of the most important characteristics of life and love: courage.

Every choice we make is a risk. Because every decision leads to a consequence. And we cannot control how the consequences turn out even when we steward our choices wisely. Not only that, but making a specific decision closes us off to the other decisions we might have made. It reveals a commitment, an element of hope that could let us down.

The harvest is in full bloom, and Boaz is celebrating. At Naomi's suggestion, Ruth puts herself in a completely compromising situation with Boaz. She trusts Naomi enough to make herself completely vulnerable to Boaz by lying beside him on the threshing floor. Naomi makes a marriage proposal, since Boaz is a close relative, and therefore eligible to be a "kinsman redeemer" and redeem Naomi's land.

Boaz commends Ruth for her actions later in Chapter 3 in two ways - he calls her a person of noble character (and includes how this is known through the community) and he commends her for not chasing the younger, good looking men. The attractive Ruth instead sought security for her and Naomi through a man of great character, Boaz.

Ruth's choices are bold, value-based decisions. Her decisions require great courage, great commitment, and great character.

Noble characters make value-based choices in difficult circumstances. Our choices reveal who or what we trust. Ruth trusted Naomi and Boaz. In doing so, it turned out she was trusting God, who blessed her immensely. She honored God with her courage, and God honored her because of her courage.

Each day we have the opportunity to make our choices according to the values of Christ and His Kingdom. When we do so, we reveal a trust in God and His ways. A true choice. And a bold one.

Ponder Today: Are your choices based on a trust in God or a love for something else?

FEBRUARY 15: DAY 4 - REDEEMED

"Furthermore, I have acquired Ruth the Moabitess, the widow of Mahlon, to be my wife in order to raise up the name of the deceased on his inheritance, so that the name of the deceased will not be eliminated from his brothers or from the court of his birth place; you are witnesses today." – Ruth 4:10

The definition of "redeem" is "to gain (or regain) possession of something at a price". Ruth is a story of redemption. She and her mother-in-law Naomi have lost their husbands and their lands.

Boaz redeems the lineage of Naomi and takes Ruth as his wife. It costs Boaz. There is another possible redeemer who is first in line. He agrees to redeem the land, but then passes when he discovers it comes with Ruth. Raising a son for Ruth means the land would go to Naomi's heirs rather than his own. But Boaz chooses to marry Ruth and redeem the land for Naomi's descendants. Boaz looks beyond what was comfortable and chooses to cast his lot with women of great character.

Jesus is the ultimate example of a life of redemption. He is the Boaz-style redeemer for every one of us who are like Ruth, in need of redemption. The result of their union is a son, Obed. Obed became the father of Jesse, who was the father of King David. The Bible promises that when we follow Jesus as faithful servants, He will reward us by including us in His kingly lineage. He will reward us as servant kings.

Ruth doesn't know what God has in store for her as she is making her decisions. As she is choosing how to live and love, she has no idea the massive impact her choices will make. The loyalty and commitment to Naomi, her stewardship and self-governance, and her courage of character impact her own story. But they also influence much more. Ruth is part of a larger narrative, a bigger story. Just like each of us.

Our choices matter. They may seem small. It may seem as though our value-based character choices have little tangible effect. Our commitment to truth may not make sense to outside observers. The hard work of stewardship and self-governance is more difficult than blaming and complaining. And sometimes our courage feels dangerous and the results uncertain.

The reality is what we do has far reaching implications. Our choices matter. Our character matters. When we are faithful with our choices, God promises to multiply them. When we are humble He promises to lift us up, just as He did for Ruth. We all have the opportunity to follow Ruth's amazing example, and enjoy great blessings, which God will reward in due time.

Ponder Today: You are a small, significant part of a big story.

This concludes our 4-day series on the character of Ruth.

FEBRUARY 16: DANGERS ON THE MOUNTAIN

"...give thanks in all circumstances; for this is God's will for you in Christ Jesus." – 1 Thessalonians 5:18

We spend a lot of our time seeking mountaintop experiences. The prevailing view is that life is about chasing circumstances that exhilarate us, that bring us exuberant joy.

But there are dangers on the mountain. For one, these types of experiences are only temporary. They are one of the terrains of life we shuffle through. No matter what we do, we cannot find a life forever on the mountaintops. Adventure junkies chase more and more adrenaline, pushing the edge a little more every time. Addicts obsess unto death. It is never enough.

The way the world is set up is to experience these mountaintops as rare and temporary joys. Believing we can do all of life there is an inaccurate and unhealthy perspective.

The danger of the mountain is that we believe life has to always be this way. That we must feel this exuberance, this high, in order to be okay. We sink into apathy or delusion to protect the unrealistic hope that all things will feel great all the time.

The truth is we can be okay throughout any of the terrains of life. It is our perception that sustains us, not the manipulation of our circumstances. We do not achieve peace by overwhelming ourselves with joy. We find peace by accepting and understanding the value of all circumstances, in any situation.

The mountaintop is not the finish line. It is just like every other kind of circumstance - a checkpoint. A chance to be thankful. A chance to learn. A chance to perceive a fuller truth of the unique journey of life.

Ponder Today: What mountaintop are you longing to get back to? What are you missing in the process?

FEBRUARY 17: UNDER THE CIRCUMSTANCES

"Christ Jesus Himself being the cornerstone, in whom the whole building, being fitted together, is growing into a holy temple in the Lord, in whom you also are being built together into a dwelling of God in the Spirit." – Ephesians 2:20-22

It's a phrase we use often. "I'm doing well...under the circumstances". The implication being that whatever is happening in our lives is lowering the ceiling. That there is a maximum closing down on us, shrinking our potential by the moment.

It doesn't have to be this way. It is only so because we choose it. This mindset is more indicative of our perspective than the circumstances they refer to.

The power of perspective allows us to live over the circumstances. It does not mean the circumstances are not acknowledged and weighed. It just means they are not the sole measure that determines our weight.

The things that happen to us can be messy and sometimes tragic. But there is a force inside us more powerful than experience, more definitive than our situations. The Holy Spirit provides us insight into the identity God has bestowed on us and invites us to see Him more clearly. The circumstances of life provide an opportunity for Jesus to grow us into a holy temple in the Lord.

A true perspective allows us to view any circumstances as a step in this process. That we are being built together by the Spirit into a dwelling of God. That is a context that places all we do above any circumstance.

Ponder Today: What if we prayer for God to change our false perceptions rather than for him to change our unwanted circumstances?

FEBRUARY 18: THE CHOOSER

"I call heaven and earth to witness against you today, that I have set before you life and death, the blessing and the curse. So choose life in order that you may live, you and your descendants." – Deuteronomy 30:19

Perhaps the most fundamental question for any person is "Who am I?" Am I an evil, debased creature, full of sin? That is certainly what many voices inside (and out) scream at us. And there is evidence to support it. We are prone to selfishness and have terrible thoughts.

But the Bible tells us we are a new creation in Christ, made to walk in good works that Jesus prepared. It also teaches that all humans are made in the image of God, created for relationship and community with the Divine.

So which is it? Are we bad creatures tempted by grace or good creatures tempted by sin? The answer is that we are both, and neither. There is a third option and it is the truth.

The third role in the drama of life is the prime actor in the play. The role of the chooser. There is evil and there is good; both exist. Both are swirling within us. Both are a part of who we are. But The Chooser selects which one gets to act within the circumstances with which we are presented.

Perhaps one of the reasons we struggle with perspective is because we have failed to accurately cast ourselves in the cosmic play.

We make choices each day about how to engage with others and with our surroundings. We can choose to follow the spirit, leading to life. Or we can choose the flesh, which leads to separation (death).

Ponder Today: Your day will be most fundamentally defined by what you choose.

FEBRUARY 19: GAS IN THE CAR

"Therefore, since we are surrounded by such a great cloud of witnesses, let us throw off everything that hinders and the sin that so easily entangles. And let us run with perseverance the race marked out for us." – Hebrews 12:1

Experience is the fuel for opportunity. The things that happen to us provide the chance to make our choices. It is like being dealt a hand of cards. You can't control what you are given but you do get to decide how to play.

We are so scared of imperfection. We are frightened because experience is also the cause of pain. To avoid being hurt, we assume we must avoid experience. But if we avoid experience, we also sacrifice the opportunity to exercise our character and influence the world around us.

In trying to control our circumstances, we kill our opportunities. We have become people of apathy. Complacency is our highest ideal. We long for easy street, comfort, predictability, security.

No matter how much we try, we cannot fully control our circumstances. We cannot keep the pain at bay. We cannot eliminate risk or silence difficulty. What we can do is adopt a different perspective about our experiences.

Circumstances are not the finish line. They arrive and we think they are definitive. Then, we seem surprised that a new set is waiting in the wings. Circumstances are more like a checkpoint than an ending. They remind us that we are on the journey and have choices to make.

Ponder Today: Our choices give us stewardship over the kind of life we live.

FEBRUARY 20: ON DISPLAY

"His intent was that now, through the church, the manifold wisdom of God should be made known to the rulers and authorities in the heavenly realms, according to his eternal purpose that he accomplished in Christ Jesus our Lord." – Ephesians 3:10

The heavenly realms are watching with fascination. We are the documentary subject everyone is talking about. We are the "animals on safari." The creatures of heaven are whispering about us at the water coolers of Paradise. They can't get enough. Why?

They are watching us to learn about Him.

How can that be? The unique ability of the beings in this earthly realm is to express trust in God through belief. It is fascinating to the heavenly beings. A sight to behold. In watching us live by faith, they are learning about the Creator of all things.

We aren't merely a spectacle. Our faith shows off the wisdom and character of The Creator. It brings the divine beings further into worship. Awe. To see this great exercise actually happen causes the angels to turn toward God with a standing ovation.

Our faith choices help display the majesty of God. They bear witness to His Greatness. We have the opportunity to be significant players in this narrative. To choose to anchor our belief in the Truth of God while living in a world filled with many other options. To pursue and discover a true perspective, commit to it, and live out of it is a fascinating and holy enterprise.

Ponder Today: In Heaven, difficult choices are no longer a possibility. That means in this life, they are a limited time opportunity. Encounter them boldly and with intention.

FEBRUARY 21: TAKING COURAGE

"But when they saw Him walking on the sea, they supposed that it was a ghost, and cried out; for they all saw Him and were terrified. But immediately He spoke with them and said to them, 'Take courage; it is I, do not be afraid.'" – Mark 6:49-50

One of the interesting things about this story is that Jesus gives the disciples the recipe for courage. We gain courage by knowing God and choosing to trust him. A lot of times we think of courage as the absence of discomfort. But it is really about choosing whom to trust in the midst of discomfort.

The disciples originally think Jesus is a ghost. It is night time and there is a figure wading across the water. They've constructed myths and narratives to explain what they are seeing.

We do the same thing. We are sure when trouble arrives that we are done for. The end has come. We are sure there is no coming back from this circumstance. We are so ready to be afraid. So ready to give up. So ready to adopt the false perspectives that are clanging around this world.

Jesus offers another way. He invites the disciples to "take" courage. How? By knowing the truth. By trusting. We get our courage from the presence of Jesus. He is extending it to us; it is something only possible through a trust in who he is, an extension of knowing The Truth.

The preceding verses say that Jesus intended to walk by them to the other side of the lake. But he stops and gets in the boat to comfort his disciples. In the most startling of circumstances, his presence is the source of our courage.

Ponder Today: If we ask God for courage, we are not asking for things to be easy but to be put in situations where we have the opportunity to rely on Him.

FEBRUARY 22: JOB'S CHOICES

"Through all this Job did not sin nor did he blame God." – Job 1:22

No matter how bad things get for Job, there is one thing Satan cannot take away. His choices. Health and circumstances decline, to tragic degrees. But Job still exercises his ability to choose. No matter how bad it gets, he keeps deciding.

Satan's bet is basically this: if circumstances get bad enough, either Job will make radically different choices that mirror his circumstances or forget he has choices and flow with the tide of tragedy.

Job's friends try to lead him to this conclusion. The common sense of worldly wisdom would lead him there.

But Job makes another decision. He chooses faith in God. He chooses to trust his Creator. His circumstances don't determine his decisions. Importantly, neither do his decisions determine his circumstances. Job's choices transcend his circumstances. And this is the magic of obedience to God. It is bigger than the events, the arenas in which we decide. It doesn't play by their rules.

We each have the same opportunity as Job. We cannot control circumstances by our decisions, but we can choose our perspective. And we can make decisions out of a place of trust.

Circumstances are a necessary setting for life to play out. But each day is about the choices we make in the drama we call "life." Nothing is more important than the choices before us. And nothing in life negates those choices and their cosmic implications. The only way we lose our choice is by forfeit, which is in itself a choice.

Ponder Today: Being able to choose is a great gift. Today is an opportunity to follow Job's example and trust that our Creator has our best interest at heart.

FEBRUARY 23: LIFE AS A SOUL

"Trust in the Lord with all your heart and lean not on your own understanding; in all your ways submit to him, and he will make your paths straight." – Proverbs 3:5-6

Life is hard and confusing. A circumstance we think is best one day might show itself to be disastrous down the line - and vice versa. We need something external to put our trust in, something to submit to. We need something that knows what is best. Someone to trust.

The only one truly capable of holding this office is God. We are spiritual beings having a physical experience. And Jesus is the King of both realms. When the adventure of our brief but wonderful life ends, we continue on as living spirits awaiting a new, spiritual body. We often say "you have a soul". The truth is: you **are** a soul. You "have" a body. Our body/our mind house our understanding and our ability to perceive.

A consequence of this reality is that true happiness will always have a spiritual foundation. An entertaining comedy might provide some moments of escape, but it will not heal a broken heart. We are made for more. We are souls made for eternity. As we are confined to this temporal journey, in these temporal bodies, we are limited.

But even the limitations of life on earth is an adventure, a beautiful opportunity. It invites us to trust the Lord in all our ways. In all our choices. In all our experiences. Trust that the Lord doesn't make mistakes. In laughter as well as sadness. His best for us is embedded within our reality, whether or not it is apparent. The choice of this adventure is to lean into the mystery of our souls and the spiritual reality of our existence. To trust God to fill in the gaps. And worship him as the creator and sustainer of our souls.

Ponder Today: You are not a body with a soul. You are a soul with a body.

FEBRUARY 24: ACCEPTED AND APPROVED

"For I am convinced that neither death, nor life, nor angels, nor principalities, nor things present, nor things to come, nor powers, nor height, nor depth, nor any other created thing, will be able to separate us from the love of God, which is in Christ Jesus our Lord." – Romans 8:38-39

Most of us grew up in a culture that taught us that acceptance and approval are synonyms. We are accepted if we perform an approved behavior. Since it's what we grew up with, we tend to treat each other this way: "I will reject you if you don't live in a manner that I approve of."

But Scripture has a clear delineation between the two. A harmonious and important one. God gives acceptance freely, although we don't deserve it. Approval however is something God gives based on the choices we make.

Jesus fully accepted the woman caught in adultery. He didn't reject her one bit. But He also did not approve of her adultery. He told her to "go and sin no more." Why? As Jesus told the man he healed "Sin no more, lest a worse thing come upon you."

Like any good father, God may disapprove of what we do. He will reward what is in our best interest. But even so, will never reject who we are. We are his children and that is something we can never lose.

The Father's acceptance and approval are twin pillars of his love for us. Nothing can separate us from His unconditional acceptance. All the while, God will be approving that which brings us life while dissuading us from pursuing that which brings us destruction. Nothing can separate us from the love of God.

Ponder Today: God's disappointment with us is not because we don't "measure up"; it is because we have yet to conceive of what is truly best for us.

FEBRUARY 25: BREVITY

"As for the days of our life, they contain seventy years, or if due to strength, eighty years, yet their pride is but labor and sorrow; for soon it is gone and we fly away." – Psalm 90:10

The human life is a brief adventure. It is over in the blink of an eye. There are two options for us in the wake of this reality.

First, we can lament. We can bemoan our mortality. There is a type of lament that is tempered with truth - death is unnatural. Death is an interloper and we weren't intended to have such a short duration on earth. It is truly sad that life is so brief.

Our other option is to rejoice. To adopt an eternal perspective. Our destiny is to live on a new earth, where righteousness dwells, and to dwell there forever. Our life is not threatened. We just have to move. We have to transfer from this earth to the next. And the next will be far better.

Meanwhile, we have an amazing opportunity here. We can say to ourselves: "if this life is but a breath, I am going to make the most of it." In Scripture, the laments about the brevity of life are also invitations. They invite the perspective of humility before the Divine and a call to make the most of the choices before us.

Jesus will physically dwell alongside us in the new earth. Hope will be fulfilled. Faith will become sight. In this life, we have the amazing, one time opportunity to know him by faith.

The human life is a wild adventure. It is the prologue for a story that stretches beyond this world. We cannot add days to our life by worrying. We cannot solve the mysteries beyond our grasp. What we can do is spend each valuable day in the presence of God, making the most of the adventure.

Ponder Today: The temporal nature of our reality can either cripple us or activate us.

FEBRUARY 26: BREAD FOR THE DAY

"Then Jesus declared, "I am the bread of life. Whoever comes to me will never go hungry, and whoever believes in me will never be thirsty.'" – John 6:35

As we search for success, blessing, and approval in this life, we are focused on method and means. We are looking for the right thing to come along, the secret recipe, the magic bullet. One of the reasons people are so frustrated is because they cannot find the right means to achieve the things they long for.

The real struggle is not that we cannot find the means for success, but that we have not rightly defined success.

Jesus is not a means to our treasure. He is our treasure. He does not provide the way for us to receive daily bread, the substance that sustains us. He is that very thing himself.

The implications of this revelation are enormous. Relationship with Jesus is the blessing we are looking for. It is both the means and the subject of achieving our deepest desires. Our highest treasure is him. We do not need Jesus to provide the circumstances that will sustain and fulfill us. We need Jesus to sustain and fulfill us.

The Treasure of Heaven is available to you today. No matter what difficulties you are facing, what gifts you have, and what challenges you'll encounter today, it is all an opportunity to perceive the true source of your daily bread. The provider who gives nothing greater than Himself.

Ponder Today: Jesus is our daily bread.

FEBRUARY 27: PRESS INTO JOY

"Cry aloud and shout for joy, O inhabitant of Zion, For great in your midst is the Holy One of Israel." – Isaiah 12:6

The freedom of the gospel allows us to press into happy circumstances. It is nothing to fear or mistrust. There is no reason to avoid pleasure just because we know it will fade. It is temporary, but we can be grateful to experience joy while it is with us.

But joy can also transcend any circumstance, if we look at it the right way. Because we can always have joy that God is in our midst. Unlike the Psalmist, on this side of the cross and Pentecost we can have joy that God is within us.

We probably don't reflect on that amazing reality often enough. The God who is so large He can hold the world in his hand has taken residence in our hearts. The resurrection power of Jesus is inside, available to help us through every terrain of life. He is always leading, always guiding. He is in our midst.

Joy is more about who God is than about how we feel. It is rooted in what we choose to value. Pressing into joy is an acknowledgement that God is not only in our midst, but he is good and has our best interest at heart.

Ponder Today: The joy of the Lord is our strength. Look for joy today. Welcome it. And press in.

FEBRUARY 28: PARADOX

"Therefore I am well content with weaknesses, with insults, with distresses, with persecutions, with difficulties, for Christ's sake; for when I am weak, then I am strong." – 2 Corinthians 12:10

One of the great paradoxes of human existence is the strength found in weakness. Often our physical weakness opens the door for spiritual strength. We can see this at work in stories like Corrie ten Boom, the Dutch woman who endured a Nazi prison camp during World War II.

In ten Boom's telling of her inspiring story, her sister is the primary hero. The sisters were plagued by lice in their barracks. Betsie exhorted Corrie to give thanks in all things. They later learned they were spared abuse from the guards who avoided them because of the lice. Corrie's bitterness melted away. She learned her sister had been correct. The weakness of the lice gave them protection from the guards. More importantly, Corrie learned a spiritual lesson that helped her develop into a woman that inspired the faith of many.

There is a kind of strength that transcends muscles and money. The strength of faithfulness, righteousness, and love. A power only available through God Himself.

For whatever reason, the Lord has set up a world that applies struggle toward developing strength. When we encounter difficulties, we have the opportunity to be strong in faith. Being strong in faith is one of our greatest opportunities this side of heaven.

Ponder Today: We ought not go looking for trouble. But neither should we fear it. The strength that comes from the Lord transcends difficulty.

FEBRUARY 29: THE PRESENCE

"Let us acknowledge the LORD; let us press on to acknowledge him. As surely as the sun rises, he will appear; he will come to us like the winter rains, like the spring rains that water the earth." – Hosea 6:3

Time is a tricky reality in this world. It makes seasons temporal and circumstances ever-changing. It requires us to move and evolve, pivot and adapt.

Although we might view this as an unfortunate reality, it is actually an incredible opportunity. It gives us the chance to acknowledge God in diverse ways. To see him through a variety of circumstances and experiences.

The presence of God is as constant as the reality of change. He is the eternal presence throughout every manifestation of our temporal experience. Said another way, he is always here. Always available. Through the highs and lows, the twists and turns, the celebrations and the lamentations, God is the God of all.

It is hard for us to fathom the eternal presence of God. He is always here, around every corner, in every circumstance, through all times and seasons. God is beckoning us to his Kingdom, inviting us to acknowledge him.

Today is a day of temporal challenges and successes. Our day might include sadness or joy, a great win or a debilitating loss. The Lord is the Lord of all. He is here. No matter what is happening today, God's presence is the ultimate reality, the guiding truth. And he wants nothing more than for us to acknowledge him at this time, in this place, in these circumstances. By doing so, we participate in the eternal truth of God.

Ponder Today: God is the Eternal that lifts meaning from the temporal.

MARCH 1: ACTION REQUIRED

"Little children, let us not love with word or with tongue, but in deed and truth." – 1 John 3:18

When we think of love, we tend to think of emotion. Or perhaps we think of words, like telling someone "I love you." But this verse exhorts us to something greater. The highest form of love involves action. Deeds. Activity. We are exhorted to love "in deed and truth."

This old saying might fit: "The proof is in the pudding." You can tell me the pudding is yummy, but I find out the truth of the claim when action occurs - when it is cooked and eaten.

John implores us here to not just say that we love something. But to show it. To have our actions match our words.

A good self-examination exercise is to take inventory of what we are doing, and ask ourselves "What does that say about what I am loving?" Does how I am spending my time reflect who and what I desire to love? Does how I am spending my money (which, like time, is just another tool for reflecting value) reflect what I want to love?

When we love others, we love God. And when we love God we are loving others. But true love requires real deeds. It is not just talked about, but done.

Ponder Today: What action can you improve upon to communicate Christ as your truest love?

MARCH 2: FAR MORE

"Now to Him who is able to do far more abundantly beyond all that we ask or think, according to the power that works within us," – Ephesians 3:20

One of the reasons we are fascinated with superheroes is because they can do far more than we can. They can run faster, jump higher, punch harder. They can fly through space and save the world from peril. We watch these characters on the big screen and our hearts stir. Deep down, we desire to be far more ourselves.

The far more lives of movie superheroes always includes a fight. The ones with the great power get the call to rescue the world from evil. With power comes responsibility. To whom much is given, much is expected.

The Kingdom of God is no different. We have far more ability through the indwelling Spirit. But we also like comfort. We like to fit in.

But far more is not about a vacation in the sun. It is about being equipped to engage in the fight. And our fight is with the spiritual forces of darkness in this world. The evil one who sows discord and reaps division.

How are we able to fight such a foe? The same way the big screen characters do. With far more power. Indwelling resurrection power.

Our power is not accessed with a magic ring or a mutated gene. We access this great power with a humble heart, a listening ear, and willingness to walk by faith.

We have far more power than we can even imagine. Power to resist evil and do good. In order to access that power, we must have the courage to fight and the humility to serve. But that's just a normal day in the life of a superhero.

Ponder Today: What specific power do you have to fight evil and uphold The Kingdom of God that you too often overlook?

MARCH 3: SAFETY NET

"But God, being rich in mercy, because of His great love with which He loved us, even when we were dead in our transgressions, made us alive together with Christ."
– Ephesians 2:4-5

Receiving unconditional acceptance can be difficult. It can wound our pride. We tend to like the idea that we have earned acceptance.

When we lean into that false perspective, it leads to unhealthy habits. We will shy away from repentance. We will judge others. We justify to ourselves that we have merited God's acceptance by outperforming the people around us.

These patterns isolate us from life-giving fellowship with God and with others. But it does not have to be. God accepts us without condition. It is true whether or not we choose to admit it. The only merit necessary is the merit of Jesus. What He did for us is sufficient.

Believing God has really and truly accepted us, just as we are, because of what Jesus has done, actually provides an incredible foundation for living a fulfilled life.

If we are accepted, no matter what, we are free to share honestly about our sin and shortcomings. We are free from having to judge others. There is no need to compare. We all fall short. We can leave comparison up to God. We can admit. We can repent.

God disapproves of sin. But approval is not acceptance. God disapproves of what is bad for us. Because he loves us. We are his children. He disapproves when we engage in self-destructive behavior because of his love for us.

God's unconditional acceptance is our firm foundation. It frees us to seek God's approval without fear of rejection. Our freedom to make choices now becomes the avenue to please God and discover a mature faith. All while leaning on the unshakeable pillar of his vast love for us. Not even our own wrong perspectives can separate us from God's unbounded love.

Ponder Today: What would look like to act <u>out of</u> the acceptance of God rather than toward it?

MARCH 4: EMOTIONS AND VALUES

"... giving all diligence, add to your faith virtue, to virtue knowledge, to knowledge self-control, to self-control perseverance, to perseverance godliness, to godliness brotherly kindness, and to brotherly kindness love. For if these things are yours and abound, you will be neither barren nor unfruitful in the knowledge of our Lord Jesus Christ." – 2 Peter 1:5-8

Since emotions alert us to values, it is easy to get the two confused. It's easy to tie them together and treat our emotions as our values. But they are not the same.

Godly values are rooted in faith. Faith that what God says is true. When our emotions flare, they are to be listened to but not obeyed. Emotions are like an alarm. They tell us we need to act. But prior to taking action, we need to seek knowledge, in self-control, with diligence. So we can act in love.

Acknowledge emotions when they ignite. And then seek knowledge. Investigate. Why are the emotions flaring? What value has been triggered? Is that value virtuous or self-seeking? Be willing to wait on the Lord. Ask God to help the self-examination.

Only after this process should we decide what to do. Emotions demand action. Godliness demands we persevere in first seeking knowledge rooted in faith before we act.

Our actions should be driven by carefully considered choices.

We can remember this approach with the acronym **LID**. "Put a "LID" on emotions." (Not to suppress emotion, but to remember the approach.)

Listen
Investigate
Decide

Emotions are God's gift. They tell us when action is needed. But freedom is an even greater gift. God has granted us the power to choose our perspective as well as our actions. Let's LID our emotions. **Listen**: never suppress. They provide important content. Then **investigate**: seek knowledge through God's guidance. Then, and only then, **decide** what action to take. When we use this approach, we allow God to direct us from a foundation of faith and love.

Ponder Today: Emotions are helpful servants but terrible masters.

MARCH 5: INVISIBLE

"By faith we understand that the worlds were prepared by the word of God, so that what is seen was not made out of things which are visible." – Hebrews 11:3

Every theory about the origin of the universe is founded on faith. They all admit or presume a beginning that can't be seen. We have ample evidence that creation magic happened. We are here. But all "how" explanations require faith. Each describes the inexplicable. Creation theories answer the question "Who or what caused the creation magic?"

It requires dramatically more faith to believe in magic without a magician. So why would people want to choose that proposition when what it involves goes against all known human experience? Perhaps because it clears a path to claim that the highest intelligence in the universe is humanity. And if we claim further that we are the highest and best of existence, then we are the best the universe has to offer. Therefore, we have a right to control.

We all believe in things we can't see. But Biblical faith is far more in keeping with what we know by experience. We know creations come from creators. No one has ever seen a creation make itself. We observe that creators are sovereign over their creations. As with us.

So, it is only a step of faith to believe that we are creatures, made by God. We are physical representations of spiritual realities. Our limitations mean our beginnings require faith. Thankfully, the True Creator Magician did not leave us to speculate who or why. We know by faith that God created the worlds, speaking them into existence. We know he gave it choice, and then redeemed its poor choices.

Faith is an opportunity. An invitation to believe that God is who he says he is. The visible and the invisible declare the name of Jesus. We are invited into the uniquely human opportunity to put our faith in Him.

Ponder Today: What will you do with God's invitation to trust Him today?

MARCH 6: PLAY IN THE STREETS

"And the streets of the city will be filled with boys and girls playing in its streets.'" – Zechariah 8:5

In Zechariah 8, God discusses what Jerusalem will look like when He restores it. What will be marvelous. What is holy. Part of the picture God paints includes play. Having fun. Children having a great time.

Play is a gift from God. Having fun should be a holy endeavor. When we play as children, we are reminded of our original design. Work was God's gift to humanity. But sin made work toilsome. "Play" can be thought of as work as it was originally designed. We can experience the sensation of accomplishment. We can experience the camaraderie of teamwork - we can even enjoy the success of others.

Playing games ought to remind us of the joy set before us for our full lives. The short time frame of games is a reminder that life is also brief. Like games, we can win at life. God wants us to win at life. God exhorts us to win at life. Seven times, to seven churches in Revelation, Jesus says "to the overcomer I will give" various rewards. "Overcomer" is a translation of "Nikao" which is also translated "victory", "conquer" and "prevail."

Let's set aside sufficient time to play. To remember what it feels like to experience joy. To laugh until we cry. To smile until our cheeks hurt. To enjoy company with the people we love. Done the right way, play is holy. It is marvelous in the eyes of God.

We tend to compartmentalize "holy" as something that is solemn on Sunday. We tend to think God is somewhat disappointed with the rest of our week. God offers His perspective, and it is a substantial departure from this common view. He loves to watch children play in his streets. And the whole world is the Avenue of The Kingdom of God.

Ponder Today: What can you do today that will include meaningful, holy joy?

MARCH 7: BEAR MUCH FRUIT

"I am the vine; you are the branches. If you remain in me and I in you, you will bear much fruit; apart from me you can do nothing. This is to my Father's glory, that you bear much fruit, showing yourselves to be my disciples." – John 15:5,8

We are made in the image of God, made to reflect his glory. We are the branches and he is the vine. When we bear good fruit, the true results of the branches and the vine, we celebrate God.

The word for glory, "doxa", means that something's essence is being clearly seen by observers. If someone runs the fastest 100-meter time in the world, but no one sees it, there is no glory. And if someone buys a gold medal won by Hussein Bolt, that does not mean they have the glory of being the world's fastest runner. Glory is not always good. Philippians 3:19 speaks of those whose "glory is their shame". These are folks whose life choices are controlled by their appetites. It is something observable and it is their "glory" because their true essence is being shown.

God does not need us to behave a certain way to display His glory. The entire creation displays His glory (Psalm 19).

However, we have this unique opportunity for others to see the glory of God through our deeds. For when we abide in Him, and follow His ways, what observers are seeing is not us, but God working through us. We get to share in God's glory by being a conduit. And this actually brings glory to us, for we were created to be God's instruments. We are fulfilling our design.

We cannot do anything apart from God. We are his. We belong to him. As we seek to discern his will for our lives, and make decisions accordingly, we do not just puff up ourselves in idolatry. We reveal ourselves as God's disciples and Him as the master of glory.

Ponder Today: We are all pursuing glory. The question is are you trying to do it on your own or in alignment with God?

MARCH 8: LIMITED ENGAGEMENT

"Man is like a mere breath; His days are like a passing shadow." – Psalm 144:4

We are only here for a little while. Life is inherently fragile, temporary. There are a finite number of days for us to walk this Earth. A finite number of opportunities and choices.

It is natural to focus a lot of attention toward trying to prolong our lives. We fight against the tide of time, the doom of death. But it is important not to set aside the chance to truly live today.

Life on Earth may be brief, but it is full of purpose. Our life here is the childhood of our existence. Eternal life is a gift, but it is also a reward. We are given life with Christ; we are new creations. But we "grow up" when we learn to make good choices.

This is a life of faith, a journey brief and powerful. Children are unaware of the opportunities surrounding them largely because their experience is limited and they have no basis to compare. It is likewise for us. The Bible tells us a little about the life ahead, but it seems clear it's like telling a three-year-old what it is like to grow up and get married.

Our brief time on this Earth is a shadow of the things to come. It is an opportunity to participate in a Kingdom that transcends time and existence. We can barely grasp what's ahead, but we can believe God's word. The reward of loving obedience is more than we can ever imagine.

Life is a limited engagement. Full of adventure, sorrow, and opportunity. Ripe with beauty and meaning. We can lament our fate or press into it. We can deny reality or make the most of it. There is little time to waste.

Ponder Today: In the midst of sorrow and joy, boredom and thrill, you are living a life of purpose today.

MARCH 9: DRAMATIC MOMENTS

"...And who knows whether you have not attained royalty for such a time as this?" – Esther 4:14

In every superhero movie, there is always a moment. The drama has built. Something significant is at stake. The camera zooms in for a close up as if to ask, "what are you going to do?"

As faith superheroes, we have such moments as well. Moments of drama and significance. The challenge is that these moments don't always let us know when they are coming. We can't hear the music change or see the camera lens zoom in on us. It could be any moment.

So we can treat every moment as being full of potential and importance. And that would be true. Faith, after all, is not one single choice, but a habit of choices.

Every circumstance we encounter is a significant moment of choice. How will we respond? What will we say? What will we do? Every choice is important.

We are royalty, sons and daughters of The King. And as God's children, we have been blessed with a life of opportunity. A chance to make choices that further His Kingdom and bring glory to his name.

We ought to be intentional about the way we wield our faith. Today is an opportunity. Now is a moment. The lens of angels is zooming in on us, wondering, "what choice will they make?" Our decisions are an opportunity to be a faithful witness. And to align our awareness with the significance of the story of God.

Ponder Today: Life is not about reacting to big moments, it is about preparing for them. And realizing that, at the end of days, the preparations were as big as anything else.

MARCH 10: FRIENDLY ADVICE

"Your words have supported those who stumbled; you have strengthened faltering knees. But now trouble comes to you, and you are discouraged; it strikes you, and you are dismayed. Should not your piety be your confidence and your blameless ways your hope? "Consider now: Who, being innocent, has ever perished? Where were the upright ever destroyed? As I have observed, those who plow evil and those who sow trouble reap it." – Job 4:4-8

Like all of us going through a hard time, Job gets a lot of advice from his friends. The majority of the book is a discussion between Job and his friends about what has happened to him, why, and how to fix it.

And although Job's friends are renowned for their bad advice, they are not terrible people who make overtly evil claims. What they say makes a lot of sense from a worldly, human perspective. And, even more, the friends often encourage Job and say things that are right and true about who he is. It is only their conclusions that are off.

We get friendly advice all the time. We are created to live in community together, to sharpen one another. So how do we know when the advice of our friends is worth following?

Job leans on his faith. He loves his friends and he hears them out. But his trust is in God alone. If a friend points you to your faith, they are offering sound advice. Otherwise, they are not. Job's friends, likely because they care for their companion, are trying to find a quick solution. They are trying to find a way out of this thing, to right the ship, to answer the question so that everything will be okay again.

Our friends want the best for us. But just like we often make mistakes perceiving our own good, friends make mistakes perceiving what is good for one another.

The example of Job is to hear his friends out but rely on his faith in God. Job's posture throughout his story is worship. When his friends' advice strays from worship for the sake of ease, their advice is no longer correct.

Ponder Today: Worship is the tuning fork for discernment.

MARCH 11: THE SEARCHING

"'For I know the plans that I have for you,' declares the Lord, 'plans for welfare and not for calamity to give you a future and a hope. Then you will call upon Me and come and pray to Me, and I will listen to you. You will seek Me and find Me when you search for Me with all your heart.'" – Jeremiah 29:11-14

Calamity does not have to define us. And it certainly does not define what God is doing. God has a plan. And that plan is for our best. For our future. Our hope.

This famous "tee shirt" verse comes right after God tells Israel He is bringing a calamitous judgment upon them. He has removed his hand of protection due to their disobedience. The proper application of this verse is in connection with calamity. Even when we bring calamity upon ourselves, God's plan is to turn that into prosperity.

One of the primary ways calamity can benefit us is to cause us to seek God. In the valleys all illusions of self-reliance are stripped away. It is in the valleys we know definitively that we need help. So we call upon the Lord.

The Lord's interest is not so much for us to escape adverse circumstances. It is for us to find Him. That is the source of our greatest riches. And we find Jesus when that is what we seek. We find him when we search for him with all our heart.

Thankfully we do not have to await catastrophe to seek and find the Lord. He is always available. The Hebrew word translated "search" means to pursue, or to inquire of. The idea is to make a focus, a priority. To search for God is to make it a front-burner item, a focal point, a necessity.

Our greatest riches, best outcomes, and true welfare comes about when we make a top priority to see God in all we do. To conform our perspectives to what is true. To seek his ways rather than the path urged by fleshly desires. When we search we find, and what we find is the greatest possible prosperity; intimacy with Jesus.

Ponder Today: When have you experienced deeper intimacy with Jesus as a result of suffering?

MARCH 12: ARENAS

"Therefore be careful how you walk, not as unwise men but as wise, making the most of every opportunity, because the days are evil. So then do not be foolish, but understand what the will of the Lord is." – Ephesians 5:15-17

Every circumstance is an opportunity we can steward. This is true at home, at work, in relationships, and in every other facet of our lives. The question is: Will we make choices that are wise or unwise?

Since "the days are evil", the path of least resistance is to make unwise choices. Our world bombards us with enticements to be unwise. Many of them boil down to some version of "Transfer your money to us and your life will be better." Whether it is a beverage, a pair of shoes, or an exotic excursion, all promise to bring us fulfillment. But of course they don't.

Any time we approach an opportunity with the perspective that "This new thing will make me happy", we are sinking into the world's deception. Happiness is not founded in changing venues or getting "more". That isn't even logical. If happiness is "getting more", then happiness is impossible. Once I get "more" then I will now need "more." "More" is unobtainable.

Happiness is rooted in wisdom. Wisdom is rooted in understanding God's will. It is rooted in following the paths Jesus has laid out for us. The path of love and service in the everyday activities of life.

Life is not about what happens to us. It is about what we do in response to what happens. Circumstances are just the arena in which life plays itself out. We are the players. Our choices are the tools. If we want to live a life of peace and joy, it won't come from complaining until we get moved to a different arena. It comes from excellent stewardship of our power to choose in whatever arena we occupy.

Ponder Today: What is the arena you find yourself in today? How can you play well within it?

This following is a 5-day series on Courage:

MARCH 13: DAY 1 - FIGHTING AGE

"These were the men counted by Moses and Aaron and the twelve leaders of Israel, each one representing his family. All the Israelites twenty years old or more who were able to serve in Israel's army were counted according to their families. The total number was 603,550." – Numbers 1:44-46

The book of numbers begins with a census. Moses is charged with counting the "men of fighting age", effectively putting a number to the generation following God in the wilderness.

Later in the book of Numbers, God renders a judgment on Israel because of their unwillingness to fight for The Promised Land. The people will have to wander in the desert until "the whole generation of those who had done evil in his sight were gone".

Who was relegated to die in the wilderness? Everyone of fighting age at the time they refused to fight. A generation of equipped battlers who were afraid, unwilling to trust God, exercise courage, and enter The Promised Land.

God is holding accountable those who refused to fight.

He still does. We are called to courage. We are called to engage in a battle. Not one of violence or insult. But one of justice and truth, standing up for what is right and good and true. Ephesians tells us to get up every morning and put on our spiritual centurion uniform, because we are called to battle the forces of darkness with peace and truth.

When it comes to the Kingdom of God, we are all men and women of fighting age. We are aware of the stakes and equipped for engagement. The foundation for the fight is courage. A willingness to fight even if it might cost us something. A boldness to act in the face of fear.

Ponder Today: How does "fighting" for the gospel look different than the world's way of insult and violence?

MARCH 14: DAY 2 - THE UNIFORM

"Therefore put on the full armor of God, so that when the day of evil comes, you may be able to stand your ground, and after you have done everything, to stand." – Ephesians 6:13

The Christian life is not just about being "nice". It certainly calls for kindness and gentleness, fruits of the Spirit. But Scripture also leans heavily on war metaphors. Not because of people, but because of spiritual forces.

Jesus was often "not nice". He was downright "rude" to the Pharisees. He turned over tables. He wouldn't even talk to Herod. He told the adulteress "I don't condemn you, but go and sin no more". In each case Jesus sought the best for those with whom he interacted. But we would not describe his behavior as "nice."

The reality is that living the Christian life is often a fight. Ephesians 6 tells us our enemy is not one another, but the "dark forces in this world". And as we unite in opposition to these forces, Ephesians tells us how to dress.

The "armor of God" follows a familiar design to the reader of Paul's time - the uniform of a Roman centurion. A warrior's garb. We are supposed to put on our spiritual centurion uniform every morning, walk out the door and start fighting. There is a war out there and we are implored to dress accordingly.

Truth is our belt, uniting the ensemble, keeping our pants up. Righteousness is our bullet-proof vest, protecting our heart. Salvation is the helmet and the Word of God is our sword. All of this to prepare us to face with courage the world and its temptations, to battle against the forces of evil and live a life of faithful obedience.

We are told that if we resist Satan and temptation, we win. That's a great thought. If we fight, we win. Evil only succeeds by our forfeit. There might be pushback. Jesus got a lot of it. But Jesus calls us to stand our ground as he did. Faithful obedience is an act of courage.

Ponder Today: When we compromise right to try to impress others, we do neither us or them any favor.

MARCH 15: DAY 3 - POSTPONING THE FIGHT

"When Pharaoh let the people go, God did not lead them on the road through the Philistine country, though that was shorter. For God said, 'If they face war, they might change their minds and return to Egypt.'" – Exodus 13:17

Courage is not the absence of fear. It is the choice to fight in the face of fear.

God has to train the newly freed people of Israel to choose trust in him over fear of their oppressors. In the immediate aftermath of their exodus, God makes an assessment. His people are not ready to fight.

Sometimes God leads us the longer way, to protect us and buy some time. To train and encourage us. To deepen our faith in him.

But the faith can only be postponed, not avoided. After years of training, the men of fighting age are still slaves to fear. At the end of Numbers, they are scared of the foes in The Promised Land and refuse the fight. For this, God holds them accountable. It is no longer time to postpone; it is time for them to make a choice - courage or fear.

We can't outrun our fear. We cannot avoid difficult circumstances. We can postpone them, and sometimes God will delay for us. But we are called to stand our ground. Postponement is not an end; it is an opportunity to prepare for the inevitability of battle.

God brings the people of Israel along with patience. He does the same with us. But he does not keep us from courage, he empowers us to choose it.

Ponder Today: Boldness is not the absence of fear. In fact, fear is a necessary component of courage.

MARCH 16: DAY 4 - A COMPANION IN THE FIGHT

"Have I not commanded you? Be strong and courageous. Do not be afraid; do not be discouraged, for the Lord your God will be with you wherever you go." – Joshua 1:9

When the people of Israel are finally allowed to enter The Promised Land, under the new leadership of Joshua, the Lord reminds them (through an admonition to Joshua) of the call to courage.

The Lord is not saying this in some casual, general sense. He is reminding them of very specific circumstances, namely their refusal to fight when they heard the spies' report of the challenges they faced.

God had prepared them to trust Him. He had shown them mighty works. He had led them to victory in battle. But their spirit crumbled in fear. The first generation refused to fight.

God reminds the second generation of this failure and admonishes Joshua's generation not to make the same mistake.

The Promised Land is a place "flowing with milk and honey". But first they had to fight for it. Part of living in The Promised Land is having the courage to possess it.

God calls us to strive each and every day. He calls us to kindness in the face of rejection. He calls us to seek the best for others who will not return the favor. He calls us to love when the dominant culture is apathy. He calls us to set aside our own desires and seek the desires of the Spirit.

In other words, God calls us to fight against being self-centric. The first generation put material comfort above obedience. And the biggest loser was themselves.

This is why Jesus told us that the way to be lifted up is to lay down our lives. It takes great courage to make that kind of investment. There is a "promised land" flowing with blessings if we are willing to slay the giants of selfishness, take down the walled cities of self-rationalization, and conquer the passions that seek to enslave.

Ponder Today: Courage is a blessing in and of itself.

MARCH 17: DAY 5 - ON GUARD

"Be on your guard; stand firm in the faith; be courageous; be strong. Do everything in love." – 1 Corinthians 16:13-14

The only way for evil to triumph is by forfeit. If we fight, we win. Evil is not strong enough to defeat God, to destroy good. No matter the temporal results, the real battle (the fight for our character, the progressing of The Kingdom) will always be won as long as we stand and fight.

For this reason, it is apathy that is evil's best weapon. If we can be lulled into a complacent daze, we will give up on courage. We will lay down our faith and the enemy can destroy us before we are even aware we are in danger.

Paul implores us to be on guard. To be aware of the circumstances of the day and the opportunities they provide. To acknowledge the choices before us and the consequences for the community around us.

How do we stay alert? How do we keep aware? By doing "everything in love". Nothing alerts us to the value of this world, our lives, and the circumstances we face more than love. Love is worth fighting for. It helps us to see things for what they are worth. It helps fuel our courage. As Paul will say later, "love conquers all". It is the choicest weapon in our fight. Love keeps us on guard by showing us life for all it is worth.

In 1 Corinthians 13, Paul tells us that doing anything apart from love makes it worthless. Even to the point of saying that if we give ourselves to be a martyr for the faith, and have not love, it is of no profit.

The path to true riches, the greatest blessings, and the richest life comes through a relentless and courageous pursuit of love. That's worth fighting for.

Ponder Today: Complacency is the opposite of love.

This concludes our 5-day series on Courage.

MARCH 18: HE KNOWS BEST

"In the same way the Spirit also helps our weakness; for we do not know how to pray as we should, but the Spirit Himself intercedes for us with groanings too deep for words; and He who searches the hearts knows what the mind of the Spirit is, because He intercedes for the saints according to the will of God." – Romans 8:26-27

This verse tells us something we might be reluctant to admit to ourselves: when we ask God for things, we often have an inaccurate understanding of what we are asking for and why. We don't even know how to pray.

When we don't pray well, the Spirit prays on our behalf. The Spirit prays at a level of intimacy that transcends language and covers our inadequacy.

Although we need to continue striving, this verse also says we can relax. Not that we can stop trying to walk in faith and obedience. Rather, stop trying to perform to an imaginary standard we've made for ourselves. We have a loving Father who wants us to succeed. Our Heavenly Father cares for us as an earthly parent cares and feeds an infant whose understanding is only sufficient to cry.

It seems counter-intuitive to say that we need to check with God to see what we desire. But the author and designer of truth, the author of our story, is a trustworthy source for discovering the truth of who we are and what we ultimately desire. We, on the other hand, are actually not a trustworthy source of self-discovery. We're too good at self-deception.

The Bible urges us to listen to God and obey him. Seek God with all our hearts. These are prevalent commands in Scripture. But as we do so, we discover our imperfection. And the Spirit asks on our behalf. When we are so lost we don't know where to begin, the Spirit is on the job, advocating for us. We are called to love God with all that we have. Yet, when all we have falls inevitably short, we can rest assured – the love of God makes up the difference.

Ponder Today: God knows us and knows what we want better than we do ourselves.

MARCH 19: MORE ROOM THAN WE THINK

"Be strong and courageous. Do not be afraid or terrified because of them, for the Lord your God goes with you; he will never leave you nor forsake you." – Deuteronomy 31:6

Nothing can prepare us for when tragedy strikes. It sneaks up like a thief in the night. And while we cannot do anything to completely avoid tragedy, we are not destined to be destroyed by it. Our inability to prepare, to control, is only equaled by our ability to respond.

When tragedy strikes, it is the way in which we reply that most determines the effect. There is room for sorrow. Plenty of room. There is room for anger and confusion and dreariness. These are natural responses to tragedy. Necessary responses. We often try to gloss over the pain, thinking there is room for either acknowledgement OR healing.

The truth is we have the capacity for both.

Negative emotions are so weighty they seem to fill our whole atmosphere. But there is room for more. Room for hope. Room for learning. Room for perseverance. Room for intimacy. Room for forgiveness. Room for growth.

We are much stronger than we think.

We cannot prepare ourselves for tragedy. But in its wake, we can keep breathing. And we find, impossibly, that our hearts, our souls, and our minds expand, revealing a capacity bigger than we would have imagined ourselves capable of.

Ponder Today: Painful circumstances are something you face not something you are.

MARCH 20: TRUTH BY COMMITTEE

"And let us consider how we may spur one another on toward love and good deeds, not giving up meeting together, as some are in the habit of doing, but encouraging one another—and all the more as you see the Day approaching." – Hebrews 10:24-25

There are a lot of reasons community is important to vibrant living. A lot. We are a corporate people, made for relationships, for participation, for belonging. One of the most beautiful aspects of corporate living is the ability for the group to pursue truth together.

Each of us sees life from a specific angle. Like a ray of sunshine kissing the Earth. The degree at which we strike the surface of reality depends on the upbringing, experiences, and relationships that are unique to each of us.

Perception is the lens through which we view truth. All of us are looking at the same world, but the filters of our distinct lives create a prism of perspectives that see the truths of the world in different ways.

The value of community is we can measure these perspectives against one another. When we are exposed to a variety of these angles striking the Earth, we open ourselves up to a fuller version of the truth. Community invites us to see blind spots, discuss contradictions, and provide feedback.

In spite of what most of us imagine, we do not have to do this journey alone. The differences among us are too often cause for consternation and disgust. When we can accept each person's perspective as valuable, just as valued as our own, we allow ourselves the opportunity to be exposed to the unique angle through which they've seen and experienced the truth. Only in doing so are we capable of perceiving a truer perspective ourselves.

The truth is too big for any one of us. We need one another.

Ponder Today: Perception is the lens through which we view truth. Community is a bi-focal endeavor.

MARCH 21: RESPONSIBILITY, CONTROL, AND WHEN TO LET GO

"Each one should test their own actions. Then they can take pride in themselves alone, without comparing themselves to someone else, for each one should carry their own load." – Galatians 6:4-5

We humans have an uncanny ability. Somehow, we try to control too much and at the same time pass on what we do have responsibility over. We want to control others and avoid taking ownership for what we actually can control. We blame when our responsibilities aren't met while we try desperately to manipulate the stewardship of others.

Innately, we recognize there is some balance to be found. There are things out of our control and things within them. An improper treatment of the balance leads to victim mentality and codependency. But a healthy understanding allows us to make our choices with confidence and let go of the things that do not belong to us.

We can only control three things in this world. Our attitude/perspective, our choices, and whom we trust. That's it. Three things for just one person out of the billions on this planet.

By naming these three things and focusing our attention, we can free ourselves from wasting so much time trying to manipulate all of the factors, people, and circumstances that stubbornly refuse our efforts to control them.

In the same vein, taking ownership of these three things will feed the longing inside of us to participate and take meaningful action. It's not that we should do nothing. There is danger on that side of the spectrum too. We should do what we are meant to do. Nothing less and nothing more.

Ponder Today: Spend some time today considering what you can control and how you might focus there instead of elsewhere.

MARCH 22: WHO? ME?

"I do not understand what I do. For what I want to do I do not do, but what I hate I do. And if I do what I do not want to do, I agree that the law is good." – Romans 7:15-16

For some reason, the most difficult life to assess tends to be our own. It's strange. The person we should know the best. The one we spend the most time around. Yet, we seem to be the most elusive mystery in our own lives.

Maybe it is because we don't really know ourselves as well as we think we do. Maybe we do things for the wrong reasons. Perhaps we're just really good at lying to ourselves. The truth of our lives is so complicated, so big and weird. We are not sure what to make of it. Perhaps we are simply overwhelmed with data.

We make a lot of assumptions. Blindly accept a lot of our own biases. Truth is so difficult to determine within our own self because we assume it is already there. When we meet with others, it is easier to see their blind spots. Sometimes painfully easy. We see how their experiences have shaped their worldview. But somehow, we overlook our own influences. We're too close.

Self-perspective is the most important because it is the most difficult. Transforming our perception is a great challenge. There is more truth out there than we currently know. More self-awareness than we are currently walking in. We need something external to help give us feedback, point to our blind spots, and encourage the better parts of us. We cannot discover truth alone.

Ponder Today: Today, pray that God will show you the truth about who you are.

MARCH 23: PERSPECTIVE AS WORSHIP

"Job stood up and tore his robe in grief. Then he shaved his head and fell to the ground to worship." – Job 1:20

There is perhaps nothing more powerful than the ability to worship in the face of suffering. The entire book of Job is an ode to the power of worship. We often talk about Job as a book of perseverance. We talk about it as an example of faith. All of these are a byproduct of Job's commitment to worship.

In the face of unbearable tragedy, Job's reaction is praise. He finds a way to be thankful, to celebrate who God is. He grieves. He asks questions. He struggles. But he holds true to a perspective that does not waiver based on these circumstances, no matter how horrendous.

We think of perspective as a way we view the world, something simple and easy that can be adjusted, blown around by the wind. But perspective is the choice we make about what we accept as true.

This is an act of worship.

Declaring truth, clinging to it, and trusting in the journey it takes us on is a difficult enterprise. It is much easier to focus on "fixing" our circumstances. It is much simpler to fight for control, to demand our own way. The mystery of the Kingdom is difficult. Trusting God in all circumstances is challenging. Like Job, we have the ability to choose a perspective of thankfulness and adoration.

Ponder Today: Worship is a gratitude that transcends circumstances.

MARCH 24: THE FULL BENEFIT OF FAITH

"Now faith is the substance of things hoped for, the evidence of things not seen." – Hebrews 11:1

Faith is the gift that keeps on giving. This is a beautiful truth. But it is also a hard one for us to understand and a challenge for us to fully take advantage of. We like gifts that thrill us for the moment. Or practical ones we can store in the shed until we need it. We're unsure how to steward an ever-present gift.

What ends up happening is that the deep significance of faith follows us around as we casually ignore it or take it for granted or forget it altogether. It becomes "normal", routine. Faith starts to blend into the everyday setting of our lives and we can no longer tell if it is really even there. We put it on layaway, calling it forward only when a circumstance requires it.

Our choices unlock the full benefit of our faith. They are the physical manifestations of who we trust and how we view the world. As we make our decisions, the ramifications of faith are put into motion, reinforced, and habitualized.

If we are waiting on our faith to show itself, we are living with a false perception of how this whole thing works. Circumstance, situation, and setting are mostly external. Faith is an internal gift. It is the hope of our spirit. And if it is lying dormant inside of us, that is nothing less than a result of our choices. If we want to see it in action, there is no solution other than making the choice to do so.

Ponder Today: What choices can you make today to more fully awaken your faith?

MARCH 25: THE GOD OF THE PLAINS

"And whatever you do, whether in word or deed, do it all in the name of the Lord Jesus, giving thanks to God the Father through him." – Colossians 3:17

We spend most of our lives on the plains. The valley terrifies us. The mountain-top exhilarates. But the majority of our existence is right in between. The long road where you can see for miles. The mundane. The ordinary.

We put a lot of faith in the mountains. As if they hold some secret key that can unlock everything. The secrets of life. The mysteries solved. But the plains still come. The mysteries remain. The mundane perseveres.

We spend a lot of time afraid of the valleys. Fighting to protect ourselves from pain, we set a system in place to keep the sorrow from destroying us.

The result is that the plains get too often neglected. The everyday becomes an arena of apathy, season upon season of complacency. Waiting for what we long for and for what we fear. Missing where we are.

God is the god of the plains. He is looking over our every day. Our every choice. Every moment, every emotion, every thought, every step. It is a valuable opportunity to see the Presence of God in our lives. There is nothing more essential for the believer than seeing God as Divine in our every day. Only then may we perceive the worth of our choices and the innumerable ways He is communicating with us.

Ponder Today: What does it look like to worship God in the routine of everyday life?

MARCH 26: SUPER CHOICES

"I call heaven and earth to witness against you today, that I have set before you life and death, blessing and curse. Therefore choose life, that you and your offspring may live."
– Deuteronomy 31:19

We watch superhero movies with a twinge of envy. What could we do with super strength or lightning speed or the ability to read minds? The appeal of these movies is the powers of otherwise ordinary heroes and their ability to use them for good.

It is a perfect escape because most of us feel so helpless all the time. So puny. So weak. So outmatched when it comes to the evils of this world and the problems in our lives. Superhero movies indulge us with the impossible fantasy - that we might be capable enough to eliminate evil.

One thing the movies get wrong is that evil is not something that needs to be punched into submission. War is neither the only nor the most effective form of finding peace. We often perceive the world on a superficial level.

Most pain, however, is deeper than the surface. Evil is more serious than the superficial manifestations. And so is our power.

For each of us, our superpower is not in the physical realm. It is not as blunt or sexy as in the movies. Our power lies in our ability to choose. It is our choices that change things. We confront evil through the courage of our decision-making.

We dismiss the power of our choices because we have bought into the lie that we are not enough and need something else, something incredible, to strike a miracle into the world. Our choices are the miracle. Our ability follows us around every day.

Ponder Today: How are you going to use your superpower today?

MARCH 27: RICHES UNTOLD

"I will give you hidden treasures, riches stored in secret places, so that you may know that I am the Lord, the God of Israel, who summons you by name." – Isaiah 45:3

C.S. Lewis talks about how we miss the extravagance of existence because we are too content playing in the mud. Joy is in such high demand, so sorely sought, that when we find any semblance of it, we set up camp and gorge ourselves.

We settle too quickly. Even in our shame, we feel as though where we are might just be the best we're going to get. We don't want to change our diapers. We don't want to face the unknown, even if we are quite sure it is better.

We run the risk of missing an opportunity to experience greatness because we are frightened of our own suffering and want to settle for the tiny shadow of joy right in front of us.

God has so much in store for us. Riches untold. But it takes a little courage on our part to follow him through what might be cold and embarrassing circumstances to get there. Our brief glimpses of joy are not invalid, just inadequate. They are meant to be encouragement, to empower us forward. We make an idol out of them when we stop pursuing the full joy God has for us.

It seems like an enigma. A paradox. To be thankful for our small glimpses of joy but to keep looking for more. But all joys, big and small, exist to remind us that the Lord is God. And he has more, so much more for us.

Ponder Today: Our brief glimpses of joy are not invalid, just inadequate.

MARCH 28: HURTING AND HELPING OTHERS

"Bear one another's burdens, and so fulfill the law of Christ." – Galatians 6:2

When deep pain finds us, we often feel very alone. Pain runs so deep it has a way of isolating us. Especially in this culture of social media, where everyone's best foot is always forward. Individually and collectively, we avoid pain. And the experience of it, along with the obvious hurts, can make us feel like we are failing, uniquely struggling to cope with the deep sorrow of tragedy.

One of the shocking things about our tragedies is that it opens our eyes to others who are struggling with similar things. Most people aren't flying flags of prenatal loss. Most people aren't raising their hands to announce struggles with addiction. We hide our hurts.

Our hearts are uniquely qualified to ache for these numerous others who are experiencing the same tragedy we are. An amazing thing happens - we serve one another in our shared pain (with helpful advice, empathy, and the general feeling that we are not alone).

Our struggles are an opportunity. Not just for us to gain a true perspective. Not just for us to grow and to learn and to persevere. Our trials qualify us to love and serve others. They invite us into unique opportunities to care for a hurting world.

Ponder Today: How is your pain an opportunity to serve others who share in your struggle...and allow them the opportunity to serve you?

MARCH 29: A SHORT RIDE

"...for death is the destiny of everyone; the living should take this to heart." – Ecclesiastes 7:2

The Bible has a thousand ways of reminding us that "every man's life is but a breath". We are "a mist that appears for a little while and then vanishes". As much as we try to fight it off, delay it, and avoid it, death is coming for us all. Life is like a two-minute roller coaster ride – it spins and twirls, sinks, and rises. And it is over before you know it.

There are three distinct ways we can approach the "two-minute ride". One is to try to make it last as long as possible. That seems to be the main approach of most Americans. The goal of life is to prolong it. An approach destined to fail, eventually.

The second is to live in fear of death, for any number of reasons.

The third is to live in anticipation of our next season of life, and look at this season as a preparation for that season. If we look at it this way, choose this perspective, then it makes sense to live by faith, for that is the way we set up to have maximum joy in the next season of life.

Our temporary stay on this Earth is an incredible opportunity. A chance to love God and cherish one another. A chance to choose faith and be the person we were created to be. Life is an abundance of opportunities. At least until it isn't.

We can spend our lives fighting the inevitable or we can accept the design of human life and make the best of the time we are given.

Ponder Today: You have one precious life. How will you spend it today?

MARCH 30: THE MEANING OF WORK

"Whatever you do, work heartily, as for the Lord and not for men..." – Colossians 3:23

It is becoming more and more fashionable to talk about the meaning of life. Why are we here? What is our purpose? Many of us tackle these transcendent questions about our soul.

Ironically, this line of questioning has not transcended into our work. Although we spend roughly half of our adult lives working, we have not brought the question of purpose into the workforce.

The reason is simple. We view work as a means to an end. It provides money to make us secure or to buy things to make us happy. We work to earn a living so that we might live the life we want during weekends, vacations, and evenings.

Work is part of the plains, the terrain of life that encompasses the mundane, everyday. As such, it is a place where we will spend most of our time. And it is an opportunity to choose a perspective. We mistakenly associate "mundane" with boring. Routines are just as essential to happiness, fulfillment, and purpose as surprises. We cannot spend the bulk of our lives waiting for an explosion. A life of purpose includes a life of intentional work.

What we do is important. Purpose is not so easy to turn off and on as punching a time clock. If we aren't living with purpose at work, it will bleed into our family and our free time. If there is no purpose in the means, the end will be found wanting as well.

The plains are not a burden but an opportunity. We cannot pursue the meaning of life without considering the meaning of our work.

Ponder Today: How does your work provide meaning to your life?

MARCH 31: BUYING SNACKS

"The Lord is my Shepherd, I shall not want. He leads me to lie down in green pastures, He leads me beside still waters. He restores my soul." – Psalm 23:1

Standing in front of a candy or soda vending machine, nothing happens until we make a choice. Which choice to make? There are desirable ones. Tempting ones. Something that might taste good, might even make us feel satisfied for a while. But one thing is certain: whatever we choose will be temporary. We will thirst again. We will hunger again.

Too often, we treat God like a Cosmic Vending Machine. We expect to "push a button" and get the treats. We expect God to satisfy us the way we want to be satisfied. Thankfully, God doesn't operate that way. Like any good parent, He has our highest good in mind. God knows our deepest desires, the ones that extend beyond mere appetite. And it is those desires God seeks to satisfy. Desires like significance, freedom, belonging, and approval.

God is not a vending machine, He is a Shepherd. And like a good shepherd leading sheep to grass and water, God leads us to the places where we can gain this deep satisfaction. But like a sheep, we might have to cross terrain that is unfamiliar, scary, monotonous, or tempting.

We still have a choice, but not what vending machine lever to pull. Our pivotal choice is the perspective we choose on how to see God. Is He the Good Shepherd who has our best interest at heart? Or a genie in a bottle to call on when all else fails? The Bible invites us to walk a path that leads to the fulfillment of our own deepest desires. The path is to follow Jesus wherever He leads through all the terrains of life.

Ponder Today: Desiring God's gifts more than we desire God Himself is the believers most tempting form of idolatry.

APRIL 1: COMPETING PERSPECTIVES

"Now fear the Lord and serve him with all faithfulness. Throw away the gods your ancestors worshiped beyond the Euphrates River and in Egypt, and serve the Lord. But if serving the Lord seems undesirable to you, then choose for yourselves this day whom you will serve, whether the gods your ancestors served beyond the Euphrates, or the gods of the Amorites, in whose land you are living. But as for me and my household, we will serve the Lord." – Joshua 24:14-15

Every day, we face a myriad of choices. They flash and jump and shout in front of us, vying for the important result of our decision. With competing agendas, the hope is to influence us to choose a perspective that benefits the parties involved.

Like the cereal aisle in the grocery store, we can be overwhelmed by the competing choices presented. Product advertisements, peer pressure, institutional suggestion, the flesh, the Spirit, the powers of darkness – all have a lobbyist whispering into our ear.

We choose a perspective whether we realize we are doing so or not. In the chorus of voices, we allow one to rise to the top. It could be we have been choosing the same perspective for so long that we don't even recognize it as a choice. It just feels like the way things are.

But the choice rises anew every single day. There are new opportunities, moment by moment, to make a better choice. A truer choice. Each day is its own opportunity to choose a true perspective.

The perspective we choose is one of only three things we can control. The essence of self-awareness is to be aware of our choices and understanding of their consequences.

Ponder Today: What perspective are you choosing today?

APRIL 2: A SEASON OF HOPE

"And we boast in the hope of the glory of God. Not only so, but we also glory in our sufferings, because we know that suffering produces perseverance; perseverance, character; and character, hope. And hope does not put us to shame, because God's love has been poured out into our hearts through the Holy Spirit." – Romans 5:2-5

The roller coaster is a ride of anticipation. Hope boils as we wait in long, winding lines for the adventure of a two-minute ride. Once we're on the coaster, it starts with the slow ascent, the track clicking along the way. From the moment it reaches the apex and plummets down until the end of the ride, it is all about hope. The surprise joy of the next turn.

The same is true for our "two-minute ride" on this earth. Our lives are brief. James calls it a "wisp of vapor". Along the way, the twists and turns can be terrifying. The waits can be excruciating. The joys overwhelming.

No matter what is happening to us, it is shaping us for the next season. The next turn. The next rise or dip. It is preparing us for the next chapter. For our existence is eternal. And that eternity is shaped by what we do during this "wisp of vapor", our two-minute ride on Earth.

Somewhat ironically, this perspective of hope is the best way to enjoy our present. Life is infused with anticipation. Things are not just randomly happening to us. There is a story at play. The track is connected. Someway. Somehow. Living in the moment requires the paradox of hoping for what is to come. Such is the nature of imperfection.

Perspective is our opportunity to harness anticipation, to see beyond ourselves, and to be filled with that most important of human qualities – hope. Life is hard and sometimes the dips can be painful. Sometimes the speed freezes us. And sometimes the joy comes bursting out. All of it is life. All of it is a call to true perspective. All of it is hope.

Ponder Today: How are your choices in today setting you up for the life to come?

APRIL 3: THE MOUNTAIN MIRAGE

"The way of a sluggard is like a hedge of thorns, but the path of the upright is a level highway." – Proverbs 15:19

One of the greatest dangers on the mountaintop is the temptation toward complacency. We long for the heights because we imagine a certain comfort there, an ease. We falsely believe reaching the mountains means we won't have to struggle, or even work.

Laziness is not the anecdote to turmoil. The belief that apathy is any sort of cure is as false as it is rampant in the modern world.

The Lord does not promise us comfortable circumstances. He promises to be our comfort. The difference is massive. Apathy is a fool's goal. Meaning requires work and sacrifice and struggle. And since God wants the best for us, He does not desire for us to sit on a throne and sleep.

This is the danger of the mountaintop and the danger of living under the circumstances. When we believe an improved circumstance will bring us happiness, we will be disappointed. "More" is the pot at the end of the rainbow - you can chase it but you will never find it.

The God of comfort is with us throughout all terrains. He is not here to ease the circumstance or deliver us into apathy. He is there to be our comfort and provide the transformational peace of His Presence in every circumstance.

Ponder Today: There are times when we must choose between comfort and meaning.

APRIL 4: THE ARENA OF CIRCUMSTANCE

"You clothed me with skin and flesh, and knit me together with bones and sinews." – Job 10:11

Many scholars believe Job is the most ancient of Biblical texts. If this is true, the story of Job serves as a kind of preface to the rest of the text. It sets the stage, as it were, for creation and the prophets and the nation of Israel and the life/death/resurrection of Jesus Christ.

It seems a poetic possibility. Because Job addresses some fundamentally tough questions. Why does God allow bad things to happen? Why do the innocent suffer? What benefit is there in all this for humanity?

When reading Job, it is hard not to feel a cringe of familiarity when Satan is allowed to play a part in the circumstances. His allowance to alter Job's settings feels very close to home.

Perhaps the reason for all of this is that God wants to communicate in this preface that the battle for humanity will play out in the arena of circumstance. Satan and his dominions will be there, including the inclinations of the flesh. So will the Spirit. And the mysterious Creator of all things. But central casting in the drama is humanity. And the drama's tension is this question: "What choices will they make?"

It is a question as relevant for us as it was for Job. The world has been created. The board has been set and the players are in position. What choices will we make in the midst of the arena, in the world of opportunity set before us?

Ponder Today: Satan can meddle in circumstances but he cannot rob us of our ability to choose.

The following is a 4-day series on Romans 1:16-17:

APRIL 5: DAY 1 - THE FAMOUS BELIEVERS

"First, I thank my God through Jesus Christ for you all, that your faith is spoken of throughout the whole world." – Romans 1:8

For the next few days, we are going to explore the profound truths of Romans 1:16-17 and the verses surrounding it. In 16-17, Paul says "the power of God brings salvation". We often think about salvation as a one-off, binary, heaven-and-hell issue.

But what is interesting about Romans 1 is that Paul is writing to famous believers whose "faith is spoken of throughout the whole world" (he sets up 16-17 with these words in verse 8). They have already received the kind of salvation we often think of. "Salvation" simply means one thing is being delivered from something else. Like money being saved from being spent. A baseball game being saved from a loss. And there are lots of things we as humans need to be delivered from. From hell to heaven for sure, but that's just one of many.

What does a group of people whose faith is so great that it is being spoken of throughout the entire world need to be saved from?

Paul will give the answer throughout Romans: we need to be saved from ourselves. Our flesh. Our sin nature. From hypocrisy. From deception. From the chains of slavery and sin. We have been delivered from sin in Christ, but in order to experience that deliverance, we must walk daily by faith.

The opposite of living by faith is pride. Living by self. And it is self that we need to be saved from after we are already believers. That is what the Romans who are famous for their faith need to be rescued from. Self.

Where do we get the power for such a deliverance? From the resurrected power of Jesus. The power that delivers us from hell to heaven is the same power that can deliver us from self to walk in the footsteps of Jesus. We have this power. But in order to tap into that vast power, we must first "unplug" from our own.

Ponder Today: In what ways is God saving you from the flesh-centered parts of yourself?

APRIL 6: DAY 2 - PUFFED

"See, the enemy is puffed up; his desires are not upright— but the righteous person will live by his faithfulness." – Habakkuk 2:4

Habakkuk 2:4 is a verse that shows up many times in Scripture, including Romans, Hebrews and Galatians. In Romans 1:16-17, its closing phrase "the righteous will live by faith" is quoted.

Habakkuk tells us the opposite of righteousness is pride. Being "puffed up." The fruit of living faithfully is righteousness. Unrighteousness comes from being self-seeking, serving our appetites.

In context, this verse is God's answer to Habakkuk's question: "Why aren't you bringing justice, judging wickedness?" God answers "I am bringing the Babylonians to judge Israel by invading them." Habakkuk then says "I'm only a man, so please don't get mad at me for asking another question. But how is that justice? The Babylonians are even worse!" God answers "The righteous shall live by faith, and the proud does not". Then proceeds to say the Babylonians will get judged in due time as well.

The world-famous believers in Rome need to be delivered from pride. Pursuing the fulfillment of unhealthy desires. Even though believers have been made a new creation in Christ, we still have the perverse desires of the flesh. We need deliverance daily.

The flesh clamors to be in control. To make sure we get our share. To seek to satisfy unquenchable appetites. Our sinful nature is an expert at justifying actions, and rationalizing against the Spirit. But if we continue to follow this, the consequence is death. The death of freedom through addiction. The death of relationship through self-centeredness. The death of our gifts through lack of use.

Paul exhorts all believers to a better way. To a life lived in the power of the gospel of Jesus Christ. Christ came to deliver us not only from eternal judgement, but also from the power of sin to destroy. His indwelling resurrection power can be used today when we are willing to set aside self.

Ponder Today: Faithfulness to God breaks us of pride.

APRIL 7: DAY 3 - RIGHTEOUS HARMONY

"For I am not ashamed of the gospel, because it is the power of God that brings salvation to everyone who believes: first to the Jew, then to the Gentile. For in the gospel the righteousness of God is revealed—a righteousness that is by faith from first to last, just as it is written: 'The righteous will live by faith.'" – Romans 1:16-17

The Greek word for righteousness is "dikeaosune". It means "Harmony". Things working together toward a common purpose. It is about being a good steward of our individual gifts in a way that benefits the entire body to which we belong

The Bible often calls the church The Body of Christ. Righteousness is not just about doing our part but doing it in conjunction with others around us. And righteousness comes through walking by faith, faith that God's way is the right way to live. It is the goal at the beginning, middle and end of the Christian life: "from first to last."

Paul might have been writing a parallel to Plato's Republic. The type of reasoning his Roman audience would recognize. Plato and Paul both address the same question: "What is dikeaosune (justice/righteousness)?" And they come up with similar answers: Harmony.

Paul uses the metaphor of a body to illustrate the harmony of dikeaosune, with all the parts doing their job. Plato uses a city state, where everyone applies their gifts for the best interest of the body. But the big difference is the head. Paul's head is Jesus. Plato's is a group of capable people, the "Guardians".

But Paul is writing about the good news of the power of God. That is the true source of unity. The energy of harmony. Christ is both the reason for righteousness and the ability to achieve it. The head is what holds and directs the body. Paul's message is astonishing: through mutual trust in him we can live the righteousness God has called us to, because we have the resurrection power of Jesus. It is a spectacular assertion with the power to transform our lives. But it requires that we set aside false perspectives, and believe and act upon what is true.

Ponder Today: How can you promote harmony within yourself and your community today?

APRIL 8: DAY 4 - NOT ASHAMED

"For I am not ashamed of the gospel, because it is the power of God that brings salvation to everyone who believes: first to the Jew, then to the Gentile. For in the gospel the righteousness of God is revealed—a righteousness that is by faith from first to last, just as it is written: 'The righteous will live by faith.'" – Romans 1:16-17

In order to live a life of justice and harmony, to do our part in the Body of Christ, we need courage. It is a necessary characteristic to avoid pride and make the choices of uprightness.

The reason courage is so needed is because righteous living is counter-cultural. Culture is a consensus by any group of people about what behavior is honorable and what is shameful. We live in a superficial world, full of fake intentions and sinful longings. We celebrate arrogance. And shun uprightness. Our society shames true humility.

So, it takes courage to live a faithful life. We will face rejection. We will face ridicule and scorn.

These attempts of the culture to get us to conform are strong. But the power of God is infinitely stronger. This is more than just good news. The power of God delivers us from futility. The power of God brings hope and harmony, justice and uprightness. It is a stronger force than the culture of this world.

It is to the Truth we must answer in the end. If we are ashamed of the gospel, we will not reap its reward. We will close ourselves off from the benefits it offers. The world promises everything, but delivers nothing. The promises of the gospel are real. They bring power and life and deliver us from futility. But they require courageous faith to receive.

Ponder Today: How does your understanding of what is honorable and what is shameful measure up to the world's standards? To the gospel's?

This concludes our 4-day series on Romans 1:16-17.

APRIL 9: A NEW DAY

"The steadfast love of the LORD never ceases; his mercies never come to an end; they are new every morning; great is your faithfulness." – Lamentations 3:22-23

There is something significant about the start of a new day. The deck reshuffles. The cycle of life starts anew. We awaken to new opportunity.

Each day has its unique challenges and frustrations. But each new day is a fresh start, a chance to begin again. In a world so full of imperfection, new days are welcome occasions.

Each new day starts with beauty, with promise. The sunrise paints the sky as dawn ushers in another chance to live our best life.

The thing that is so beautiful about each morning is the consistency of God and His love for us. We do our best every day.

But many sunrises go unseen. We make mistakes. We fall short. And instead of making a fresh start, perhaps we despair. But God promises we can begin anew. His forgiveness is limitless.

What might be cause for shame and frustration has been redeemed for joy, peace and freedom. What is required is for us to request it, receive it, and embrace it.

Our hope is in the Lord. And although we may not make the best choices every day, He is there to steady us with His Grace and to motivate us with His Love. He is consistent every day. And every day he offers us a fresh opportunity to make new choices. Better choices. Redeeming choices.

The sunrise is a daily reminder that today is a day we can begin anew, and make choices rooted in the reality we can gain from seeing life from God's perspective, the perspective of a new dawn.

Ponder Today: Take a deep breath. Reset your countenance. Make the best of today.

APRIL 10: THE FEAR OF DEATH

"There is no fear in love. But perfect love drives out fear, because fear has to do with punishment. The one who fears is not made perfect in love." – 1 John 4:18

There are a few options for us during this brief yet meaningful existence on earth. And one of the most popular choices is fear. Particularly, the fear of death. Not knowing what happens next bleeds into a general concern for what is around every corner.

Our two-minute-ride will one day end. That much we cannot avoid. There is no evading death. It is a natural part of life. But the inevitability of death does not have to destroy us. It could, if we so choose, motivate us.

Although there is not a way to avoid death, there is a way to defeat it. Jesus Himself did not avoid death. He was not afraid of its inevitability. He did not flee from it. Neither did He submit and just let death have its way. Jesus confronted death with courage, intentionality, and purpose. He turned it on its heels by taking away its power.

The only way death wins is when it intercepts life. The inevitability of death can cripple us. It can birth apathy. Or it can remind us of the unique importance of this brief existence and the opportunity of today.

Death is prowling, looking to steal our choices. Hoping to lull us to sleep with whispers of fear. But today is a new opportunity. A new chance to live this brief life as best we can, while we can.

We spend so much time trying to avoid death rather than trying to overcome it. We overcome death by living life to its fullest. By taking away its power, refusing to allow fear to rule over us, define us, or disqualify us from the opportunity of today.

Ponder Today: What we fear is the flip-side of what we trust. If we fear death, it is because we trust comfort (avoiding pain) or our own immortality (pride). Death is not worthy of your trust or your fear.

APRIL 11: "WE'LL NEVER USE THIS"

"For in him all things were created: things in heaven and on earth, visible and invisible, whether thrones or powers or rulers or authorities; all things have been created through him and for him. He is before all things, and in him all things hold together." – Colossians 1:16-17

A common refrain from high school students goes something like this: "Why do I need to know algebra?! I'll never use this in real life." I would guess that most (if not every) parent and teacher have fielded this question.

The answer, of course, is that school is not just about math... or science or English. It is about teaching us how to learn, how to solve problems, how to think.

We spend a lot of time waiting for big, romantic moments. We're looking for lightning to strike. And we mope through our days in the meantime, thinking, if not saying, "what is the point of this?"

Everything in life matters. Everything. Whatever circumstance or setting we find ourselves in, it is an opportunity to choose. And the choices we make slowly mold our character.

Mundane life is not inherently mundane. We make the ordinary dull as a result of our perspective. We convince ourselves that because a thing has happened many times before, it is not exciting. Because we don't fully understand, it is useless.

There is value in all we experience. All we see. All we do. The only thing that voids this meaning is our unwillingness to see, to search. What we choose, even in the moments when we cannot see the end fruit of our choices, helps shape the life we are living.

Ponder Today: Our decisions not only affect the circumstances around us, they develop and reinforce patterns for how we choose, how we think, and what we perceive.

APRIL 12: AN INVITATION

"You unbelieving generation," Jesus replied, "how long shall I stay with you? How long shall I put up with you? Bring the boy to me." – Mark 9:19

We love Jesus' miracles. They wow and inspire us. They do everything a mountaintop experience should do – awaken something within us, provide a sense of the extraordinary, and motivate us.

The downside is that we often think of the miracles as the end, the result, the goal. Jesus' physical miracles are only the beginning. Just like every mountaintop experience, they are gifts meant to transform us. They are invitations to change, opportunities to prepare for the majority of life (the plains) and the most difficult phases of life (the valleys).

The physical miracles are an invitation. They call us to the table and provide a mysteriously beautiful taste of what the feast is all about. But it is not enough to take our invitation, to treasure it, to frame it and tell people about it. The invitation quickly becomes meaningless if we do not take advantage of the offer.

Jesus is offering relationship. He is offering to share a meal together. A feast! The mountain tops are just to get our attention, to hint at what might be possible if we commit to belief.

Sometimes you can hear Jesus' frustration in the midst of His miracles. In Mark 9, he is prepping for a miracle but is frustrated with the lack of belief.

The mountaintops are not the end. They are not the destination, or the goal. They are terrain for the journey, meant to equip us, to inspire us, to invite us. The real heart of the journey is a meal at the table. The truest miracle is the possibility of intimacy with the Lord, the opportunity to participate in His Kingdom.

Ponder Today: How has your last mountaintop experience transformed your day-to-day living?

APRIL 13: HAVE HIS WAY

"As the heavens are higher than the earth, so are my ways higher than your ways and my thoughts than your thoughts." – Isaiah 55:9

When we approach God solely as The Giver of gifts and the provider of solutions to our problems (as we perceive them), we are trying to turn Him into a Cosmic Vending Machine. We want Him to give us exactly what we ask for.

God does not need more of our perspective. We need more of His. When we aren't ignoring Him, we spend so much time trying to explain ourselves to God, making a pitch for the longings of our flesh to be fulfilled.

The problem is we do not really know what to ask for. We need to ask Him what we ought to ask for. God does not exist to hear from us and provide resources so we might have our way. He exists so we might hear from Him and be resourced to participate in His Way.

The issue is not that we ask too much of God (or even that we are asking Him for things). The issue is we are asking too little of Him. We are asking for our perspective to be validated through changed circumstances. But what if God wants to redeem our circumstances through changed perspective?

Scripture is full of pleas for us to die to our false perceptions, to see past our superficial desires, and to discover The Way, The Truth, and The Life.

Ponder Today: God does not need more of our perspective. We need more of His.

APRIL 14: NO RESCUE FROM CIRCUMSTANCE

"Shall we accept good from God, and not trouble?" – Job 2:10

The story of Job is not about God rescuing him from tragic circumstances. Tough as it may be to deal with, God authorized those awful circumstances. Job is not about ease of situation or salvation from setting. It is about the opportunity for humanity to make choices. Most particularly, choices about who to trust and how to choose a true perspective.

The circumstances we can see are the arena in which these choices play out. However, as we learn from Job there are also many circumstances we do not see. Angels are watching to see what we decide. We are allowed to see this in Job's story. Job had to decide who to trust and what perspective to choose even without knowing what he could not see.

We have all encountered difficulty and can resonate with confusion and pain. Difficult choices in the face of hard circumstances hits close to home. Like Job, we must choose before all is known. And we cannot wait around for the arena to change. The choice must be made now, today.

The circumstance of today is the setting, the people we interact with are the players. What remains are the choices before us. Our choices determine who we become. Our essence is intertwined with knowing and being known, and that takes place through daily decisions. Job shows us that choices rooted in faith create a lasting benefit not available in any other way or any other time. It is a benefit that befuddles angels and shakes the cosmos. It is a benefit we can secure when we live life above the circumstances.

Ponder Today: The circumstances of today are just the backdrop against which your choices must be made.

APRIL 15: UPS AND DOWNS

"Can you find out the deep things of God? Can you find out the limit of the Almighty?" – Job 11:7

Life is like a roller coaster. There are ups and downs. Twists and turns. Terror and glee. Although at times it feels it might last forever, it is truly over in the blink of an eye.

There is no way to fully prepare for what comes next. Part of the design of a roller coaster is the exhilaration of not being in control. Similarly, life is full of mystery and surprise.

The only thing we can do to prepare is to understand the journey we are on. An accurate perspective allows us to adapt to the changes, enjoy the best parts and endure the worst.

One twist leads to another. One dip sets up a rise. The whole of life is a beautiful journey. We did not design the ride. We cannot control its architecture. But we can make choices to control the perspective we will have along the way.

Observation is an avenue for preparation. It informs perception, setting the standard of awareness within us. We might not know exactly where we are or what's next, but we do know God is in all places, and is the designer of our "ride."

If we wrap our minds and hearts around the value of the ride, understanding the incredible investment God makes to teach and prepare us for a lasting joy, we are set free from getting lost in every loop. The terrains of life are opportunities to probe the infinite depths of God.

Ponder Today: Life is a brief, but epic, adventure.

APRIL 16: A FORK IN THE ROAD

"...strengthening the disciples and encouraging them to remain true to the faith. 'We must go through many hardships to enter the kingdom of God.'" – Acts 14:22

One of the effects of pain in our lives is that it interrupts our path. The impact of suffering causes a fork in the road. Our expectations and the reality we face crash together like two tectonic plates and it changes the terrain of our journey.

If our pain is not addressed properly, it can lead to dysfunction. This is one choice in the fork of the road. We can choose to make poor decisions in the wake of pain. We do this for a variety of reasons: trying to punish our pain, in rebellion to a life we felt betrayed by, through defensiveness, out of shame or embarrassment, or trying to short-circuit the pain by ignoring it - just to name a few. Pain feeds insatiably on blame. And we can choose ourselves down a path of recurring pain, inevitably spiraling into dysfunction.

The other choice, the alternate path, is to learn and grow. Just like in exercise, pain is how character strengthens. We should never go looking for pain, but we need to understand that the earthquake it causes is not meant to destroy us but to develop us. We can't stay on the path we were on before. A new development has caused a fork. And we must choose.

These choices are not easy. We had a straight path. We could see the horizon. And pain has shifted the journey. It's not that pain knocks us off course, it just realigns the track. Making the choice to journey toward true perspective is the subtle, yet powerful opportunity of life in the midst of pain.

Ponder Today: Are your choices compounding or redeeming pain?

APRIL 17: THE IN BETWEEN

"Then he went down to Nazareth with them and was obedient to them. But his mother treasured all these things in her heart. And Jesus grew in wisdom and stature, and in favor with God and man." – Luke 2:51-52

It is easy for us to forget that Jesus' ministry begins in earnest when he is well into adulthood. There is the account of his birth. Then the scene with him and his parents at the temple when he is twelve. And then these two little sentences at the end of Luke 2 that account for the majority of Jesus' life on this planet.

Before the fanfare. Before the miracles and the parables. Before disciples and death and resurrection. Jesus spent most of his life on the plains.

He does not enter the scene at the wedding at Cana out of a Divine vacuum. His ministry begins after years and years of growth. Wisdom. Stature. Faithfulness in the mundane.

Our best moments are the result of years and years of character development, healthy living, and growth. If it is so for Jesus, how much more so for us?

Life is not just the big moments with lots of lag time in between. Life is what happens in the in-between. It is the decisions we make on the plains that determine who we are.

When Jesus' ministry is marked by His baptism, His Father comments on the thirty years Jesus lived on the plains: "This is My Beloved Son, in Whom I am well pleased." The Father was immensely pleased that Jesus grew in wisdom and stature being faithful at work, home, and in the neighborhood.

Do not overlook the years of everyday life. It is an opportunity to grow in wisdom and stature. An opportunity to live a great life. An opportunity to please God by being faithful in the small things; small things that turn out to be big things.

Ponder Today: What do your everyday thoughts, actions, and attitudes reveal about your relationship with God?

APRIL 18: TEAM SUPER

"From him the whole body, joined and held together by every supporting ligament, grows and builds itself up in love, as each part does its work." – Ephesians 4:16

We often think of superheroes as lone wolves. Their true identities are secret. Their powers misunderstood by those around them. They live lives of extreme responsibility and loneliness. They are marked by angst and a heroism we associate with carrying the weight of the world by oneself.

Recent hero movies have shown another side of what it means to be super. Living in community. Movies like The Avengers and The Justice League (even The Incredibles) explore what it looks like for a team of supers to band together. To spread the responsibility and know one another.

This is a more accurate picture of life in the Kingdom of God. We are meant to be faith superheroes. But not alone. We are called to steward our own responsibilities. But our impact is magnified exponentially when used in tandem with other faith superheroes.

God's call on our lives is not just to employ the vast power He placed within us to serve others. It is also to partner with others who have diverse strengths. Unifying for the cause of goodness.

Life is a team sport. Discovering our super ability is just the beginning. The next step is to team up with others toward a common goal.

Ponder Today: Who is on your immediate team of superheroes and how are you serving The Kingdom of God together?

APRIL 19: A LACK OF UNDERSTANDING

"Listen carefully to what I say; let my words ring in your ears. Now that I have prepared my case, I know I will be vindicated."
– Job 13:17-18

When difficult circumstances find their way into our lives, we often react the way Job has in these verses. We petition for a trial. If God could just hear our case. If he would listen to our perspective on the matter...

It's a tempting course. Our perspective on justice is inevitably biased and we are very likely to begin with the case already decided in our favor. We believe if we could just explain our situation to God, he would surely change things.

But God does not need more of our perspective. We need more of His. Even if our evidence makes a certain amount of sense, as it does with Job, the Lord understands what is going on at a deeper level than we do. He eventually tells Job as much in the verbal perspective-overhaul that closes the book.

A secret to living above our circumstances is to understand that God knows where we are coming from. He understands. He knows what we think and what we want even better than we do.

The circumstances of life are not accusations. They are simply the arena in which we must make our choices.

Job's circumstances are tough. Really tough. So are many of ours. Like Job, we cannot wish away circumstances. And demanding our own verdict won't work out the way we hope.

But we can always know that our Creator is present with us to teach and guide us through every circumstance. It is natural to seek comfortable circumstances, but the Eternal Judge offers us a better deal: we can seek our comfort in Him.

Ponder Today: It is foolishness to try to push our perspective onto God when the whole point of life is to receive perspective from Him.

APRIL 20: PERCEIVE THE GOOD

"You intended to harm me, but God intended it for good to accomplish what is now being done..." – Genesis 50:20

Whether we realize it or not, we always choose a perspective. Choosing a perspective is like knocking over the first domino. It leads to more decisions that follow the effect of the same line of perceiving.

In Genesis 50, Joseph chooses to understand, forgive, and influence his brothers by acknowledging the deep truth of his story. His brothers decided to kill him out of jealousy, then relent and instead sell him into slavery. Joseph recognizes the reality that harm was intended. But Joseph chooses to see that God used this evil to save the family. Joseph chooses grace toward his brothers.

Too often perception is something that just happens to us. We choose a perspective without even knowing. That causes a false reality. We aren't able to distinguish between emotions and reality. We are quick to blame, to justify our anger, to defend our feeling. What is often lost in the midst is the reality that we are making choices.

If we want to live intentional, purpose-filled lives, we have to be aware of the choices we make concerning our perception of events, our own self, and the world at large. Like Joseph, we can choose a perspective that recognizes the good God intends.

Ponder Today: Pray that God will help you navigate and, if necessary, overcome your biases, predispositions, and sufferings to perceive Him more clearly.

APRIL 21: MORPHING TROUBLES

"Therefore we do not lose heart. Though outwardly we are wasting away, yet inwardly we are being renewed day by day. For our light and momentary troubles are achieving for us an eternal glory that far outweighs them all." – 2 Corinthians 4:16-17

There are unavoidable pains and avoidable ones. Too often we allow the latter to follow the former. We act out, blame, and reciprocate in order to either rationalize, punish or pacify the hurt.

Sometimes difficulty is unavoidable. Circumstances are tough or confusing due to no fault of our own. Our fallibility struggles to make sense of things. Certain aspects of life we cannot control.

We can also have avoidable pain. Ironically, avoidable pain often stems from attempts to circumvent unavoidable suffering. The paradoxical solution is to feel our pain honestly, for all it is worth. That can be a positive step toward discovering what is real and true.

In either case, avoidable or unavoidable, our pain is an opportunity. To learn. To grow. To see in new ways. To develop character and intimacy with God and others. When pain finds its way into our lives, we can make the choice to acknowledge it truthfully.

The pains of life can be pathways to blessing, if we have eyes to see. The momentary afflictions of this life can achieve an eternal benefit for us when we embrace the daily renewal offered by the resurrection power of Jesus residing within us.

Ponder Today: What can you do to break the cycle of avoidable suffering in your life and view pain as an opportunity to grow?

APRIL 22: SEEKING JUSTICE

"He has shown you, O mortal, what is good. And what does the Lord require of you? To act justly and to love mercy and to walk humbly with your God." – Micah 6:8

Faith superheroes, just like the heroes in comics and movies, are called to a purpose. They are tasked with upholding justice.

The responsibility of our power brings us to the question of justice and our part to play in upholding truth. Both individually and corporately, we have been given the gift of faith, not solely to feed the internal desires of our own flesh but to pursue the greatest good available to all of us. And to do it together.

Justice is much more than upholding the laws of the land. And it certainly is not about the arbitrary judgment and sentencing many comic book heroes employ.

Justice is harmony. It is each member of the body of Christ doing what it was made to do to the best of its ability. If the arm is acting like the leg or the toenail like the elbow, the body is out of harmony.

We were each created to do our part. With Christ as the head, we are a body designed to uphold the system by participating properly in the Kingdom of God. The justice we seek cries out in our bones. It is the harmony of a chorus all of creation sings together. Placing things in their proper place is the heart of justice.

Ponder Today: If justice means harmony, we begin the pursuit of just by playing our part - stewarding our own lives - as best we possibly can.

APRIL 23: DANCE

"In the land of Uz there lived a man whose name was Job. This man was blameless and upright; he feared God and shunned evil." – Job 1:1

The story of Job begins with Job's faithfulness. It ends with the faithfulness of God.

Everything in between is about this difficult, but beautiful dance between creature and Creator. Job and God are in this together. They are not adversaries, though at times it may feel that way.

Intimacy is not predicated on things going our way. Any married person can testify to that. It is a central theme to traditional vows. An intimate relationship is about personal togetherness.

Job and God experience this dance of togetherness throughout the difficult story of Job. His friends tempt him to abandon the relationship. They question its nature and the pain it causes. In the end, Job discovers the truth. He discovers oneness. And the Lord demonstrates His faithfulness to His servant.

Life is hard. Things rarely go the way we expect. Sadness and difficulty and disappointment are a ready part of each day.

Through it all, the Lord is faithful. And He calls us to be faithful. The reward is not an ease of circumstance but a relationship of intimacy. A unified relationship filled with communication, perseverance, and perspective.

We are dance partners with God, just like Job. We have the opportunity to explore the difficult challenge of intimacy alongside the Creator of the cosmos.

Ponder Today: God is not just Father and Judge; He is Groom. And we are His bride. May He have this dance?

APRIL 24: COMFORT AND CONTROL

"So do not fear, for I am with you; do not be dismayed, for I am your God. I will strengthen you and help you; I will uphold you with my righteous right hand." – Isaiah 41:10

Choosing a true perspective is not the same as the cultural fad of "positive thinking".

Positive thinking is just another way we try to control our circumstances, believing we can manifest the good and expel the negative by focusing on one and ignoring the other.

This is not pursuing truth. Some circumstances are hard and some are easy. Some we label good and some bad. Some we want to hold on to and some we long to cast aside. Adopting a true perspective is about acknowledging all circumstances as terrain for the journey.

The aim is that we might see above the circumstances into what God is doing. His comfort is not in eliminating negative circumstances but in his persistent presence. Comfort comes by adjusting our proximity to Him, not by controlling our proximity to specific circumstances.

In order to discover truth, we need to face the very real and very challenging reality of negative circumstances. Just like we need to evaluate positive ones. We cannot control life by obsessing over one kind of circumstance or another.

Our only hope is to find rest in him. In the presence of Jesus, our comfort abounds. No matter what is happening around us.

Ponder Today: You do not need comfortable and controllable circumstances in order to worship God.

APRIL 25: ISSUES OF TRUST

"No temptation has overtaken you that is not common to man. God is faithful, and he will not let you be tempted beyond your ability, but with the temptation he will also provide the way of escape, that you may be able to endure it." – 1 Corinthians 10:13

Choice is the great power and the great responsibility of each person. The most vital choice we make is about where we place our faith – the landing pad for our trust. There are a thousand choices we make every day that inform and reflect that vital decision.

When we choose to trust God, it is like knocking over the first domino. We can then move through the world, one foot in front of the other, one decision at a time, with effective purpose.

When, instead, we choose to trust our circumstances, it is like wrapping ourselves in a straightjacket. We are forfeiting our ability to choose. The circumstances choose on our behalf. We cast ourselves as the victim and can't seem to get the dominoes to line up right.

God is trustworthy. He remains faithful. He invented faithfulness. His patience guides and directs us, catching us when we fall. He protects us from being tempted beyond our ability.

Trusting in God prevents our hearts from drifting into oblivion. It frees us from the shackles of bondage, most often self-imposed. It gives us confidence to face whatever lies ahead.

Trust is a decision. And it allows us to decide.

The only way to break free of the straightjacket of trusting circumstances is to perceive God for who he is, put our trust in him, and perceive our circumstances for what they are worth – the arena for continued choices.

Ponder Today: There is no greater choice today than this: in whom will you place your trust?

APRIL 26: LITTLE BECOMES BIG

"And whoever gives one of these little ones only a cup of cold water in the name of a disciple, assuredly, I say to you, he shall by no means lose his reward." – Matthew 10:42

We often think a successful life of faith requires credentials or an extensive skill set. We compare ourselves with the accomplishments of others and feel inadequate.

Brother Lawrence became famous for discovering the depths of faith while performing ordinary tasks in the kitchen. His life of devotion was focused on the "little" things. The everyday, mundane tasks we so often take for granted or approach with annoyance.

God provides all we need to live a life of meaning, joy, service, and fulfillment even in the routines of life. Success does not come through comparison, but through faithfulness in small things. When viewed over a span of time, the accumulation of small tasks performed faithfully looms large.

Every day we face the decision to perceive God in our lives and in the world. Each sweep of the broom. Each line at the coffee shop or morning walk to the mailbox. Each step and each breath. They are all ripe with opportunity.

The key is not the perceived importance of the task, but our motive. Even a tiny thing like providing a cup of water for a "little one" is huge in God's eyes when it is done in the service of discipleship.

The plains are an arena, a terrain of life, in which this perspective can display who we are and who God is. We do not need a massive event or season. Daily activities performed in faithful service are great events in God's Kingdom.

Ponder Today: There is nothing bigger than the little things we do.

APRIL 27: BOASTING

"This is what the Lord says: 'Let not the wise boast of their wisdom or the strong boast of their strength or the rich boast of their riches, but let the one who boasts boast about this: that they have the understanding to know me, that I am the Lord, who exercises kindness, justice and righteousness on earth, for in these I delight,' declares the Lord." – Jeremiah 9:23-24

The mountaintops are dangerous terrain for one very specific reason. It can lead to misguided boasting.

We are created to celebrate. And we are created to participate. Boasting is where these two collide, the intersection of purpose and thankfulness. Although boasting gets a negative connotation, the idea in and of itself is not bad. We are made for it.

The reason boasting gets a bad rap is not because it is bad but because we do it badly. We boast of our strength, of our wealth, our achievements and our ability. We celebrate wrongly. Boasting that is not rooted in the truth looks bad. It is bad. It causes us to wrinkle our noses because it reeks of inaccuracy.

Our boasting belongs in our ability to know God. That he has made a way for us and we have reciprocated with understanding. This is not an excuse for exclusivity and arrogance. Those are different things – boasting perverted in yet another way.

The Lord wants us to celebrate. To cheer. But he wants to do it based on the truth, the accuracy of what is going on. Adopting a true perspective leads to true celebration. If we celebrate in falsity, we are fools. But to celebrate in the fullness of truth is a sign of the faithful.

Ponder Today: From where and to where is your boasting aimed?

APRIL 28: GRACE FOR DAYS

"For from his fullness we have all received, grace upon grace." – John 1:16

If we step into the pursuit of truth, we will find some things that make us uncomfortable. This can cause some of us to bail on the quest. Self-awareness leads to the inevitable truth that we are broken and wretched, miserable, blind, and in need.

Yet, a continued pursuit of truth allows us to find that we are also okay, accepted, loved, and adored. How is this so? How can these two realities live side by side?

The answer is one word: grace. We are okay not because we decide we are okay or because we choose to ignore the reality of our brokenness. We are okay because Jesus makes us okay in the sight of God. Through his life, death, and resurrection, he mends the brokenness. The fullness of Jesus fills in our gaps.

As heirs, sons and daughters of his family, we are now freed and empowered to pursue the experience of grace. Grace is not only the water in the desert for dying, imperfect beings. It is the fuel in the car. Once we are rescued, it is the thing that enables us to drive forward, to excel, to act according to the grace given us.

Ponder Today: Grace resolves the paradoxical truth of our brokenness and our worth.

APRIL 29: MOVED BY VISION

"Where there is no vision, the people perish." – Proverbs 29:18

The key motivator in life is purpose. Meaning. A goal to achieve. An end to accomplish. A proper vision propels us through life's challenges.

Without a vision to grab hold of, to tether us to the person God has made us to be, we will find ourselves tossed back and forth by the waves of circumstance. Every wind of teaching becomes our new source of motivation.

The reason adopting a true perspective is so important is because there is nothing more vital than knowing who we are, who God is, and how we are to think, act, and believe as a result. All of life is a pursuit of this end.

We find what we are looking for. And so many of us are unsure where to look. Like Peter hopping over the side of a boat, our vision is meant for Jesus. Our eyes are made to lock with His. We can do incredible things, live incredible lives, and overcome impossible circumstances with a proper vision in place.

Without this vision of life, we are destined to perish. We might be overwhelmed by circumstances, led astray by falsities, or lulled into an apathetic sleep.

But with the vision of true perspective, we can see the world through the eyes of God's wisdom. We can discover the purpose He has for us. We can participate in the fullness of meaning.

Ponder Today: What is your vision?

APRIL 30: HANDS IN THE AIR

"For the Spirit God gave us does not make us timid, but gives us power, love and self-discipline." – 2 Timothy 1:7

One of the greatest tests of fortitude for a youngster is putting one's hands in the air during a roller coaster. The handlebar in front of the seat is a safety net, a sense of control. Hold onto it and you might feel further from danger. Let go and you are inviting unnecessary risk into your ride.

There are a lot of things in the adult world that take the place of the metaphorical handlebar. Money. Sex. Power. It is there, right in front of us every day. Impossible to ignore. The world puts it in place to help us feel more comfortable. To give us a sense of control. And if the ride gets wild, we hold onto it with white knuckles.

If you ask a youngster why they love putting their hands in the air, they will likely say "it is more fun". How can this be the case? It's the same ride. And more dangerous, more unknown, more out of one's control! Yet there does seem to be an element of joy that accompanies the risk, an element of freedom that comes in letting go.

Our life on earth is a short ride. It comes with twists and turns, surprises and drops. Holding the handlebar won't change the ride. It won't prevent the twists, the turns or the drops. It might make us feel more in control but it won't fundamentally change the ride. If we adopt a true perspective, however, it can add to the fun.

Ponder Today: What would it look like to release your grip on the world-provided safety bar today?

MAY 1: MADE WHOLE

"Then he said to him, 'Rise and go; your faith has made you whole.'" – Luke 17:19

We have narrowed the word "miracle" to mean "something physical we are not used to seeing". We talk about the physical healings of Jesus as his miracles. What Jesus does to the physical elements of this world are only a shadow of the truly miraculous work of his life.

The primary focus of Jesus is the healing of souls. Physical miracles are a manifestation of his power – so that others might have a glimpse of what he is capable of and come to him for the main event.

When Jesus says "it is your faith that has made you whole", we often assume he is talking about cause and effect. You had faith so now your physical body is healed.

Perhaps he was saying something much deeper.

Jesus makes this statement about wholeness only to the leper who returned to thank him. The leper had already been physically healed, but he wanted the man behind the power. He returned to Jesus in gratitude. He recognized that the "mountaintop" of being physically healed wasn't a place to remain. His faith pursuit of Jesus led him to wholeness. Faith is not what leads to healing; faith is the healing.

No matter whether we are sick, battered or broken or whether we encounter a physical blessing, a faith pursuit of Jesus is the path to wholeness.

Ponder Today: You might be longing for a physical miracle while God is working on a spiritual one.

MAY 2: PAIN AND JOY

"Consider it pure joy, my brothers and sisters, whenever you face trials of many kinds, because you know that the testing of your faith produces perseverance. Let perseverance finish its work so that you may be mature and complete, not lacking anything." – James 1:2-4

Imagine you walk into a coffee shop and see a person buckled over at the waist, tears streaming down their face. Is this person experiencing extreme sorrow or immense joy?

There are definitely clues that might help you determine whether it is sorrow or joy. But isn't it strange that our body has the same responses in extreme cases of either? Closed eyes. Tears. Holding our stomach.

In a lot of ways, joy and pain are opposites. But if we take the perspective offered by James, they are more like cousins, descendants from the same family. The family of opportunity.

James 1 tells us we ought to see all trials as opportunities for our faith to be tested and proven, like gold or silver being refined. Although not pleasant, when we take this view, we can actually see all trials as related opportunities, terrains of our journey.

Suffering is a part of persevering in faith. A deep sense of hope, love, and joy that we have been gifted, the amazing opportunity to live by faith during the two-minute ride that is our life.

Of course, we should not go looking for pain. And we certainly should not create it for ourselves. But when it inevitably arrives, we have an opportunity to see its presence in the context of a true perspective that puts our lives on earth into a much greater context. Our current life is a once-in-an-existence opportunity to know God by faith. We can embrace joy in that, even during times of difficulty.

Ponder Today: Opportunities come in all shapes and sizes. Make the most of yours today.

MAY 3: LITTLE OFFERINGS

"Each of you should use whatever gift you have received to serve others, as faithful stewards of God's grace in its various forms." – 1 Peter 4:10

Sometimes we have a hard time naming what we are good at. It seems obvious to others. But for some reason, we have a hard time seeing the gifts that have been given to us.

Perhaps it is because we live in a culture of "more". And thus, we think we are always lacking. We see the talents of others and imagine we need to be a little more like them (even as others might do the same when looking at us).

Our own talents seem so...lame. Boring, inadequate, simple. What is closest to us becomes easy, familiar, and monotonous. And we spend days (weeks, years) trying to be who we aren't rather than making the most of who we are.

Each of us has gifts. Physical, intellectual, emotional, and spiritual. They have been endowed to us by our Creator. It is tempting to imagine our gifts as somehow lesser than the gifts of others. But there are no wasted gifts in God's design. The only wasted gift is the un-utilized one.

We have been equipped for every day. Each opportunity is uniquely suited with the person God has made us to be so that we might participate in His kingdom. We cannot be someone else. We cannot trade our gifts. But we can make the choice to adopt a true perspective surrounding our capacity and responsibility.

Ponder Today: What are your gifts? Have you been overlooking them lately?

MAY 4: LIGHT IN THE DARKNESS

"You are the light of the world. A town built on a hill cannot be hidden. Neither do people light a lamp and put it under a bowl. Instead they put it on its stand, and it gives light to everyone in the house. In the same way, let your light shine before others, that they may see your good deeds and glorify your Father in heaven." – Matthew 5:14-16

One of the reasons we are so mired in complacency is because we are waiting to be a majority. We hide or silence the hope within until we see a tipping point, the moment in time when it becomes popular or at least acceptable to be purveyors of truth.

A light shines in a dark room and it changes the atmosphere. The lamp itself takes up only a small volume, yet it transforms a vast space around it from dark to light.

Similarly, each of us takes up a very small part of the planet. But when we choose to follow Jesus' way, it has a disproportionate impact. It can change the environment. We are called to take our place and do our part.

How are we to do that? What is the difference between being light and dark? Doing good deeds to be approved by the Father, rather than by people.

And what does He want us to do? Help people that can't pay us back. Help the Samaritan in the road in front of us rather than stepping over him. Be kind to someone who can't "do anything" for us. Serve those who cannot repay (in this life). A little light transforms the darkness.

Ponder Today: What can you do to add a little light to the darkness today?

MAY 5: CONVERGING PATHS

"For you were called to freedom, brothers. Only do not use your freedom as an opportunity for the flesh, but through love serve one another. For the whole law is fulfilled in one word: "You shall love your neighbor as yourself." – Galatians 5:13-14

When Tony Stark finds himself dying in a cave, he is desperate for survival. And Iron Man is born. Through his experience he discovers the responsibility to serve others. And he is surprised when he discovers, through serving others, a purpose he had not previously known.

It is the same with us. In actuality, our greatest self-interest lies in serving others. Focusing externally is the best (and only) way to gain internal fulfillment.

We typically view pursuit of purpose as two diverging paths – serving self or serving others. This is correct in one sense. We cannot serve others if we use life's opportunities for indulging our flesh or our superficial passions. But there is another sense in which this is not the case. There is an "us" that is separate from the flesh. We are a new creation in Christ. He wants the best for the "new us". Jesus wants us to pursue our self-interest. But in order to do that we must know which "self" we are pursuing the best for.

This verse presumes we already love ourselves. Which means we were designed to pursue our self-interest.

Our flesh's view of "self-interest" leads to self-destruction. It leads to devouring and being devoured. A true perspective of ourselves lays the foundation for the pursuit of our true self-interest.

Ponder Today: What is truly best for you involves what is truly best for others.

MAY 6: QUICK LISTENER

"This you know, my beloved brethren. But everyone must be quick to hear, slow to speak and slow to anger; for the anger of man does not achieve the righteousness of God." – James 1:19-20

Listening is an important and often overlooked part of communication. We all tend to vie to be seen and heard. It's easy to forget that we need to fight to hear what others say and see what others see.

When we refuse to listen to others, we only see one way. Our way. And the odds are we do not have a monopoly on the truth. Even if our facts are right, there is something that is more important than just knowledge: loving someone by hearing them.

Not listening leads to wrath. Anger. We become incensed that our way is not being accepted. We raise our voices. We use manipulative tactics to try to turn an argument in our favor. If we refuse to listen, we become trapped in our own heads. Our insecurities feast and the chaos forms like a tornado. We try to displace it, blame the other for their inability to listen, or make everyone around us hurt in equal measure.

It is easy to see how this kind of anger does not produce the righteousness God desires. The Greek word translated "righteousness" includes the idea of community and harmony. Listening leads to harmony, anger does not.

If we cannot listen to others, it probably means we cannot listen to God either.

When we make the effort to listen, to slow down the fleshly impulses of pride, we can hear what others have to say. Not only hear what they say, but also to see what they are seeing. That opens the door for us to know God better.

Ponder Today: God is using others to speak truth to you just as He is using you to speak truth to others.

MAY 7: REQUEST AN AUDIENCE

"Rejoice in the Lord always; again I will say, rejoice. Let your reasonableness be known to everyone. The Lord is at hand; do not be anxious about anything, but in everything by prayer and supplication with thanksgiving let your requests be made known to God." – Philippians 4:4-6

God is available. It is a beautiful reality in the Kingdom of God. The Lord is at hand.

In the midst of Job's suffering, he requests an audience. Moses enters the temple. Even Jesus sought solitude to pray.

In our pursuit of truth, the beautiful reality of the Lord's proximity is omnipresent. We often try to figure out how to stop sin or overcome obstacles, how to understand our setting or solve our problems. We try to figure out how to read Scripture or be a good friend. In all our striving, we forget the one essential truth that serves all this and more: God is available.

We strive and strive without asking or praying. We search without seeking. With just a turn of perspective, a simple reminder of the simple Truth, our journey finds new breath. The God of the universe has seen fit to make Himself available to us.

Like Mary when Jesus visits her home or Jesus himself on the mountain, we have the amazing privilege to sit at the Lord's feet. Let's come and ask, to make our requests and our very selves known before God.

We will never discover a true perspective without encountering The Truth. He is available today.

Ponder Today: The Lord is in every place at every time. We do not need to invite Him in; we need to accept His invitation and transform the way we perceive.

MAY 8: WE

"But when they measure themselves by one another and compare themselves with one another, they are without understanding." – 2 Corinthians 10:12

We live in a world full of gifted people. Everywhere we go we are surrounded by the beauty and skill and passion of others.

Unfortunately, our responses to the greatness of others are not always healthy. Jealousy. Comparison. Envy. Wrath even. We sometimes feel as though the ability of others is a condemnation of our own ability. As soon as someone succeeds, we can feel stifled and limited, as if our own success is being subsequently pushed out of the way.

We forget that we are all in this together. We are made to work as a team. Counter-Intuitive as it seems, celebrating others actually allows us the opportunity to be ourselves. Others are great. We can't stop that (and shouldn't). The prison is not the ability of others but the perspective we adopt in response.

Unhealthy responses are a treadmill that waste our energy and keep us from progressing. An untrue perspective can poison us, creating unnecessary obstacles and paradigms that are unproductive.

Celebrating the greatness in others is part of participating in greatness. It frees us to be encouraged and contributive. It leads to understanding. Choosing to value others unleashes power to unlock the potential within ourselves. It is an act of love. Acting in love taps in to the unlimited power of the Spirit.

To see others as valuable is an opportunity to also look within and see how we might partner with the good going on in the world.

Ponder Today: The people around you are not enemies or competitors; they are partners (or potential partners) in God's grand design.

MAY 9: COUNTING LIFE

"Teach us to number our days, that we may gain a heart of wisdom." – Psalm 90:12

We count what matters. And what we count expresses what we value. We count time in our schedules and dollars in our bank account. Counting is a way of keeping track, a way of paying attention. A way of valuing.

What we don't count tends to drift to the back of our mind. What we are not tracking won't get our attention.

In the arena of life, we often spend time counting painful situations. We keep track of what hurts. Worse, we keep track of who hurt us. We also count the moments of euphoria, the highlight reel of life.

What we may not count often enough is everyday occurrences. During the mundane part of living, the routines of life, we can be lulled into a sense of complacency. During life on the plains, days and weeks and months slip by. Perhaps a high or a low arrives and awakens us to the seriousness and the joy of life like an alarm clock going off. But without that stimulus we tend to lose track of the amazing opportunities hidden in the plain sight of the every-day.

The Psalmist is asking for the wisdom to see every day as valuable. To count it. To name it. To see it for the opportunity it is worth. Life is as much what we do in the mundane times as what we do in the highs and lows. Maybe more so.

Ponder Today: We need to learn to count every day, every opportunity. Because they all matter.

MAY 10: OVERCOME

"Who is the one who overcomes the world but he who believes that Jesus is the Son of God?" – 1 John 5:5

We want to win. Something within us innately desires victory. We want to be on top. We want to succeed.

There are many different ways to look at winning. If the world is tricking us, it gets us to accept its definition of winning. But we can trick the world back. You might call this "beating them at their own game". We can do this by realizing that winning is overcoming the world itself.

And that happens through faith.

The Apostle John tells us that to overcome, we need to make our choices based on faith. Faith, belief, is the thing that defeats evil and the powers of 'the world'. Not faith in just anything. Faith that Jesus is the Son of God.

Who or what we believe is one of the three things we control. Living a life of choices that shout out, "Jesus is the Son of God", is the very essence of how we can win at life. That life will look like serving others in love, even when that love is rejected.

We don't need darkness to disappear to defeat it. Trials, pain, and challenges will always be a part of life. The key to overcoming is to adopt a true perspective.

Ponder Today: A true perspective comes through the opportunity of faith, over and above our circumstances.

MAY 11: ABIDING

"We are foreigners and strangers, as were all our ancestors. Our days on earth are like a shadow, and there is no abiding." – 1 Chronicles 29:15

There are many places in Scripture that talk about the brevity of life. One fascinating truth about time is that there is no abiding in time. Like Peter on the Mount of Transfiguration, we are often trying to plant ourselves in a moment of time. But time refuses. It marches on.

There is no abiding. One step leads to another. One season, one circumstance, one setting, bleeds into the next. That means there is also no abiding in circumstance.

We are transient beings. Time makes it inevitable. This world is not our home. We are carrying passports to another Kingdom. Time marches on, but truth remains.

The reason truth is so important is because the truth is stable. It is transcendent. It is eternal.

Circumstances are not our home. They are terrain in the passage of time on this earth. They provide a context for eternity but they cannot be eternal themselves.

A true perspective allows us to think of ourselves, our situations, and our choices in light of the eternity into which we will abide. Making choices in service to our circumstance is like trying to pitch a tent in a hurricane or on the moon. It has neither the gravity nor the patience to abide.

Ponder Today: Are you trying to anchor in things that are temporal?

MAY 12: PREPARED

"Beloved, do not be surprised at the fiery ordeal among you, which comes upon you for your testing, as though some strange thing were happening to you." – 1 Peter 4:12

Pain is inevitable in this world. Nothing will eradicate it from our lives. Not even faith. The flesh loves to whisper this lie: if everything were adequate, you would never have to feel pain.

If we believe this lie, pain can control us. It can make us believe it is a condemnation of who we are. But a true perspective is that pain brings opportunity. Hurt comes with powerful potential.

If the pain is self-induced, there is an opportunity for self-examination and positive change. Hope is not about believing things will always be easy but believing that there will always be a path to good.

A true perspective is not shocked by the existence of pain. Knowing that pain is part of the journey (and not letting it shock us when it arrives) helps us have a healthy view of ourselves, our world, and the choices we make before, during and after the pain.

Truth is not bridled by 'positive' circumstances. It does not need things to be a certain way. Truth celebrates our expectations but leaves room for the inevitable moment when reality does not match up. In those moments, we are granted the opportunity to grow, to extend, and to discover more of the truth than we previously grasped. And with the truth comes freedom, and a greater and more fulfilled life.

Ponder Today: Pain is a path to growth.

MAY 13: PRAYER AS CONVERSATION

"But He said, 'On the contrary, blessed are those who hear the word of God and observe it.'" – Luke 11:28

Our prayers often resemble giving a speech in a freshman year public-speaking class. We're trying to sound formal. Presenting the facts with rigidity. Presenting a petition we don't really believe in – fulfilling an assignment.

Prayer is designed to be communication between us and God. He invites us to his table for a meal, into his presence for a convorsation.
Listening is an essential part of conversing. Jesus implores us to hear his voice. How else will we obey? How else will we know who He is?

The spirit is calling out to us. It beckons us to discourse. There are times and places for the petitions, the speeches, the pleas. But what prayer is really about is a daily conversation, equal parts listening and speaking.

One challenge is that we don't really converse very well, even with one another. A lot of our conversation is just waiting until we can talk about ourselves. Always on standby with a story or a point that displays our knowledge and gets the conversation back into our favorite arena – ME.
Listening is the key to any conversation. Otherwise, it is just two entities giving self-aggrandizing soliloquies to one another.

Today is an opportunity to pray. To listen and hear the voice of God. To respond in kind. To interact with Divinity. There is no greater gift than the chance to be in communion with Jesus.

Ponder Today: If we do not listen to God, we are not truly conversing with Him.

MAY 14: A COVER UP

"Even in laughter the heart may be in pain, And the end of joy may be grief." – Proverbs 14:13

We all have an aversion to pain, and tend to avoid it. We may run from it, hide from it, or deny it. We desire a life of happiness, so, not surprisingly, we tend to view pain as an enemy from which we must flee.

One problem with this perspective is that today's pain often leads to tomorrow's joy. Child bearing inevitably leads to pains of many sorts, but it is also the source of happiness. Any loving relationship comes with a share of pain. The cost of avoiding pain can be the loss of our greatest joy.

Another source of pain comes from suppressing truth. Humans are naturally adept at pretending "everything is ok." Suppressing pain behind a mask unnecessarily perpetuates suffering.

We can be strategic about pain. We can avoid the self-inflicted kind, while embracing the unavoidable kind as an opportunity. When we encounter pain of any sort, the joy of the Lord provides a way out.

Joy and grief, pain and happiness, swirl around one another. It is a complicated dance we can either relish or dread. The key is to allow ourselves to acknowledge what is real. The truth of what is happening, even in pain and sorrow, is an advocate. It allows a perspective that moves us toward growth, intimacy, and peace.

Ponder Today: We avoid truth for the sake of comfort, but avoiding truth is more disastrous than encountering the reality of discomfort.

MAY 15: THE SOURCE OF GLORY

"How can you believe, when you receive glory from one another and you do not seek the glory that is from the one and only God?" – John 5:44

In our pursuit of purpose, joy, and peace, our biggest mistake is settling for small rewards when great rewards are available. Gaining glory from other people is fun and satisfying, for a while. Until it fades, is forgotten, or the same people who cheered us are now booing.

The approval of God is more constant and more significant than the approval of man. It is not only more desirable, it is lasting. It is permanent and dependable. The glory of man tricks us by providing a shot of adrenaline, like a junkie getting a high, before the bottom drops out.

The lasting glory that only God can give transcends joy. It persists even through sorrow and boredom, suffering and malaise, the valleys, and the plains. The glory of God is not dependent on the mountaintops.

When we pursue glory, purpose, joy, or peace, the key is to pursue it in its true form. The infusion of truth into our journey vaccinates us from the illusions of the world's fake substitutes.

God is the King of Glory. All other attempts to gain what only He can give are a mere shadow. They may hint at the glory of God, but they are fleeting phantoms.

The glory of God rises each day like the morning sun. It beams through our circumstances (even the tragic ones) like a warm opportunity. It brightens our surroundings, bringing an ineffable clarity to the choices we need to make.

Ponder Today: The key to vibrant living is pursuing glory, joy, and peace in their purest form.

MAY 16: KNOW YOUR ENEMY

"For our struggle is not against flesh and blood, but against the rulers, against the powers, against the world forces of this darkness, against the spiritual forces of wickedness in the heavenly places." – Ephesians 6:12

The Bible often uses the metaphor of life as a conflict, a battle, a war. Ephesians 6 encourages us to get up each morning and put on the spiritual armor of a Roman Centurion.

If we fight in a war, but can't tell the difference between our allies and enemies, we're in real trouble. This verse makes something crystal clear: people are not our enemies. Not a single human is our true enemy. Our real enemies are spiritual forces of wickedness. The true enemy of our souls promises us life but only delivers death.

When we choose to see the truth, we are more apt to make choices in alignment with what God wants for our lives. And the truth is that neither circumstances nor others are ever our root problem. Each human has that spark of Divinity within from having been made in His image. Our real enemy is the whispering manipulation of darkness (both internally and externally). The flesh wants us to turn on each other, and on ourselves.

But God provides a better way. When we properly name our enemy, we can fight effectively. The demons flee at Jesus' name. Believers have the power of the Spirit. We are in this together. God has provided us all the weapons we need. It is our choice to put them on. Our faith is our defense. Truth is our sword. If we resist, we win.

Ponder Today: Nothing derails a battle like confusing an ally with an enemy.

MAY 17: FUNNEL

"We know that all things work together for good to those who love God, to those who are called according to His purpose. For those whom He foreknew, He predestined to be conformed to the image of His Son..." – Romans 8:28-29

The circumstances of our life are a funnel. The slippery slopes and the rocky terrain propel us forward.

We tend to get lost among the rocks. As we slide along, experiencing "all the things" of life, we can't help but grab the jutting slopes of circumstance, trying to stop, to make sense of it all.

How can this slope lead to the same place as that rocky crag? How can pain and joy be instruments of the same purpose?

The Personhood of Christ is the thing we are catapulting toward. It is eternal. It is not swept away by the tides of time. He is unmoved, consistent, and true.

All of our circumstances are funneling us toward being conformed to the image of the Son. We can fight against it, close our eyes, or imagine a false alternative, but the truth is that all things are working together to direct our hearts toward the steadfast love of Christ.

As difficult circumstances arrive, our comfort and peace lie in this truth: that God holds all things in the palm of his hands. Each thing that comes into our lives is shaping us. Like a sculptor with his chisel, God is chipping away all that does not look like Jesus.

It is not peril into which we are being called, but love. If we pursue the truth and see our circumstances as a part of the funnel, a journey toward the truth and toward Christ, that will not explain everything along the way. But the destination will make sense of the journey.

Ponder Today: What if you viewed everything you have ever encountered or experienced as one more step closer to the heart of God?

MAY 18: RED LIGHT, GREEN LIGHT

"Throughout all their journeys whenever the cloud was taken up from over the tabernacle, the sons of Israel would set out; but if the cloud was not taken up, then they did not set out until the day when it was taken up." – Exodus 40:36-37

The Israelites in the wilderness must have had expectations of how the journey to the Promised Land would unfold. They likely would have been in a hurry to experience the joy of having their own land. To be clear of danger and feel secure.

It might have been quite frustrating for them to then have the LORD ask them to sit and wait.

Faith is an incredible calling on our lives. We are called to assess the evidence and make logical decisions. We are called to trust in the God of mystery when logic needs to be transcended. We are called to listen, and to follow.

One challenge of faith is to be asked to wait when we are ready to go, or to have to go when you are ready to wait.

When the gap between God's leading and expectations widens, faith becomes paramount. Whom (or what) do we trust? What do we lean on? Where do we place our belief, our hope?

The angels know what is at stake. They are like spectators watching a World Cup goal. They know the deep truth that sometimes eludes us: the presence of God is the truest Promised Land. That whether He is calling us to wait or to go, He is with us. And in this truth is the security we seek.

Ponder Today: Whether you are waiting or going, what is most important is that you are with God.

MAY 19: COURAGE IN DISAPPOINTMENT

"The wicked flee when no one is pursuing, but the righteous are bold as a lion." – Proverbs 28:1

Throughout life, we will face seasons of disappointment. Times when things do not go according to our plans. When events just don't make sense. When we are hurt, confused, or angry.

Courage is perseverance in the face of disappointment. It is continuing in the face of loss. Courage is rooted in faith - faith that pursuing the path Jesus lays out for us has rewards that go beyond mere circumstance. The boldness commanded in Scripture is an edict to continue sailing to the true north when it isn't easy - in the face of obstacles.

Courage is not the absence of pain. We can spend a good chunk of our time trying to avoid danger, confusion, or mystery. But pain will come.

Boldness does not eliminate our fears; it overcomes them. We can't show courage if all is going as we hope and expect. It is only during disappointment or danger of loss where we have the opportunity to be courageous.

There is no reason to feel ashamed for being afraid. Courage is naturally accompanied by fear. And being disappointed does not mean we failed. In fact, we succeed when we face down disappointment and continue striving.

Ponder Today: Boldness does not eliminate our fears; it overcomes them.

MAY 20: THE FULL JOURNEY

"You will make known to me the path of life; In Your presence is fullness of joy; In Your right hand there are pleasures forever." – Psalm 16:11

The path of life is a long and winding road. The terrains change, from valleys to plains to mountains. Seasons change. We never know what lies ahead. But we do know that as time marches on things will change. There is no planting. No way to pause the journey.

We live in the present. So understandably, our tendency is to focus our attention on the little plot we currently occupy. And when things are going well, when we occupy a mountaintop, we tend to try to freeze the journey.

But, just as the disciples weren't allowed to build dwellings on the Mount of Transfiguration, we are not meant to stay put, even in the best of circumstances. Tomorrow is always a new day. And the path of life continues.

A true perspective helps us to see the fullness of the journey we are on. It allows us to view living by faith as the true opportunity of this life. It shows us how to have comfort in God, rather than in circumstance. It shows us how to have joy, even when life's journey takes us off the mountaintop. Like the disciples, we can follow Jesus into the valley to minister to those in need without regret.

Because God's presence goes with us, He is manifest on every step of the path. No circumstance is constant enough to fill us. But the one who abides with us is eternal enough to fill our souls, and satisfy our deepest longings.

Ponder Today: In a world where everything changes, our hope and trust belongs to Him who is Eternal and transcends the tides and seasons.

MAY 21: THE WILDERNESS RIDE

"Then Moses led Israel from the Red Sea, and they went out into the wilderness of Shur; and they went three days in the wilderness and found no water." – Exodus 15:22

There is no metaphor more apt to describe the journey of Moses and the Israelites in the desert than a roller coaster ride. We may think of wandering through the desert and assume an aura of gloominess. And there is plenty of that.

But there are some really incredible highs as well. The Israelites were rescued from Egypt and a land of slavery. They were led by a pillar of fire while food appeared on the ground miraculously. They received the Ten Commandments and viewed manifestations of God coming from Mount Sinai.

Moses himself was used by God to part the Red Sea. The Bible says he was the most humble man in the entire earth. But he disobeyed God's command. For this, he was disqualified from entering the Promised Land.

The next generation entered the land of milk and honey. They possessed the inheritance that was their promised land. But the roller coaster continued. They had great victories when they were faithful and courageous, and great defeats when they were not.

In short, the general pattern is that the Israelites' could not endure the trial of success. The mountains led to valleys and plains, and back to mountains. The salvation of the Israelites was not found in the geography of the Promised Land. It is in obedience to God, available in the wilderness as well as the mountains. So it is with us.

Ponder Today: The riches of God are available in the wilderness and in the Promised Land.

MAY 22: WELL DONE

"His master said to him, 'Well done, good and faithful servant. You were faithful with a few things, I will put you in charge of many things; enter into the joy of your master.'" – Matthew 25:21

"Glory" in the Bible is a translation of the Greek word "doxa" and it means "the essence of something being clearly displayed and observed." Our great privilege is to exhibit God's truth through the way we live, in a way that it is clearly seen by others. We are promised that if we show God's true essence through our lives, God will grant us the glory of his approval.

The greatest end of our life will be to sit with Jesus as he reviews our life and continually hear "This was very well done." That is a glory that will never fade. Life is an opportunity where we can display to others the essence of God by the way we live. The choices we make. The perspective we choose.

We participate in glory when we make decisions that manifest the goodness of God.

The whole process is modeled in this parable in Matthew. The voice of the master speaks and makes clear the connection between the master and the servant, the joy of approval, and the blessing for continued action.

In all our striving, this is what we truly desire. We all long to hear "well done" from an earthly father. Even more, each of us, is longing for the approval of the Heavenly Father. We want to be counted among His faithful servants. We want to be entrusted with His vision. We want to participate in His kingdom.

Each day begins anew, and is an opportunity to walk in obedience, and hear "well done."

Ponder Today: Our need for approval is meant for God and can only be fulfilled by God.

MAY 23: A SHEEP WITH EARS

"My sheep hear My voice, and I know them, and they follow Me." – John 10:27

There is no better way to discover truth than listening to God. When we listen, we quiet what we already know to make room for what we might discover.

Humans are crowded with wickedness. The flesh is not a candidate for reform. It needs to be weeded out. Replaced. We do this by planting the word of God in our hearts, minds, and souls.

Listening is a risk. It asks us to step away from ourselves, to open up to the possibility of others. We risk our wickedness being exposed.

But too much of life is trying to cover up our weaknesses rather than naming it and replacing it. There is wickedness in each of us. When we expose and name the rot within, we have a chance to change. An opportunity to make different choices.

The Bible tells us the first step in listening to God is to listen to one another. It teaches us to set self aside. When we set self aside, we are then able to truly listen to God.

Listening to God helps expose our blind spots. It shines a light on the parts of us that do not look like God. That gives us the opportunity to replace counterproductive thoughts and behaviors with those that look more like Jesus.

Ponder Today: Learning to listen to others is the gateway to learning how to listen to God.

MAY 24: THE ART OF WAITING

"Rest in the Lord and wait patiently for Him." – Psalm 37:7

Scripture admonishes us to wait on God. It goes against most every aspect of our current culture. If cell coverage causes our phones to take ten seconds to load, we feel terribly inconvenienced. We can't stand to have to wait [to watch cat videos].

We want to move, shake, get things done, take control, and achieve. The last thing we want to do is wait.

Yet waiting is a beautiful opportunity. It is commanded. It is a chance to pause, to worship, to trust, to exercise faith, the very same faith that fascinates angels.

Waiting allows us to confront and embrace our lack of control. It allows us to reflect on what is true, and real. It allows us to reassess our role, and God's role, and make sure we are not sitting in the wrong chair, and trying to do God's work of being the judge of the world.

Righteous waiting is an art. To be expectant yet involved; both hopeful and participative. The power and love of God is our strength, and waiting is an act of obedience.

A true perspective helps us toe the line between avoidance and patience. It can be difficult to discern between times when good stewardship means taking responsibility to act and times when good stewardship means waiting patiently for God to act. It can be difficult to move. And difficult to wait.

Waiting is not apathy. The subject of apathy is self. We are told to wait on a person, to wait on the Lord.

Ponder Today: It is often holy and wise to press into waiting rather than fight against it.

MAY 25: WHAT DO WE REALLY WANT?

"Trust in the LORD and do good; Dwell in the land and cultivate faithfulness. Delight yourself in the LORD; And He will give you the desires of your heart." – Psalm 37:3-4

The Lord desires to give us all the gold we want. He longs to shower gifts and blessings and goodness upon us. But we have to recognize the difference between blessing and burdens.

When we seek money, power, and fame from the world, we are not seeking lasting treasure but trivialities that will be eaten by moths or rust away. That satisfies a desire, but not our deepest desire.

The infinite gold and great wealth that Jesus offers is considered foolishness by the world, but is actually a true and lasting wealth that will not perish. This is what our hearts truly long for.

We sense this and perceive it in some deep place within us. Yet because we confuse our desires, this verse is perhaps one of the most misused and misquoted verses in Scripture. Psalm 37 is not about God giving us the desires of our flesh. These desires are a mere shadow of the things for which we truly long. The desires of our flesh are not our purest desires. The spirit is the seat of our deepest longing, and the place our true treasure is stored.

What we really value is spiritual treasure like peace, belonging, and acceptance. The issue is not that God doesn't give us the things we ask for; the issue is that we don't really know what we want.

If we are distracted by the perversions, the shadows that we cannot name, we can lose sight of what we truly desire. How do we discover what we really want? Trust in the Lord. Delight ourselves in him.

He will show us the source of our longings, the deepest desires of our hearts. The water he gives will cause us to thirst no more.

Ponder Today: Our problem is not that God withholds what we desire but that we do not know what our heart truly longs for.

MAY 26: OUT OF THE STORM

"Then the Lord spoke to Job out of the storm. He said: 'Who is this that obscures my plans with words without knowledge? Brace yourself like a man; I will question you, and you shall answer me.'" – Job 38:1-3

After all Job has been through, the Lord finally speaks. And he speaks "out of the storm".

For any of us who are hurting, who are experiencing loss or confusion or pain, we can relate to the story of Job. We can relate to unhelpful solutions from well-meaning friends trying to solve our problem. We can relate to uncertainty and angst.

The hope of pain is that if we can relate to Job's circumstances and his suffering, perhaps we can relate to his hope.

In the midst of the storm, the Lord speaks. He calls down to us. Even if it produces conviction. Even if it is rhetorical. Even if it adds to the confusion. Even in the midst of all these things, there is comfort in the Lord's voice. Truth in the turmoil. Stability in the storm.

Like an outstanding coach that is hardest on his best player, God uses difficulty to call Job to a higher place. This interaction with God does not make Job happy, or comfortable. This interaction with God causes Job to see God as he has never seen him before. Through immense difficulty, a door opens to the greatest of treasures.

Job-like circumstances show up every day. We are threatened with pain and apathy and falsity. But in the midst of the storm, the Lord speaks.

Ponder Today: If a storm is raging around you, perk up your ears. Somewhere in the midst of it, the Lord is speaking.

MAY 27: EXILED

"For I know the thoughts that I think toward you, says the Lord, thoughts of peace and not of evil, to give you a future and a hope." – Jeremiah 29:11

There is a lot behind this verse that might not be apparent when you see it on a bumper sticker, tee shirt, or plaque. A few verses earlier, God tells his people they are about to be exiled from their home. They will return, but while they are in Babylon God tells them to:

"Build houses and dwell in them; plant gardens and eat their fruit... And seek the peace of the city where I have caused you to be carried away captive" (verses 5-7).

The unique vocation of humanity does not get washed out in the receding tide of The Fall. Humanity has been exiled from the Garden. The Garden is our true home. The Garden is a physical place with physical manifestations of this vocation. But the Garden is much more than that.

The Garden embodies the relationship God intended to have with humanity. And we are commanded to cultivate that Garden. During this period of exile from the physical Garden, our task remains. We are to dwell on this earth as the exiles of Israel lived. God instructed them to build houses and dwell in Babylon as though it was their home while awaiting their promised return to their true home in the Promised Land.

While we live in exile in this fallen world, we are to make it our home. We are to build houses and establish relationships. Since we are exiled, we must do this by faith. And we are to seek the peace of our current world. The best way to seek peace is to live our lives in harmony with the original intentions of the Garden, because we carry its vocation with us.

Ponder Today: We are all exiles, trying to retain a semblance of home.

MAY 28: TRAINED SENSES

"For everyone who partakes only of milk is not accustomed to the word of righteousness, for he is an infant. But solid food is for the mature, who because of practice have their senses trained to discern good and evil." – Hebrews 5:13-14

It is easy to think of mountaintop experiences as the height of spiritual maturity because of how it feels. But feelings don't determine maturity. A child getting a piece of candy is happy for the moment, but that doesn't make them mature. Feeling mature doesn't make us mature.

True spiritual maturity is the ability to discern good and evil. To choose between the flesh and the spirit. True spiritual maturity stems from the capacity to choose a perspective that is true.

Maturity takes practice. Learning to choose a true perspective doesn't happen overnight. Like a high-performance athlete training their sport, studying the word of God and learning to apply it takes time and effort. Spiritual maturity is a product of the hard work of daily choices made to pursue what is true.

Mountaintop spiritual experiences, in all their splendor, are more likely to be encouragement than equipping. They can be more like milk than meat. We can tell from the Apostle Peter's writings that he never forgot what he saw and learned on the mountain. But it was the application of that knowledge on the plains and valleys that cemented his legacy as a great man of faith.

The mountaintops can be so encouraging that it can be difficult to come down. But no matter what terrain of life we find ourselves in, God wants us to grow and mature. And we do that by learning to apply His Word to train our perspective to see what is true and make choices out of faithful obedience.

Ponder Today: The heights of experience are not a finish line. They are a checkpoint, an equipping station.

MAY 29: ACTIVE WAITING

"Wait on the LORD: be of good courage, and he shall strengthen thine heart: wait, I say, on the LORD." – Psalm 27:14

The Hebrew word "quavah" is used here as "wait". And it has a root that means "bind together" or "gather". It has the sense of collecting oneself. This waiting is not apathy, or even inactivity, but part of the journey of proper action.

It is like a running back who takes slight steps, or sometimes none at all, as he waits for a hole to open up in the line. He is waiting, but not inactive. Sometimes he will just pump his feet, running in place. He is gathering himself. Collecting his energy. Doing so with vision, with purpose.

Our society tends to hate waiting. When the Internet takes five seconds to load we get irritated. When we want something, we want it now. But of course, getting it now only makes us want something else. Perhaps we need a little more waiting to help remind us that happiness is not in our circumstances, but in our choices. If we spent more time shuffling our feet until we find the right hole to run through, perhaps we would gain a lot more ground toward our destination.

Waiting helps us be deliberate rather than reactive. If we bind the truths of our circumstances with the truth of God's Kingdom, we can make choices to take maximum advantage of the opportunities we encounter.

Ponder Today: Sometimes waiting is the proper action - patience is a fruit of the Spirit.

MAY 30: PLACED IN THE GARDEN

"Then the Lord God took the man and put him into the garden of Eden to cultivate it and keep it." – Genesis 2:15

The Lord has placed us in the world. He created the parameter of time and the opportunity of community. He created the concept of relationship and the beauty of nature. The swirl of emotions, the depth of thought, and imagination are intentional tools of His making. He made the process of choice and consequence as well as the capacity for belief.

This is our arena. Even though mankind was cast out of Eden, we still live in a world of God's creation. A shadow of the garden, but a manifestation of the Lord's will nonetheless.

We live in exile, but we are still designed to cultivate. All of his creation is ripe for cultivation. We have the opportunity to cultivate the garden within ourselves. We can cultivate relationships with other humans. And we can cultivate the earth as stewards of God's creation.

The soil in which we have opportunity to cultivate is the circumstances we encounter each day. We can't cultivate in soil we don't have, only the soil we do have.

It is ours to sow, and God's to grow. When we do the job of cultivating unto the Lord, we are doing what God made us to do. We are being his instrument.

The world is a beautiful garden. But gardening takes work and time. The calling to cultivate is a calling to utilize our circumstances as tools for the Kingdom. And trust God with the reaping.

Ponder Today: What are you doing today to cultivate The Kingdom of Heaven?

MAY 31: NEW LIPS

"Woe is me, for I am ruined! Because I am a man of unclean lips, And I live among a people of unclean lips; For my eyes have seen the King, the Lord of hosts." – Isaiah 6:5

Have you ever wondered what it would be like to enter the presence of Jesus? Isaiah got to do that very thing. Isaiah is a righteous man, but this is what happens to Isaiah: He hears the heavens declaring the holiness of God and it exposes a truth about him he had not previously seen. He sees the beauty of God and how he stands in comparison. He discovers he needs a lip replacement.

This is just the beginning of Isaiah's journey. He discovers more truth, adopting a perspective and making choices of obedience that help him grow in faith. All of this requires change.

This is the "problem" of seeing ourselves truly - it might mean we need to change. But the right perspective is the one Isaiah chose - he gladly sought cleansing. If we are dirty, why would we not want to be clean?

Knowing the truth is a blessing. Truth sets us free. Isaiah was set free from unclean lips. One reason we might avoid truth is because we don't want to change. But God implores us to be transformed by the renewing of our minds.

By listening to God, we receive a great gift. We gain perspective. New avenues of truth are exposed. We learn how to be cleansed. We receive instruction on how to set aside "me" and walk in newness of life.

Ponder Today: The reason we hesitate listening to God is because it often requires change.

JUNE 1: BETWEEN YOU AND ME

"So Peter seeing him said to Jesus, 'Lord, and what about this man?' Jesus said to him, 'If I want him to remain until I come, what is that to you? You follow Me!'" – John 21:21-22

When angels gather to watch over the earth, they look with anticipation to see the choices we make in faith. They nudge each other and point down at us as we make judgments without benefit of tangible evidence, trusting in a God we cannot directly see or touch.

Down here on earth, we find the choices difficult. It is hard to make decisions based on faith. It is tempting to direct our attention elsewhere. Rather than focusing on making the best choices, we often prefer to pursue distractions. One of our favorite distractions is to focus on the choices to be made by others. Point to their story instead of ours. We prefer to see and judge how they are doing, rather than focus on how we are doing.

We are not meant to know the journey of another. Each person's story is uniquely precious to them and to God.

Our own faith is enough for us to work out. Our own obedience is enough of a task to concern our hearts and minds. The story of others is theirs. But our story is ours. And Jesus invites us to walk in the obedience and faith within our journeys he has graciously gifted us. We could easily get lost in watching others. But the command of God is clear: "Follow me!"

Ponder Today: The quickest way to a transformed life is to clarify within oneself what is mine to steward and what is not.

JUNE 2: SHREWD

"Behold, I send you out as sheep in the midst of wolves; so be shrewd as serpents and innocent as doves." – Matthew 10:16

God calls us to be as shrewd as the world in the way we fight darkness, but to be completely innocent of its evil. We are called to fight a better way, for a better cause, with a better source of power.

All evil is a perversion of good. There is nothing evil creates. All evil is a disruption or a perversion. The prince of darkness twists and perverts what God created for our good into that which harms. The enemy steals, kills, and destroys. He does not create.

Our challenge is to use the resources God has given us without perverting them. As tempting as it may be to pursue shortcuts, relying upon our own power, and our own sense of control, we must be diligent to pursue the better way. God's way. But God's way includes being a shrewd warrior.

Jesus, the Lamb of the World, was killed by his enemies. But Jesus secured the true victory. Our tempered shrewdness is a better method of fighting for a better cause, in obedience to the best source of power in the universe. Our victory is sure. What victory looks like is up to God.

We cannot back down from a fight with darkness. The sword of the spirit is truth, and needs to be wielded every day. But neither can we let the fight dictate our identity, and twist us into being of the world. We fight out of who we are in Christ, and who sent us forth. It is Jesus who sent us out to be shrewd sheep in a world with many wolves, equipped, empowered, and defended.

Ponder Today: The Gospel is not just a call to fight, but a call to reimagine what fighting looks like.

The following is a 7-day series on James Chapter 1:

JUNE 3: DAY - ORE TO GOLD

"And let endurance have its perfect result, so that you may be mature and complete, lacking in nothing." – James 1:4

The worldly perspective about winning is clear. We measure winning by what we accumulate. Fame. Money. Followers. Our success is measured by the physical treasures we put in our storage sheds.

On the other hand, the Biblical view of winning is not about what we can accumulate but who we are. Character. We win life by being, not by getting. True victory is about learning to encounter our trials with character.

Only by taking this view of success can we celebrate struggle. Like ore refined by pressure, we become who we are by facing our trials with courage and a proper perspective. Coal is turned into diamonds by the stress put upon it. And the same is true for us.

If we take the earthly view of success, it makes sense to avoid pain as a priority. What accumulation is there in suffering? What tangible prize do we get from our sorrow? In a strictly practical sense, our suffering has no market value. It is a setback. Endurance is an obstacle to be diminished rather than an opportunity to grow.

But in God's economy, suffering is a path. Trials are a testing ground, an arena to develop and exercise our character.

James tells us to "consider it joy" when we encounter trials because winning requires a test. James presents life as a championship match. An opportunity to overcome self-seeking and choose instead to walk with the Lord. To endure and persevere and overcome when we encounter trials.

We are ore being refined into gold. We are not pirates gathering treasure. We are people becoming treasure. Pursuing the character and perspective of God. The opportunity presented is for us to become complete, to be all God created us to be. Material wealth ends up in a landfill, but spiritual wealth is a gold that endures.

Ponder Today: Success in life is about being; it is not about getting

JUNE 4: DAY 2 - ALL CIRCUMSTANCES ARE TRIALS

"But the brother of humble circumstances is to glory in his high position; and the rich man is to glory in his humiliation, because like flowering grass he will pass away." – James 1:9-10

When we think of the word "trial", we often think of a very specific type of circumstance. One that is hard, that we don't like. Something negative we have to overcome. But James says all circumstances are trials.

These verses reference both the trial of want and the trial of plenty. We are familiar with the trial of want. The struggles with feeling like something is missing. The pain of loss; even the malaise of the mundane. When in the valley or on the plain, it is important to realize the perspective that "This is an exalted opportunity" to be faithful and depend on God. To endure and win the crown of life.

The mountaintops of life are traditionally viewed less as a trial and more as a triumph. We think winning at life is ascending the mountains. But winning is about who we are not where we are. And mountaintops have dangers of their own, a kind of trial to endure. On the mountaintop, we have to choose to adopt a different perspective. "This is only fleeting. It won't last. Enjoy, but don't depend on this. Depend on God." This is difficult. Our senses tell us we are winning. We must have the eyes of faith to believe "This is fleeting, do not trust it." If we make an idol of prosperous circumstances, we have lost our way just as effectively as if we cower under difficult circumstances.

All circumstances are trials. Tests. Championship games. Olympic trials. The valley, the plain and the mountaintop. Each has their struggle. And each is an opportunity to win gold. Life is not about avoiding one trial for the sake of the other. It is about navigating all trials through a Godly perspective.

Ponder Today: We cannot avoid trials, but we can overcome them.

JUNE 5: DAY 3 - TRIAL VS TEMPTATION

"Blessed is a man who perseveres under trial; for once he has been approved, he will receive the crown of life which the Lord has promised to those who love Him. Let no one say when he is tempted, 'I am being tempted by God'; for God cannot be tempted by evil, and He Himself does not tempt anyone. But each one is tempted when he is carried away and enticed by his own lust." – James 1:12-14

As we journey toward understanding what it takes to win at life, it is important to see what James says about the difference between a trial and a temptation. The clear difference is intent. A trial is something you are meant to overcome, to succeed against. A temptation is something you are meant to fail. The difference is in the intention of the source.

A temptation is a lie to rebuke. A trial is a truth to navigate.

God allows trials. They give us an opportunity to choose. Our acceptance in God's eyes is unconditional. But there is more for us! A "crown of life". The fruit of our love for him. For this, he allows trials. He wants us to succeed. He longs for us to succeed.

We love to blame God. To call him out for "tempting" us. But only Satan (via our flesh) tempts, because Satan is the one who wants us to fail. We are dragged away by our own desires toward sin and temptation. It is not God's fault. Our own lust tempts us, dragging us away and enticing us with our desire for things other than God. Satan has his part to play, but sin is "conceived" when we choose our lust over God's love. When we chose our temptations over his trials. Once conceived, our unchecked sin can "give birth to death".

If winning at life is overcoming our trials, it is important to distinguish between trials and temptations. God is the author of life. He is rooting for our success. Stewarding trials and rebuking temptations develop the Image of God within us.

Ponder Today: A trial is something we are designed to overcome. A temptation is something designed to overcome us.

JUNE 6: DAY 4- THE SURPRISING POWER OF LISTENING

"This you know, my beloved brethren. But everyone must be quick to hear, slow to speak and slow to anger; for the anger of man does not achieve the righteousness of God." – James 1:19-20

At first glance, this verse on listening seems out of place. What does listening to people have to do with taking in God's word?

As James has already pointed out, temptation is not God's fault. It is the responsibility of our lusts. The evil desires of our flesh. Although we are made in God's image and have His spirit dwelling in us, we are also cursed with a sin nature. That sin nature pits us against not only God, but against others. We want what they have. We desire to have power over them. We seek to control.

In order to truly listen to another person, we have to first set aside these lusts. We have to set aside "anger" that stems from not getting our own way, and see what they see. Walk in their shoes. Understand their perspective.

When we do this, we are exercising an incredibly important skill: to separate ourselves from our flesh. To recognize that there is a third character in the boxing ring; the referee. Like a referee, we can decide to set aside our flesh for the sake of the spirit. And listening to other people actually prepares our hearts to listen to God, and to hear His word and transplant that word into our hearts.

God is the author of the word of life, which has been planted within us. The only thing capable of suffocating its fruits is ME. My flesh, lusts, and narcissism. The first step in transforming that dead way of living with true life is a surprise: learn to effectively listen to others.

Ponder Today: Listening invites learning, from others and from God. none of us has a monopoly on the truth.

JUNE 7: DAY 5 - A TRANSPLANT

"Therefore, putting aside all filthiness and all that remains of wickedness, in humility receive the word implanted, which is able to save your souls." – James 1:21

The "Therefore" of verse 21 tells us what the first 20 verses are there for. The point is to let us know that God gives us trials, but not temptations. Every circumstance is a trial. Temptations don't come from trials. Temptations come from within. James tells us that first our lust is conceived within our hearts. Lust then gives birth to sin and then, when sin is full-grown, it results in death. Separation. The most tragic separation may be when we are separated from the life we could be living.

What is the solution? The solution does not lie in reforming our old selves. The cure comes from a transplant. As with any transplant, the first step is to put away the old. James tells us to put aside our inner wickedness. Move it out of the way. Render it inoperative. Tell our old self, our flesh, "no thanks." And in its place implant God's word. His perspective of our best interest. His perspective of winning at life.

Just like a heart transplant saves the life of someone whose heart is failing, implanting the word saves our lives. The word translated "soul" is the Greek word "psuche" which is translated "life" about half of the time it appears in Scripture ("soul" the other half). Living under the control of our dead self's passions is like living as a zombie. Transplanting God's word frees us to become all we can be. To encounter every circumstance as a champion. And win life's gold by living in godly wisdom. Listening to others trains us to listen to God. Listening to God gives us a life transplant.

Ponder Today: Truly submitting to God's perspective transforms the way we think, feel, and act.

JUNE 8: DAY 6 - DOERS OF THE WORD

"But prove yourselves doers of the word, and not merely hearers who delude themselves. For if anyone is a hearer of the word and not a doer, he is like a man who looks at his natural face in a mirror; for once he has looked at himself and gone away, he has immediately forgotten what kind of person he was. But one who looks intently at the perfect law, the law of liberty, and abides by it, not having become a forgetful hearer but an effectual doer, this man will be blessed in what he does." – James 1:22-25

To truly overcome trials (the Bible's definition of success), we have to align our thoughts, emotions, and actions with God's word. It is not enough to set aside the old self (verse 21), we have to put on the new self. A transplant begins with removing the bad heart, but if it stops there, what good has it done? We need a new heart, a new perspective, a new way of doing things.

This is how the law is fulfilled within us. Only through a transformed heart. And we are only transformed if the change makes its way into our behavior.

James talks about a man (the translation doesn't mean "human"; it means "male") who looks at himself in a mirror and then walks away, forgetting what he looks like. Women are more focused, more intent when they look in the mirror. They don't leave until they look exactly right. Men tend to do only the minimum.

James says we delude ourselves when we think we are growing in godliness but give our character only a passing consideration.

There are three things we control: our actions, who we trust, and the perspective we take. Are we going to trust the world or the Lord? Will we adopt the world's perspective that success is accumulation and earthly prestige? Or will we adopt a true perspective and invest in something that brings peace and will last forever?

Choosing to trust God and adopting a true perspective about life lays a foundation to actually do good deeds. To not only hear and implant the word, but to choose to put it into action. The goal of a healthy inner life is to have it overflow into our actions.

Ponder Today: What we do is perhaps the truest indicator of what we really believe.

JUNE 9: DAY 7 - THE ENIGMA OF PERSEVERANCE

"Consider it pure joy, my brothers, when you are involved in various trials, because you know that the testing of your faith produces endurance." – James 1:2-3

We finish our series on James 1 by returning to the beginning. James 1 begins with an enigma. It tells us when we encounter bad circumstances, we are to make a choice. Choose a perspective to view them as "pure joy." This tells us that perspective is something we can choose, which is a huge revelation. And the Bible does not ask us to do things unless we are capable of doing them.

It also tells us that life has difficulties. As we have discovered later in James 1, all circumstances are trials. Prosperity being perhaps the most difficult to endure. And endurance is the chief benefit to us in life. Why? Verse 12 tells us: "How blessed is the man who endures temptation! When he has passed the test, he will receive the victor's crown of life that God has promised to those who keep on loving him." Endurance is the means by which we gain the "victor's crown of life." This is the way to win.

James does not pretend this is easy. He acknowledges we will need some help. Which is why he tells us to ask for wisdom. How are we supposed to see life from this perspective? James answers: ask God and he will reveal how. Interestingly, James says to ask with no doubt. If we believe God will give us a true perspective, then we will gain it. But if we doubt, we are "double minded." If we try to have the mind of God and the world, James tells us we will be "tossed by the wind" - like a paper blowing in a gale, being swept along by the surrounding circumstances.

James tells us, conclusively, that we can choose a godly perspective. If we ask, believing, God will give us the wisdom to know it. This is a key foundation to a truly successful life.

Ponder Today: We are adept at asking God to change our circumstances, but struggle with the more important ask - that God would awaken our own ability to choose.

This concludes our 7-day series on James Chapter 1.

JUNE 10: INVESTING IN LOVE

"And though I bestow all my goods to feed the poor, and though I give my body to be burned, but have not love, it profits me nothing." – 1 Corinthians 13:3

1 Corinthians 13 is inspirational and romantic. But it is also very practical. These verses tell us something that is often overlooked. It tells us why we should choose to love.

Why I should just bite my lip instead of yelling at the referee. Why I should answer for the hundredth time the question my four year old is asking. These verses give us not only the instruction, but the reason behind it.

Love is profitable to us. It is a sacrifice, but it is also an investment that has a great return. When we invest money in stocks, we sacrifice getting to spend it. But we lay the foundation for future returns. Love is similar, except when we invest in love, we always get an outstanding return. But if we "invest" without love, we get worse than a bear market. It "profits me nothing." "Nothing" is a really bad return.

Paul tells us that even the greatest of all sacrificial actions are of no benefit without love. Feeding the poor is great. But if we are doing so without love, there is no return. Being a martyr is the ultimate sacrifice. But if we do so without love, we gain no lasting benefit.

The Bible is the Truth. It reflects the Living Word. It reflects reality.

People always pursue what they perceive to be in their best interest. The Bible is full of admonitions that inform us what is truly in our best interest. None is greater than Paul's admonition to love. Love is seeking the best for others. And when we love, we also seek the best for ourselves.

Ponder Today: In giving, we participate in the blessing of love. We get as we give. It is a profit to all.

JUNE 11: YES AND AMEN

"For as many as are the promises of God, in Him they are yes; therefore also through Him is our Amen to the glory of God through us." – 2 Corinthians 1:20

There is a Golden Rule in Improv Comedy. Actors never say "no". Everything is "Yes, And…"

The reason for this is that a "no" kills the momentum of the story. If you negate what another actor says or does, you have slammed the brakes on the energy of working together. The story cannot progress. This doesn't mean Improv actors have to agree on everything. One could say "Yes, and there is another noise over here". There is a way to redirect that doesn't stall the cooperative effort.

We live in a world of "no". There is negativity, skepticism, and cynicism. "No" is the default position of the flesh and the world when we seek harmony with others (what the Bible calls righteousness).

Perhaps we can learn something from Improv actors. Perhaps instead of seeking to focus on what we don't like in our everyday activities, we can focus on what we appreciate, what we enjoy, even while we redirect from things that annoy us.

The particular thing this verse provides as a "yes anchor" are the promises of God. We can seek truth or opportunity in any circumstance. This can be true whether it be an annoyance, like a car battery that dies, or a genuine loss, like a loved one passing.

We can "redirect." We can say "yes" to the promises of God. We can say "amen" to Jesus who is shaping and molding us as we walk by faith in this life.

Ponder Today: What does it look like to say Yes to Jesus even when things are not going our way?

JUNE 12: IDOLS

"The idols of the nations are but silver and gold, the work of man's hands." – Psalm 135:15

We all serve something. When we fear or submit to anything, that is worship. The human spirit has no choice but to submit.

We can play mind games to try to get around this - so we can say we serve ourselves. But as hard as we might try, this doesn't work. The source of satisfaction of our desires, whether shallow or deep, will always connect to things outside ourselves.

A danger of the mountaintops of life is that momentary pleasant circumstances can perpetuate an illusion of self-dependence. We can, for a moment, believe we have validation that a false belief is true.

Life's mountaintops can be a hard place to see what is true. Since the foundation of worship is what we believe to be true, mountaintop experiences can lead us to worship falsely.

A true perspective allows us to see things as they are. We can choose to see what is true in the midst of mirage and illusions.

It is reasonable to say that the greatest trial of all is the mountaintop of prosperity. The illusions of the idolatry of self-dependence lurk. But that also means that the greatest opportunity lies there as well. Choosing to depend on Jesus when all we see surrounding us say that isn't necessary might be the greatest act of worship.

The truth is that Jesus is the truth. He is the way, and the truth and the life all the time. Even on the mountaintop.

Ponder Today: Our successes invite us into a grand delusion that we have done this ourselves and no longer need God. They also invite us into thankfulness and stewardship. It is up to each of us which invitation we accept.

JUNE 13: TREASURES

"'Do not store up for yourselves treasures on earth, where moth and rust destroy, and where thieves break in and steal. But store up for yourselves treasures in heaven, where neither moth nor rust destroys, and where thieves do not break in or steal; for where your treasure is, there your heart will be also.'" – Matthew 6:19-21

There are two kinds of treasures. Temporary ones that disintegrate in our hands. And eternal ones that stick to us forever.

So much of our time is wasted on temporal things. Their value seems to melt as soon as we touch it and this makes us think we just need a little more. And we can spend the entirety of our lives grasping for sand.

The treasures of heaven are real and eternal. Obedience to God is full of reward. All the reward we can handle. And the thing about heaven is that it is not that far away. We aren't just putting our treasure on layaway. We get to experience the benefits of God's kingdom now with hope of an even fuller experience on the other side of this temporal life. The nature of the Kingdom of Heaven is that it is something we can know fully now by faith, and will know in the future by sight.

We are so used to fading treasures, it is sometimes hard for us to imagine ones that are permanent. It is hard to trust that a treasure will stick around. We can be tempted to dismiss the pursuit of treasure because we have seen how it leads to dissatisfaction and corruption. But it is not the search that fails us; it is the thing we are searching for, the nature of the treasure.

God wants the best for us. He longs for our highest good. And our highest good nests in the intimacy of walking in relationship with Jesus in all we do each day. God promises the gift of his presence, the everlasting reward of relationship with Him. It is ours to receive daily. It remains for us to choose to have the perspective to see, the faith to believe then make the choice to follow.

Ponder Today: Are you chasing temporary treasures or eternal ones?

JUNE 14: HOME AWAY FROM HOME

"For we know that if the earthly tent which is our house is torn down, we have a building from God, a house not made with hands, eternal in the heavens. For indeed in this house we groan, longing to be clothed with our dwelling from heaven, inasmuch as we, having put it on, will not be found naked." – 2 Corinthians 5:1-4

As we pursue truth and meaning in our lives, there is something important we need to acknowledge: This is not our home.

We long for a new earth, where righteousness dwells, peace reigns, and war is no more. But this verse speaks of a new home for our souls, a new body. As we age, as we encounter sickness or injury, or as we contemplate mortality, we groan. We long for a body that does not suffer. A body that does not decay.

The great news is that such a body awaits us. The blessed hope of the new life in Christ is the resurrection. Living in a new, spiritual body that is incorruptible. Living in a new earth that is free of corruption.

Meanwhile, we dwell in an earthly tent in a fallen world. We live in hope, but we also live in purpose. We have an immense responsibility before God to be good stewards of the opportunities He has given us to live this life, on this earth, in this body.

As we pursue purpose in this fallen world, it is essential for us to keep in mind our eternal destiny. Our current life is but a season. We long for a better day. Our purpose spans well beyond what we can currently see. When we walk in the obedience of faith, we are laying up treasures that do not rust. A true perspective makes the most of this life while setting the stage for the life to come.

Ponder Today: The difficulty and the joy of this life is balancing a unique opportunity with a longing for something more.

JUNE 15: MYSTERIOUS JOY

"Then our mouth was filled with laughter, and our tongue with joyful shouting; Then they said among the nations, 'The Lord has done great things for them.' The Lord has done great things for us; We are glad." – Psalm 126:1-2

Roller Coasters are a strange source of adventure. We stand in line for an hour so speeds and dips can jostle us for a few seconds. We have the sensation of being out of control, while in reality we are quite safe. In a strange way, we gain joy from experiencing that which we fear, while trusting the theme park construction and operation. Or, we can choose not to trust the theme park, in which case we can experience genuine fear and dread, and hate every minute of the ride.

We can learn a lot from the roller coaster. Our 2-minute adventure ride of life has a lot of standing in line. A lot of waiting. We can enjoy the wait, or fret. It's our choice. Fretting won't make the line any shorter. We might as well choose a perspective of hope and just enjoy chatting with the people standing in line along with us.

The 2-minute adventure ride of life can also make us feel out of control. When this occurs, we can choose to trust the maker of the adventure. God is the builder and operator of the theme park of life. He is more dependable than Disney. Even when it frightens us, even when we aren't in control, it is a journey made for our benefit. Whether or not we enjoy it is a matter of perspective.

Perspective helps us enjoy the journey. We can choose a perspective that accepts that the turns and turmoil of the ride are a part of the adventure. Even if our heart drops to the pit of our stomach, in the end, there will be joy. No theme park maker worth their salt would have it any other way.

Ponder Today: If we truly trust God as Creator, all of our twists and turns move from moments that could derail us to opportunities to observe His provision.

JUNE 16: BEYOND OUR IMAGINATION

"Eye has not seen, nor ear heard, nor have entered into the heart of man, the things which God has prepared for those who love Him." – 1 Corinthians 2:9

The Bible tells us we ought to love God. But it doesn't stop there. The Bible also tells us the enormous benefit of loving God. It is a benefit so great it goes beyond anything we can imagine.

Loving God simply means obeying God no matter our circumstances, living in the manner the Bible tells us to live. This is often hard. We don't feel like serving, we feel like being served. We don't feel like waiting patiently, we want what we want now. Why should we do what we don't feel like doing? What is the benefit?

This verse tells us plainly that the benefit to obedience is so vast that we can't conceive of it on our own. This glory comes from loving Him by walking in faith, following His Spirit, living counter to the flesh and choosing to serve in truth.

God wants us to lay aside our flesh so He can bless us beyond our imaginations. God's gift of new birth is an unconditional gift that is received solely by faith. This is something different. It is an unimaginable blessing that is reserved for those who love Him. Loving God means listening and obeying. There are many who think blessing comes from getting God to listen to us. But unimaginable blessing comes when we listen to Him and obey His commands. Loving God is the most profitable of all human activities, leading to the greatest blessings.

Ponder Today: The greatest you can imagine is far from the greatest there is.

JUNE 17: DELAYED GRATIFICATION

"Let us not lose heart in doing good, for in due time we will reap if we do not grow weary." – Galatians 6:9

Our world is obsessed with instant gratification. We want to be satisfied NOW! We don't want to wait for the Internet to load or our coffee to brew. If it can't happen the instant we want it, we move along to something that promises to satisfy more quickly.

Studies have shown that the ability to pursue delayed gratification is a personality trait of the world's most successful people. Why? Because perseverance is a key component to learning and success. We grow by reaping the benefits of struggle rather than by ignoring or avoiding it. Seeking something big, pursuing something greater than our limited scope, takes time and patience. It takes hope.

We ought to pay particular attention to the Bible's story of Esau. Esau wanted to eat now, and worry about inheriting the mantle of leading the family later. He was impoverished as a result. The Bible calls Esau "profane." He considered the opportunity God had given him as something of no value. Similarly, God grants us each day as an opportunity to plant the seeds of doing good, trusting Him to grow and cultivate the crop while we patiently await the blessing of harvest.

The deepest joys are those for which we patiently wait.

Faith in God's promises is an exercise in delayed gratification that provides a wonderful opportunity. It gives us a truer perspective. It is a beautiful thing that distinguishes the Kingdom of God on this planet from the manifestation of eternity to come.

Ponder Today: The greatest joys require a season of waiting.

JUNE 18: A TRUE WIN

"Do you not know that those who run in a race all run, but only one receives the prize? Run in such a way that you may win. Everyone who competes in the games exercises self-control in all things. They then do it to receive a perishable wreath, but we an imperishable." – 1 Corinthians 9:24-25

Like the Greeks Paul was writing to, our culture loves competition. There is, indeed, something Biblical about competing. However, there is more to the passage. And more to competition than we often acknowledge.

As faith superheroes, the Lord is the source of our power and the One who determines the cause for which we contend. The spiritual race is not a competition of one person against another. It is about the cause of advancing justice. The Greek word translated "justice" is usually translated in the Bible "righteousness." The Bible describes "righteousness" as being like a well-functioning body, where every body part plays its role to maximum design.

So what does it look like for a faith superhero to "win" while having an argument with your spouse? Is winning getting the other spouse to concede a point? That's worldly competition. Winning the spiritual competition is taking one step further toward the marital goal of oneness. Winning in marriage is each party playing their role to best serve the whole.

It is good to compete. Right to compete. But we need to be very careful how we view competition and how we define opponents. If we choose a worldly perspective, we will get a fleshly result of biting and devouring. If we fight, contend, and contest for truth and justice, the reward is spiritual unity.

A true win consists of more than being the first to break the tape. A true win is about stewarding influence, exercising character, and pursuing vision. Faith superheroes pursue God's truth, and Biblical justice, which is harmony through service. This is a race we are called to run and to win.

Ponder Today: If we are not clear about who are true enemy is, we will never win.

JUNE 19: TOMORROW

"So do not worry about tomorrow; for tomorrow will care for itself. Each day has enough trouble of its own." – Matthew 6:34

We are constantly looking ahead. Especially during the seasons of life on the plains. We are concerned about the next problem. The next downturn.

Our culture is addicted to drama. We treat stress as some sort of nutrient, necessary for our survival. A secret value.

We do not know what it means to be content. We need a high. And in the absence of a high, a low serves. It makes more sense than contentment. In fact, a low is just an inverted high. We live on the extremes. We don't know how to just be without a turbo-charge of emotion.

Our perspective on trouble multiplies exponentially as we hold on to past problems and count all possible future ones. Ironically, we lose sight of our current troubles. Their true nature is hiding under fears for the future and wounds from the past. We are angry today but can't really understand why.

Life on the plains is an opportunity for self-awareness. An invitation to ownership. Worrying about tomorrow won't negate the necessary choices of today. We cannot avoid stewarding today's opportunities. We can choose to look beyond it and thus let it pass us by. But that is a choice.

Tomorrow has its own choices. Opportunity awaits. But it is also here. Now. Today is a day of challenge. A day of beauty. A day of choice.

Ponder Today: Contentment is a choice.

JUNE 20: ABUNDANCE ON THE MOUNTAINTOPS

"The thief comes only to steal and kill and destroy; I came that they may have life, and have it abundantly." – John 10:10

Life on the mountaintops is dangerous. It is where we can most easily adopt the perspective that we are in control and don't need to depend on our Creator.

Mountaintops are about abundance. Like everything else, our perspective determines what that abundance turns into. We can convert material abundance into spiritual abundance. Or we can become a slave to our material abundance.

The mountaintops can help us see the care of God in our lives. It can be advantageous. We can choose to view the mountaintop as our greatest test. If we can see what is true while circumstances scream all that is false, the mountaintop becomes a great place to know God. The mountaintops can give us a glimpse at abundant life. They can provide great encouragement. The mountaintop comes with the opportunity for increased responsibility.

We can also have the illusion that mountaintop experiences bring fulfillment. Inevitably, we discover that material wealth does not bring true comfort. Dependence on "stuff" crowds out that which brings true prosperity. Serving others with our mountaintop prosperity leads to love, purpose, and connection. Hoarding "stuff" leads to isolation; we can love stuff but it can't love us in return.

Peter and John were allowed up the Mount of Transfiguration. It is clear from Peter's writing that it made a permanent impression and greatly shaped his ministry. Peter learned not to camp on the mountain, but to invest what he learned. We are invited to do the same.

Ponder Today: Your success is not about hoarding victory but an opportunity to serve others with your resources.

JUNE 21: PATIENT EMOTIONS

"He who is slow to anger is better than the mighty, and he who rules his spirit, than he who captures a city." – Proverbs 16:32

Patience is a virtue and a fruit of the spirit. To be patient is to exercise the art of waiting, to rest for a moment and consider all one's faculties before taking an action.

Our emotions are reactive by design. They alert us to the importance of the occasion. They let us know something of value has been ignited. They serve an important function, but are too often allowed to serve functions for which they are not suited.

There are two possible responses when we feel emotions. The first, and counterproductive way is to immediately react. To treat our emotions as king, and serve their biddings. If we're angry, we scream. If our emotions register offense, we fight to avenge their perceived offender.

If we react like this, we act before we take time to listen and understand. We short-circuit truth. We short-circuit choice. We become a slave to our emotions.

The second, and more constructive way to respond to emotions is with patience. Wait a second and figure out why we feel the way we do. Count to ten. What is the cause, the value being threatened? Ask "Why do I feel this way?" Emotions tell us "Something needs attention, and action." We should always listen. But while emotions are helpful in telling us action is needed, they are not constructive in making good decisions about how best to act.

Ponder Today: You cannot control your emotions but you can keep them from controlling you.

JUNE 22: SABBATH REST

"Remember the Sabbath day, to keep it holy. Six days you shall labor and do all your work, but the seventh day is the Sabbath of the Lord your God. In it you shall do no work: you, nor your son, nor your daughter, nor your male servant, nor your female servant, nor your cattle, nor your stranger who is within your gates. For in six days the Lord made the heavens and the earth, the sea, and all that is in them, and rested the seventh day. Therefore the Lord blessed the Sabbath day and hallowed it." – Exodus 20:8-11

The Bible makes a considerable point of the Sabbath. Jesus was chastised by the Pharisees for not following their Sabbath rules, and Jesus answered that God made the Sabbath for man, not man for the Sabbath. Which brings a question to mind: "Are we taking full advantage of something God made specifically to bless us?"

The principle of the Sabbath rest is a lot bigger than eliminating some buying options on a particular day of the week. It is about unplugging. It is about focusing on what truly matters in life. It is about giving our bodies a break from adrenaline, pursuing physical and mental renewal.

As with all disobedience, when we don't follow God's directives, we are the loser.

The cool thing is that we don't have to wait for a designated day of the week to practice the Sabbath principle. Sabbath rest, no matter when we take it, allows us time and space to reset our perspective. When we are busy, when life is hectic, we often allow our perspective to be shaped, without realizing it's happening.

When we take a Sabbath rest, a pause from the circumstances of life, we can reflect on what is true. What is beautiful. What is lasting. We can reshape our perspective to what God would have us think.

Our world is so obsessed with circumstances that stepping away from them has been equated with "doing nothing". It's like we slip into a void. But the truth is that Sabbath rest is as much a rhythm of life as anything else we do. We need to take time off when training for a marathon or we will over-work ourselves and do damage to our bodies. The same is true for our souls.

Ponder Today: Sabbath rest is not limited to a day or a lack of circumstances; it is about perspective, intention, and trust.

JUNE 23: A WILD ADVENTURE

"You will make known to me the path of life; In Your presence is fullness of joy; In Your right hand there are pleasures forever." – Psalm 16:11

Life is an adventure. Somewhere in the struggle of every day, we often lose the perspective that life is really a crazy, beautiful ride. We get tunnel vision concerning the problems of the day. We aren't sure how we will make it through. We get addicted to highs and terrified of lows.

The path of life is windy. It is wild and unpredictable. It is beyond our control. But all of the things that make it terrifying make it thrilling. It wouldn't be an adventure without risk, without danger, without the joy of triumph and the hard lessons of defeat.

The Lord is watching over us. He has placed us on this planet not to suffer and toil but to thrive and live (even as we suffer and toil). He has placed us in an epic journey. We are a novel of His creation, a character of His authorship.

The thrill of adventure never looks the way we imagine. And what can seem like a long journey is actually a flash in the pan when measured against eternity. We get one chance at this adventure. We can sleep through it, waste it, lament it, or enjoy it.

Only through knowing God is it possible to perceive the journey of life. The path is windy and arduous. But it is thrilling. It is an adventure.

Ponder Today: Zoom out and appreciate your life as an epic journey.

JUNE 24: MINDSET

"Set your mind on the things above, not on the things that are on earth." – Colossians 3:2

Our mind focuses on where we set it. If we go on a walk through the woods looking for the quickest path to our destination, our eyes will drift toward worn paths and cleared obstacles. If our motivation is to bird-watch, our eyes will be up toward the tree branches, and we will eagerly scale any obstacle so we can view the aviators.

In the same way, we have to be aware of our mindset as we traverse through the journey of life. What are we seeking? Because that is what we will see.

Are we seeking to maximize physical comfort? If so, then we will see the most expedient paths. Conversely, if we seek to have God as our comfort, while watching for the "birds" God sends, we are prepared to see what is truly beautiful.

There are so many things calling for our minds to be set on them. So many voices and temptations calling out to us. We can't really control what thoughts come to us. We will see many things that create thoughts along the way, as we "hike" through life. But we can choose what to look for.

Ponder Today: Where is your vision set and how does it affect your steps?

JUNE 25: FOR FREEDOM

"For you were called to freedom, brethren; only do not turn your freedom into an opportunity for the flesh, but through love serve one another." – Galatians 5:13

Freedom is the opportunity to make choices. And the defining choice of a person's life is whether we are to live by the flesh or by the Spirit. Both are within us.

If our primary choice is the flesh, then we will either act as the flesh, or rationalize that we are somehow "getting better" rather than acknowledging that the flesh is an unredeemable force that needs to be set aside each day. If we think we are good, we are likely to either wallow in the guilt of moral failure or rationalize our failings. But if we live in the reality that our primary choice is to trust that Christ has set free, we are empowered to live our best life.

The freedom granted to us is a unique opportunity. It makes us into beings capable of faith and a certain kind of love. The love of service and unity. A love of trust and truth. These are the manifestations of the spirit of God alive within us. The ripples of his glory.

But our flesh is screaming at us. It wants us to use the agency granted us for other means. It wants us to chase idols that make sense to us and are more self-contained.

The infinite joys are only available through the proper exercise of our freedom. The faithful refusal of the flesh's constant tempting is the only way to unlock the treasures we most long for.

Ponder Today: What is your flesh inviting you into? What about the spirit? What will you choose today?

JUNE 26: THE RESPONSES

"For as long as life is in me. And the breath of God is in my nostrils. My lips certainly will not speak unjustly. Nor will my tongue mutter deceit." – Job 27:3-4

The book of Job uses most of its ink talking about Job's choices. The circumstances come pouring down in the first couple chapters. God's response and the redeemed circumstances are in the last couple. In between, there are more than thirty chapters about Job's struggle to respond to his circumstances.

This, more than anything, is what makes Job so famous and so relatable. Like Job, we deal with challenging, even tragic, circumstances. Like Job, we know God is good. And like Job, we struggle with how to live in a world where both of these things are true at the same time. How do we respond? What are we supposed to think, do, and say?

The quality of our life on earth (as well as our accounting to our Maker) will be determined not by our circumstances but by the way in which we respond to those circumstances. Life is going to throw all kinds of things at us. Pain. Joy. Boredom. And like Job, we have choices to make. The choice about how to respond to the circumstances we find ourselves in.

Job is an inspiration. Job chose to worship. Job chose to trust God, even when he could make no sense of what was occurring around him. Job chose to maintain his integrity, even when those closest to him urged him to despair. But all along Job asked questions. He pursued God for answers. The end result was riches that will never fade, a name that won't be forgotten, and the highest praise from his heavenly Father.

Ponder Today: Your circumstances are invitations to choose. How will you respond?

JUNE 27: THE BENEFIT OF PROFIT

"For what will it profit a man if he gains the whole world and forfeits his soul? Or what will a man give in exchange for his soul?"– Matthew 16:26

The Bible is full of verses that talk about the true nature of profit. It tells us to "store up treasures in heaven" (Matthew 6:20) and warns "profit without love is vain" (1 Corinthians 13).

We tend to view the word "profit" through a worldly lens, with a temporal understanding of gain. We say things like "you can't take it with you" and "money doesn't buy happiness", but often our behavior makes it seem we don't really believe this.

It is a deep issue, what we truly believe about "profit." We all pursue profit. But what is true profit?

The Biblical treatment of profit suggests that true riches are not money or possessions. It is love and wisdom and truth. Not just because they are commanded of us but because they are the most significant benefit to us. Love is sacrificing for others, but it gains us the greatest possible profit. Profit that lasts. Profit that enriches our lives. Gaining wisdom is uncomfortable. It means we have to learn the truth about ourselves we don't like to admit, and change as a result. There is no greater benefit to our lives than truth and wisdom.

Profit is that which truly benefits us. All we need to do is take a sampling of the world's biggest bank-account holders to see that income and character do not work hand in hand. Neither do income and relationships or income and peace. Money is no guarantee of true profit or significant benefit. We'd do better to pursue those things that create a true and lasting benefit.

Ponder Today: How you determine what is profitable will determine how you spend your life.

JUNE 28: GIRD YOUR LOINS

"Stand firm then, with the belt of truth buckled around your waist, with the breastplate of righteousness in place." – Ephesians 6:14

Paul has an interesting suggestion for how to start out the day: put on our spiritual uniform. Paul wrote during the Roman era, and takes from the dress and armament of the most fearsome warriors on earth at that time as an illustration of how believers ought to approach each day.

The first item listed is one of prominence. A belt to hold up our pants. Some translations say "having girded your loins with truth". In the ancient near East, both men and women wore long, flowing tunics. It could get in the way. They didn't have "belts" as we know them. So when battle or hard work was on the horizon, they "girded their loins" by pulling the hem of the back of their tunic between the legs then tying the tunic into a knot near their waist. They could run and work and fight without the cloth constantly getting in their way.

Until we gather up the truth, we are going to get in our own way. We will trip over our lack of self-awareness, our inaccurate perceptions, and our improper use of emotions. The truth binds these in an effective way so that we might go into the world and work the fields and fight the battles we are called to.

We often prefer our own assumptions. But the truth binds everything else together. Without it, we flutter in the wind. Everything crumbles to the ground, shackling our ankles and leaving us in naked embarrassment. Each day we do battle with the world, and with our own flesh. As you engage in the fight God has called you to, make sure you have girded your loins with truth.

Ponder Today: If you haven't gathered yourself around the truth, you will constantly find that you are getting in your own way.

JUNE 29: FORTRESS OF SOLITUDE

"After He had sent the crowds away, He went up on the mountain by Himself to pray; and when it was evening, He was there alone."

– Matthew 14:23

Every good superhero has their Fortress of Solitude. Batman has his bat-cave. Superman has his... Fortress of Solitude. Ironman has Stark Tower.

As faith superheroes, the same tool is necessary for us. We need a safe place to retreat. To pray. To recharge. A place to reconnect to the source of our strength.

Solitude is an asset because it allows us the opportunity to catch our breath. It allows us the chance to contemplate, to re-calibrate our perspective so that we can ensure we are stewarding our gifts and opportunities well.

Jesus retreated. He went away by himself to pray. He needed the time away to connect himself to God. Away from the noise, the expectations, and the responsibilities. Just a son with his father.

If we want to live transcendent of our circumstances, we need to be able and willing to step away from them from time to time. Into a safe place. A chalice for the soul. A fortress of solitude. In the era of social media, perhaps one of the most important things we can do is to unplug. To "send the crowds away." To stop engaging with what all the people surrounding us think, and focus on what our Creator thinks.

Jesus' life is our model. He is the truest and best faith superhero. He gives us permission, leads us, provides an example to unplug, to "send the crowds away." When we make a focused solitude a regular rhythm of our lives, we are leaning in to a necessity for any faith superhero.

Ponder Today: What is your life-bringing, soul-stirring fortress of solitude?

JUNE 30: THE REWARD

"Whatever you do, work at it with all your heart, as working for the Lord, not for human masters, since you know that you will receive an inheritance from the Lord as a reward. It is the Lord Christ you are serving." – Colossians 3:23-24

It has become conventional for modern Christians to think that God somehow wants us to serve Him without gaining anything in return.

The Bible is clear that God's intent is to reward us for even the smallest things we do if we do it for Him. Our life on the plains can feel mundane and humdrum. But if we adopt the perspective from this verse, it becomes clear that every single thing we do can be done "as unto the Lord." That means God cares about everything we do. He cares how we care for our home. How we treat one another. How we drive. How we manage our time. How we care for our bodies and possessions. "Whatever you do" is a comprehensive description of life.

Humans naturally seek self-interest. We are designed that way. The Bible doesn't tell us not to seek our self-interest. It tells us to believe that God's way is in our self-interest, while following our flesh, or the world, is self-destructive. We often think our choice is between serving God and serving ourselves. But that is an untrue perspective. The choice is actually between serving God and serving the flesh and the worldly system to which it is connected. If we serve God, we gain life now and the "reward of the inheritance" later. If we serve the flesh, we get destruction now, and can lose all or part of the reward of the inheritance later.

Ponder Today: What is best for you is what God wants for you.

JULY 1: HE IS RIGHTEOUS

"Little children, make sure no one deceives you; the one who practices righteousness is righteous, just as He is righteous." – 1 John 3:7

The plea for righteousness is an essential theme in the Bible. The word righteousness is not something we use in everyday speech, so it has lost some of its flavor.

"Righteousness" is a translation of the Greek word dikaiosyne. It is also translated "justice". Plato's Republic focuses on the meaning of dikaiosyne. The dialogue concludes that dikaiosyne occurs when a group of people serve one another to the maximum benefit of all. Not because they are compelled, but because they choose to do so.

Dikaiosyne is teamwork. When a group of talented people all choose to use their gifts to play their position to their utmost ability, they are practicing dikaiosyne. Righteousness is a beneficial harmony that we choose.

Another English word we use to translate dikaiosyne is "justice". Justice in English means to " line up with a standard". Like "right justify" lines up with a right margin.

The Biblical standard of justice or righteousness is unity. But not unity for the sake of unity. People can unify around evil. True righteousness is when each of us chooses to do what we do best to benefit others. To serve. To love.

Righteousness is choosing to serve others, to seek their best interest by living and speaking the truth. When we choose this perspective, listen to God and act accordingly, we are following this admonition. Righteousness is living in a manner that serves others. We either do it, and in so doing follow Jesus' example, or we don't. It is not about talk. We can deceive with claims. But true righteousness is following the Way in our daily lives.

Ponder Today: Righteousness is a habit, a pattern, a way of life.

JULY 2: SPEAKING THE TRUTH

"These are the things you are to do: Speak the truth to each other, and render true and sound judgment in your courts."
– Zechariah 8:16

A lot of the time, when we think about speaking the truth, we are really talking about having the brashness to voice an opinion. In our self-centric culture, opinion often substitutes for fact. When we say things like, "I'm just telling the truth" we are really saying "I get to determine what truth is."

This verse is not talking about opinion. It is talking about truth. The truth. Reality as it is. Reality as God establishes and reveals. And the uncomfortable fact is that truth is an acquired taste for us all. The gumption to share our opinion is a small step along the path of seeking truth, not the decisive end. The courage and patience to listen to others is one of the greatest keys to uncovering what is true.

The call laid out in Zechariah is not to boldly proclaim what we think. It is to dialogue together until we discover what is right. Which is why it is accompanied by a reference to sound judgment. The proper application of truth discovered through community is to apply sound judgement among the community members.

As we strive to speak the truth to one another, let us have the humility and courage to adopt a proper perspective. God is infinite, and sees all perspectives at once. By sharing among one another, we gain the benefit of seeing multiple perspectives. We need one another to seek and apply truth. When we share with one another, we are walking as God leads, and He always leads toward our best.

Ponder Today: Expressing your honest opinion may be a step toward truth, but it is far from the last one.

JULY 3: TRACK LAYER

"For we are His workmanship, created in Christ Jesus for good works, which God prepared beforehand that we should walk in them." – Ephesians 2:10

We have a race marked out for us. A journey prepared beforehand to which we've been called. An adventure that's been laid upon us, a path for good works. We have a job to do, a special assignment.

In the adventure of life, Jesus is the tracklayer. He lays out the path. He guides us through the twists and the turns. He fires the starter's pistol to get us out of the blocks and run the race. He is also the judge that pulls the tape to let us know we've finished.

Along the way we have jobs to do. People to touch. Stewardship to embrace. Responsibilities to discharge. Service to render.

The only way we even begin to fulfill this divine calling is because we are given the strength to perform great deeds by God's grace. This is what we were made to do. He's already prepared the way. What remains is for us to choose to follow the path he has forged.

How do we know we are walking in the path God prepared? Certainly not by our circumstances - that's just terrain. We walk in Jesus' way when we engage with whatever circumstances we have with faithfulness. When we walk in obedience to the chances we've been given.

Ponder Today: Serve with the opportunities you have. Follow the track laid before you. It is your divine occupation.

JULY 4: SHAKEN BY THE TRUTH

"This is what the Lord Almighty says: 'In a little while I will once more shake the heavens and the earth, the sea and the dry land. I will shake all nations, and what is desired by all nations will come, and I will fill this house with glory,' says the Lord Almighty. 'The silver is mine and the gold is mine,' declares the Lord Almighty. 'The glory of this present house will be greater than the glory of the former house,' says the Lord Almighty. 'And in this place I will grant peace,' declares the Lord Almighty." – Haggai 2:6-9

The prophet Haggai is speaking to a desperate people. They have recently returned from exile in Babylon. Their previous temple, the splendor of Solomon's reign, was destroyed by an invading army (as had been prophesied).

And the Israelites have finally been allowed to return home. Even so, they discover the truth of the Kingdom of God is an acquired taste. It is not ease and simplicity. It is work, stewardship, and trust.

Like them, we seek the shortcuts. The quick path. The easy answers. We are looking for the magic wand to wave and make everything comfortable.

Truth does not always go down so smooth. And the truth Haggai shares throughout his book is a difficult one. On first returning, the Israelites tend to their own homes, desperate to repair their destroyed neighborhoods. Understandable. But the temple of God remains in ruins. Haggai has to share with them the hard truth that the temple of God is more important than their own dwellings. And then, once work begins, the people are discouraged at the meager progress - they are a long way from Solomon's temple.

But there is hope ahead. The truth is that life in the Kingdom requires hope. It requires work. It requires trust. We want a gospel of ease rather than the gospel of truth. We want to ensure our circumstances are okay before we jump into the hard work of obedience. Haggai's message is for us just as much as for the returning Israelites - there is no greater truth than trusting in the Lord and stewarding the work before us.

Ponder Today: The goal is truth, not comfort.

This following is a 5-day series on The Book of Revelation:

JULY 5: DAY 1 - A SIMPLE MESSAGE

"The revelation from Jesus Christ, which God gave him to show his servants what must soon take place. He made it known by sending his angel to his servant John, who testifies to everything he saw—that is, the word of God and the testimony of Jesus Christ. Blessed is the one who reads aloud the words of this prophecy, and blessed are those who hear it and take to heart what is written in it, because the time is near." – Revelation 1:1-3

Revelation is an instruction to His servants. That means any believer can benefit from the message of Revelation. God wants to give a blessing to His servants and the word He uses for "blessed" is makarios which means happy. We all want to have a happy life. God tells His servants three things they need to do to be blessed, or happy: 1) Read this letter, 2) Hear (or understand) this letter, and 3) Keep (or do) the things written in this letter.

Perhaps the biggest key to understanding that Revelation is a simple book with a simple message is the next word: keep. Would it make sense for God to give us a prophetic word for us to keep, or do, then not give us anything to do? If God gave us a prophetic word so that we could read, understand, and keep or do, then it must be readable, understandable, and doable.

Revelation has many predictions about the future, but we cannot do in the future. We can only do in the present. The main purpose of Revelation is not to give us a future-events puzzle to untangle. Rather, the primary purpose is to reveal to us what to do now, in the present.

The great blessing of happiness promised to God's servants in Revelation is a great reward from Jesus that He has reserved for faithful servants. In other words, for followers who do what God asks us to do. Blessing or happiness comes from obedience.

The bottom line of Revelation is very simple: being a faithful servant, living in obedience, brings great happiness - real happiness, the kind that lasts forever and no one can take away. No matter the circumstances, God calls His servants to walk in faithful obedience so that they can receive a great blessing.

Ponder Today: What happens in the future is not as important as how we choose to steward today.

JULY 6: DAY 2 - THE KEY TO HAPPINESS

"Look, I am coming soon! My reward is with me, and I will give to each person according to what they have done. I am the Alpha and the Omega, the First and the Last, the Beginning and the End. "Blessed are those who wash their robes, that they may have the right to the tree of life and may go through the gates into the city." – Revelation 22:12-14

The simple message of Revelation is this: to be a faithful witness, no matter our circumstances, and not fear any sort of death, including rejection. If we do that, He will reward us beyond our imagination. This verse from the very last chapter echoes the message from the first chapter.

Many difficulties lie ahead, ranging from severe persecution to the siren song of great riches. But no matter how crazy events on earth get and no matter what we are tempted to rely upon, God is still on His throne. God's throne is specifically mentioned 39 times in Revelation. The message is clear, nothing happens on Earth that He did not authorize.

No matter how crazy events on Earth become, He is still in charge, No circumstances occur without His permission.

This encourages us to keep being faithful and courageous witnesses because we can trust that History is still in His hands.

Accordingly, no matter the circumstance in which we find ourselves, we can still be blessed. No events can stand in our way. We have the unilateral choice to gain blessing. Only we can stop ourselves. The simple message of Revelation and the key to happiness is this: Be a faithful witness, and walk in obedience, no matter the circumstances. Jesus possesses the throne, and will reward His faithful servants. If we walk in obedience, we win - God says so.

The Greek word translated "blessed" in this verse refers to those who "wash their robes" from the filth of the world and the flesh by walking in faithful obedience. It is the same as in the opening promise of Revelation in Chapter One. This repetition emphasizes that the greatest blessing available in life requires us to adopt a perspective that walking in obedience is the path to great happiness - a perspective that defies that of the world.

Ponder Today: The only thing that can keep you from God's blessing are your own choices.

JULY 7: DAY 3 - MARTYRS ARE BLESSED

"I, John, your brother and companion in the suffering and kingdom and patient endurance that are ours in Jesus, was on the island of Patmos because of the word of God and the testimony of Jesus." – Revelation 1:9

One of the main things Revelation directs us to do Is to "keep the words of this prophecy". To make a primary life goal to be a faithful witness. To not fear death of any sort. To have a good "testimony" for Jesus.

The word translated "testimony" in this verse is a Greek word from the root "martyria" from which we get our English word "martyr." The Apostle John experienced a form of death because of his "marytria", his "testimony of Jesus." That form of death was exile.

We tend to think of a martyr as someone who has their physical life terminated as a result of their witness for Jesus. But a faithful witness for Jesus can experience many different forms of death. Faithful obedience can cost His servants the death of relationships, the death of opportunities, or the death of status when we are rejected for our witness. It caused John to be separated from all he knew and loved.

Being a "martyria" is not determined by how we physically die. We live a good or poor "testimony" based on the way we live our lives.

If we live the life of a faithful witness, we set up a life completely at odds with the world system. There is a price to pay; it could cost us our life. But most likely it will cause us to be separated from something else. Perhaps a position or a relationship. We should expect it to cause us rejection by the world. To not fit in or belong in the dominant culture.

Jesus instructs the churches through the book of Revelation: Difficult things are going to happen; it is going to be pretty tough, but hang in there. Keep trusting. Keep obeying. Keep walking faithfully. Have a good "martyria". If you do, you're going to have amazing blessings.

Jesus promises to make all our obedience worthwhile. This message applies to any of us who read, understand, and keep, or do what John admonishes - to live a good testimony for Jesus.

Ponder Today: The choice to follow Jesus comes at a worldly price, but is worth it eternally.

JULY 8: DAY 4 - GOD IS ON HIS THRONE

To the one who is victorious, I will give the right to sit with me on my throne, just as I was victorious and sat down with my Father on his throne." – Revelation 3:21

The Greek word thronos shows up an astounding 46 times in Revelation. Most of the time, thronos is translated as "throne" and the vast majority of times it underscores the reality of God's sovereign rule over all things. No matter how bad and out of control things appear on earth, God is still in control. God is on His throne and nothing threatens that rule.

In Revelation 3:21, thronos appears and we are told something mind boggling: those who "overcome" as He "overcame" will be given an unthinkable reward: the reward of sharing His throne. To participate in ruling the earth as servants of Christ.

Jesus left us to be His faithful martyreo or witnesses. He sits on the throne of Heaven. Meanwhile, Satan still sits on an earthly throne of power. But only for a time. Jesus is coming back to take that throne. And when He does, He will invite His faithful martyria (witnesses) to share the throne with Him.

What makes a faithful witness? One who obeys His commands. What is Jesus' primary command? To love others. To serve with our gifts to the benefit of the Body. Jesus, the King, came to earth and exhibited the life of a servant. His faithful servants who demonstrate they are willing to serve others during this life are the ones He desires to rule the New Earth, where righteousness dwells.

Throughout the book of Revelation, disasters prevail—famine, war, and death among them. But none of these things surprise the One sitting on the Throne of Heaven. In fact, most of the time the disasters are authorized.

No matter how bad things get, God exhorts us to be faithful and endure difficulty. He is not surprised and is still on His throne. We can trust that He is in control, whether or not we can see how His ways are leading to our best. If we are faithful witnesses, we are pursuing our best, and nothing else comes close.

Ponder Today: Nothing surprises God. Nothing.

JULY 9: DAY 5 - WINNING AT LIFE

"Look, I am coming soon! My reward is with me, and I will give to each person according to what they have done."
– Revelation 22:12

The first three chapters of Revelation are addressed to seven churches that existed during John's time. Each address ends with a promise, "To him who overcomes I will give a reward." The rewards vary for each church. What does not vary is the exhortation to "overcome."

What does it mean to "overcome" and how and what did Jesus "overcome?"

The Greek word translated 'overcome' is nikao which is derived from the Greek god Nike, goddess of victory. It is translated as overcome, conquer, prevail, defeat and get the victory. It means to come out on top, to win. Jesus overcame temptation. Philippians 2:8 tells us that Jesus had to learn obedience through difficulties and trials. He overcame a desire to avoid the cross and endured the cross.

What does Jesus desire to do with the authority He won to reign over all the earth? He desires to share it with His servants who prove themselves faithful. Jesus desires His servants to enter His joy, but they must first prove themselves faithful.

Lasting happiness, the greatest fulfillment available to any human, is to function as we were created and accomplish what we were made to do. Jesus redeemed us by His grace and sent the Spirit to dwell within us, filling us with His power, that we might be restored to the glory He intended for us. The best and truest happiness possible is available and will be given to all believers who are faithful servants. Those who serve others in love and who continue to trust that God is on His throne.

Ponder Today: What does it mean to overcome and how are you being invited to do it today?

This concludes our 5-day series on The Book of Revelation.

JULY 10: HOW GOD SPEAKS

"But I tell you, in this you are not right, for God is greater than any mortal. Why do you complain to him that he responds to no one's words? For God does speak—now one way, now another— though no one perceives it." – Job 33: 12-14

It is common to wonder if God is using circumstances to tell us something.

God condemns what Eliphaz and two of Job's friends had to say about God, but is silent about Elihu. Which likely means that Elihu is on point. And here Elihu makes a startling claim: God is speaking all around us, but we can't really hear.

The Bible conforms Elihu's first point, that God is always speaking in a number of places.

Psalm 19 tells us that the heavens declare God's glory. Romans 10:18 says the heavens declare the gospel. Revelation 12 speaks of a sign in heaven of a woman giving birth and a dragon seeking to destroy the child. God also speaks through dreams - he told Joseph to take Mary as his wife. And God, further, speaks through circumstances - he sent a storm to divert Jonah to go to Nineveh.

Certainly the heavens are filled with wonder. Which reflects a God of wonder. The problem is not that God is silent. Elihu puts his finger on the core problem. We lack perception.

We tend to become oblivious to the wonder around us. The wonder is still there, we just grow hardened to it. But we can choose to take time each day to slow down and re-engage with wonder.

We can look for God in our circumstances. We tend to look for God to fix our circumstances. To bend them to our will. But the real opportunity is to seek to learn what God has for us within our circumstances. To find ways we can know Him. To learn lessons and exercise faith. God might occasionally use a circumstance to direct our path. But most often we should view a circumstance as an invitation. An invitation to know Him better. To walk in faith.

Ponder Today: God redeems circumstances not by fixing them but by empowering us.

JULY 11: GRACE UPON GRACE

"Grace and peace be multiplied to you in the knowledge of God and of Jesus our Lord; seeing that His divine power has granted to us everything pertaining to life and godliness, through the true knowledge of Him who called us by His own glory and excellence." – 2 Peter 1:2-3

The word grace that begins this passage is a translation of the Greek word "charis." "Charis" is also translated "favor," as in "...Jesus continued in favor with God and men" (Luke 2:52). We get our English word "charisma" from "charis". Charisma is used to describe someone with a persona that is viewed by others with favor. There is merit, or a reason, for the favor.

God's favor comes to us through two distinctly different paths. He receives us as His children, through no merit of our own. We need only to accept it by faith. There is merit involved, but it is not ours. The only merit involved is the merit of Jesus. There are no other strings attached. This is God's acceptance, and it is given to us without condition.

The other way God grants favor is when he approves of what we do, as in "God resists the proud but gives grace (charis, favor) to the humble" (1 Pet 5:5). God approves the behavior of his children when he deems it appropriate. God decides what he approves. God, not us, will decide what is humble or service. There will not be an opportunity for an appeal.

However, God clearly gives guidance that shows us his heart. God is merciful and, like the perfect parent he is, really wants us to succeed. Hebrews tells us that without faith it is impossible to please God. Fortunately for us, this life is full of opportunities to live by faith.

Ponder Today: God, not us, decides what is good. Our job is to hear and obey.

JULY 12: A TIRED SUPERHERO

"Let us not lose heart in doing good, for in due time we will reap if we do not grow weary." – Galatians 6:9

It is a popular narrative in the modern superhero movies. After the sixth installment of the franchise, the hero is starting to tire of doing good. He/she is underappreciated. The world is saved only to need saving again. Fighting the bad guys has the hero bruised and cynical. And he/she isn't getting any younger.

We resonate with this storyline because we all feel weary. We tire of having to make the difficult choices. Like Judas Iscariot, we are disappointed that a life of faith does not just make all the bad things go away, does not propel us to wealth and fame and the easy life.

Faith is a grind. A holy and joyful grind, but a grind nonetheless. And if we aren't careful, just like the superheroes of the big screen, we will get so tired of doing good that we question whether it is worth it or not. We might even turn bad. Or give up the fight altogether and join the "wonderful" bliss of apathy.

Life is tiring. The plains are difficult to traverse day after day. But good is available to us. The results may not be what we hoped or imagined, but the life of faith is not about the result of circumstances, rather the development of character. And the relationship we have with the Father.

Ponder Today: Do not give up. Today's grind is tomorrow's glory. Heaven is waiting and watching.

JULY 13: WISDOM AND GLORY

"We do, however, speak a message of wisdom among the mature, but not the wisdom of this age or of the rulers of this age, who are coming to nothing. No, we declare God's wisdom, a mystery that has been hidden and that God destined for our glory before time began." – 1 Corinthians 2:6-7

Wisdom is the wealth of the Kingdom of God. It is the currency of glory.

When Jesus, the Lord of Glory, came to the Earth, the wisdom of God made its way to center stage. The glory that was in existence before time began made itself known to us and invited us in for a meal.

The world's wisdom takes many forms. Earthly fame, riches, and power. These are juvenile benefits that fade away. But the wisdom of heaven is a mature wisdom. A prize of eternal value. It does not feed as the world does; it saturates us with the glory of eternity.

Jesus is the wisdom of Heaven, the Good News of the gospel. And he beckons us into himself. He invites us to take more of his wisdom, to feast on the joys of the Kingdom of God.

Abundant life is not found in superficial trinkets but in the wealth of heaven, the wisdom of the ages, the glory of eternity. Jesus came, died, and resurrected. He made himself known to humanity. He revealed the wisdom of glory. God reveals truth to us through His Spirit, that we might know the things freely given to us by God.

Ponder Today: There is a distinct difference between the world's way of wisdom and God's way.

JULY 14: SHINY LIGHT

"You are the light of the world. A city set on a hill cannot be hidden; nor does anyone light a lamp and put it under a basket, but on the lamp stand, and it gives light to all who are in the house. Let your light shine before men in such a way that they may see your good works, and glorify your Father who is in heaven." – Matthew 5:14-16

One of the beautiful things about living in this world is the way we affect one another. This can also be the worst thing. Our greatest desire is meaningful relationships, but that often becomes our greatest source of problems.

At our best, we emanate God's goodness, inspiring the goodness of God to pour out of one another. At our worst we steal life from others and make it our own - we are spiritual cannibals.

Believers have the Spirit of God dwelling within and can choose to unleash the Spirit's power like a light on a hill. Each human is made in the image of God and carries a reflection of Divine glory. But the Spirit that dwells within transcends human limitations.

Being a light starts with taking ownership, choosing a perspective of stewardship and responsibility. Recognizing that choosing to walk in the Spirit by faith is what truly brings life to our surroundings. Owning our decisions and stewarding our gifts. Investing our talents to benefit others. Trusting God's promises for our benefit, not demanding the benefit appear in a particular time or place.

We have the true source of light within us, ready for us to let it shine forth. We let that light shine when we follow Christ's example and walk in serving obedience.

Ponder Today: What are you doing to spread the light of God's goodness throughout your sphere of influence?

JULY 15: CLINGING TO FAITH

"What strength do I have, that I should still hope? What prospects, that I should be patient?" – Job 6:11

Job is renowned for his faithfulness. But in Chapter 6 of the book bearing his name, Job is struggling. In earlier verses, he wonders if it might be better for him to go ahead and die. He is out of energy. He longs for something tangible to grab onto and be the source of hope.

When our circumstances are dire and our long-suffering feels way past an expiration date, how do we hold on? How do we continue to endure when we are past our breaking point?

Job has no strength to muster hope. No prospects to justify patience. And so, he does all he can do. He cries out to the Lord. The rest of Chapter 6 is a plea for God to make himself known.

It is God who allowed Job's trial, and it is God that delivers Job. Not Job's strength. It is not the redemption of Job's circumstances that is Job's true deliverance. It is Job's deepened knowledge of God. A knowledge gained by faith.

Life is full of challenges and tragedies. It is too much for us to bear on our own - too much for our own strength, too much for our circumstances. By trusting in the God of the Universe, we allow for more than we can do on our own. More than we can comprehend. More than we can endure.

Faith is the gateway to abundance. Riches beyond measure. Not a materialistic, superficial treasure, but the invaluable glory of coming to know God by faith, as we walk through the terrains of life.

Ponder Today: When you are at the end of your rope, remember your hope is not in the rope or your grip on it. Your hope is in God.

JULY 16: EVEN SO

"But God demonstrates His own love toward us, in that while we were yet sinners, Christ died for us." – Romans 5:8

"While we were sinners, Christ died for us" means He has accepted us completely as we are. It doesn't make sense; it doesn't seem fair. Why would God accept us completely while still sinners? The answer is cosmically astonishing: Because of His love toward us.

God's justice was satisfied in Jesus. Jesus' death merited for us what we could never merit for ourselves. God's acceptance of us is not rooted in our behavior. Its foundation is the cross.

All that remains for every human is to receive His acceptance by faith. His complete acceptance of us has been fully provided, if we will only receive it. It is tragic that many reject such an amazing gift. But it is also sad that those of us who accept this free gift behave as though it must still be earned.

God's love is a love that cannot be earned or lost. So we can relax a little. God will never reject us. His love is too great. What to do then? It depends on the perspective we choose.

If we adopt the truth of the Bible as our perspective, we realize that what the world calls "life" is actually "death." We see that our self-interest is best served by faithful obedience in serving Christ. This is the way to experience our best and most fulfilled life. We know we are accepted, so we now have a foundation from which to pursue what is truly best for ourselves.

Ponder Today: All of our choices, whether we realize it or not, are in response to God's acceptance.

JULY 17: PERSPECTIVE MATTERS

"Look, you make my days short-lived, and my life span is nothing from your perspective. Surely all people, even those who seem secure, are nothing but vapor." – Psalm 39:5

Perspective is arguably the most powerful of the three things we can control. How we view God will have an enormous impact on our ability to choose to trust Him. And the actions we take will inevitably be shaped by the perspective we choose.

It is quite interesting that the actual English word "perspective" is used so little by biblical translators. We did a search of 20 translations and found only one that uses the word "perspective." The NET (New English Translation) uses it twice. In all the other translations, the perspective is presumed. Which is quite illustrative of the core issue with choosing perspective. It is a challenge to be intentional in choosing something that is so easy to presume. The NET translation of Psalm 39:5 (above) provides an illustration.

The NET rendering of 1 John 4:5 is also quite informative: They are from the world; therefore, they speak from the world's perspective and the world listens to them.

The world has a perspective. And if we adopt the world's perspective, it is inevitable that we will choose actions that are worldly. Which will result in great loss for us.

Perspective is powerful. It informs our decisions. It influences the way we think. And the way we think determines the way we act. Choosing a perspective that is true transforms us from the world to God's kingdom. It is a necessity if we are to achieve intentional living that leads us to meaning and fulfillment.

Ponder Today: Perspective is a choice, perhaps the most powerful one we can make.

JULY 18: AWAKEN

"Wake up, and strengthen the things that remain, which were about to die; for I have not found your deeds completed in the sight of My God." – Revelation 3:2

Complacency is perhaps the greatest danger facing the growing Christian. The temptation to coast. To be satisfied with what has already been, to feel stuck, unable to do more. When we stop striving we forfeit the journey.

If we have the wrong perspective about daily life it naturally leads to complacency. If we expect circumstances to bring us happiness, we inevitably miss the opportunity for fulfillment.

We can mistakenly think that joy comes from a new romance or experiencing a particular emotion. In our pursuit of mountaintops, we can miss the amazing opportunities all around us.

The Lord is not waiting for a big moment, a grand reveal, a high emotion. He is whispering today. Shouting in the mundane. Pleading through the everyday: "Follow Me." The important thing about "Follow Me" is not the specific destination we are being led to but the One whom we are following.

It is the Who not the where that truly matters.

There is an immense cost to complacency. It results in a forfeiture of opportunity. When we awaken our perspective to the truth of Christ all around us, in every moment, through every decision, we awaken what is incomplete, what we have that's been losing steam. We adopt a perspective that leads to joy.

This is the invitation of life on the plains. To perceive the divine all around us. To see the truth in all things. To be awakened to the fullness of the Kingdom of Heaven. And to rejoice in the fullness of life, even (perhaps especially) in the everyday, mundane routines.

Ponder Today: Do not let complacency compound in your life. Awaken to the choices before you today.

JULY 19: THE TAPE MEASURE

"'Consider carefully what you hear,' he continued. 'With the measure you use, it will be measured to you—and even more.'" – Mark 4:24

Jesus proclaims something in this verse that is quite sobering. When we sit down with Jesus in heaven to learn the lessons we failed to learn in this life, and have our life's work evaluated, the "tape measure" Jesus will use is the one we sent ahead. The standard will have been set based on the measure by which we had judged other people. If we hold them to a strict standard, then Jesus will hold us to a strict standard. If we are lenient with others, giving them grace, so will Jesus be with us.

Once the truth of this verse sinks in, we ought to be reluctant to judge others. We should hope Jesus pulls out our "tape measure" and says "What do you know, there's no tape inside this thing. Guess you did great."

The key to properly judging others is to stand in their shoes. Everyone has a story. We can only learn their story by listening. We tend to put a higher standard on others than on ourselves. We tend to be very good at standing in our own shoes, but not too competent at standing in the shoes of others.

When we have the humility to hear what others are saying, we might discover things within ourselves that need cleansing. Listening to God is essential for character development, self-awareness, and growth. When we view others to learn from them rather than to judge them, we gain a double benefit. We live with greater wisdom and understanding, and we shrink the measure by which we will be measured.

Ponder Today: What is the tape measure by which you judge others? How would you stand up under your own scrutiny?

JULY 20: A RESPONSE TO INJUSTICE

"Indeed, all who desire to live godly in Christ Jesus will be persecuted." – 2 Timothy 3:12

Fighting for justice is something we applaud. But for most of us our power to right wrongs is quite limited. But what do we do when we confront injustice in our daily existence? Perhaps we are falsely accused. We are shunned for not participating in shady dealings. We are slighted. Perhaps our accomplishments are overlooked. Our honesty is used against us.

This verse makes clear that our primary goal should be to ensure we are living an obedient life. If we suffer for doing well, we should count it a win.

In the midst of difficulty, we still have agency to make our own choices, even in the midst of injustice. The unjust circumstances of this world can only hold us hostage if we let them.

We should expect difficult circumstances to come as a worldly reaction to faithfulness. This does not apply to self-inflicted wounds. When we fall, consequences provide a teaching opportunity. Rather, it applies to genuine godliness. God promises to give us power to endure persecution. When we adopt a true perspective, we will understand that God does not eliminate difficult circumstances, he gives us the power to overcome them.

Ponder Today: The fight for justice begins within.

JULY 21: THE CLEFTS

"But He said, 'You cannot see My face, for no man can see Me and live!' Then the Lord said, 'Behold, there is a place by Me, and you shall stand there on the rock; and it will come about, while My glory is passing by, that I will put you in the cleft of the rock and cover you with My hand until I have passed by. Then I will take My hand away and you shall see My back, but My face shall not be seen.'" – Exodus 33:20-23

Moses asks to see God's glory, but God tells Moses this is impossible. If Moses were to see God's face, the brilliance would destroy him. He is too great to behold straight on. This is a message in the book of Job as well. God is bigger and greater than we can fathom.

Moses doesn't gain his request, but is by no means left empty handed. Not by a long shot. He is shown all of the Presence of God he is able to bear. It is for Moses' own safety and wellbeing that it was a limited reveal. A partial "yes". But even this limited revelation caused Moses' face to shine so brightly that the people feared him, causing Moses to cover his face with a veil.

If we, like Moses, seek to follow God as we exercise our gifts to serve in obedience, we have the opportunity to see God's glory. It will be a limited facsimile. But everything that happens in life – the way we feel, events, our relationships – is an opportunity to see the glory of God.

We can choose to lament that our pride is not being fed or our compulsions are not being filled. Or we can appreciate the glimpses of God's glory with which we are blessed. Within each circumstance of life, we can steward our participation and trust The One more brilliant than we can comprehend.

Ponder Today: Sometimes our complaints that we cannot see God more clearly keep us from seeing Him where we can.

JULY 22: WISDOM'S REWARD

"If you are wise, your wisdom will reward you; if you are a mocker, you alone will suffer." – Proverbs 9:12

The character traits that accompany obedience to God are the secret ingredients to making the most out of life.

Wisdom may not change your immediate circumstances. Like Jeremiah the prophet, your wisdom may fall on deaf ears. The world around you will continue to make their own choices. And wisdom may not completely change your emotions. They are still going to alert you to values being threatened or celebrated.

Yet wisdom is its own reward. It is the currency of the kingdom. Wisdom is the crossroads of truth and perspective. And it colors the way we view the world, ourselves, and the Lord of it All. When we walk in the true perspective of wisdom, we are empowered to trust God, to place our faith in him. There is no greater exercise of the human spirit. No greater reward.

On the other hand, if we choose to mock the realities of the world around us, we will find ourselves fractured. We will fully commit to a fake world while the spirit inside us longs for something more. Something true.

If we seek wisdom as a way to manipulate our circumstances, we make a mockery out of what wisdom has to offer. And we add to our suffering. But if we seek wisdom for all it is worth, diving into a godly perspective, we reap the benefits of God's approval and a life full of reward.

Ponder Today: Wisdom is about aligning oneself with the truth of reality.

JULY 23: REFINED PASSIONS

"So flee youthful passions and pursue righteousness, faith, love, and peace, along with those who call on the Lord from a pure heart." – 2 Timothy 2:22

The world has a clever scheme. It feeds the lusts of the flesh. A flaming arrow of the enemy. The goal is to lure us like moths to a flame. The Bible's recommended response is "flee".

The trap is a scheme of half-truths and superficial substitutes for our true longings. It is a scheme of short cuts. Like Satan offered Jesus. "Bow down and worship me and I will give you the kingdoms of the earth. Why wait and suffer when you can have it now?"

The flesh sells the idea that we can gain great profits without making investments. We can eat our seed corn and still have a harvest. Jesus knew better. He separated from Satan and followed the road of obedience - a road that led to the true fulfillment of his destiny as the King.

The path of Jesus is the way of life. Paul urges us to flee lusts and pursue righteousness. The Lord calls us to put away superficial attempts to feed our deepest passions. Instead, we are to do the hard work of chasing righteousness.

When we exercise the difficult decision to walk in the obedience of faith, our reward is peace, love and the fruits of righteousness. And the seed of this great blessing begins with fleeing that which is incompatible with a life of faith.

Ponder Today: Evil often presents itself as a shortcut to good.

JULY 24: FIRM FOUNDATIONS

"But the one who has heard and has not acted accordingly, is like a man who built a house on the ground without any foundation; and the torrent burst against it and immediately it collapsed, and the ruin of that house was great." – Luke 6:49

One of the reasons God is not a Cosmic Vending Machine is because we do not always know the best thing to ask for. We are so limited in our understanding. We have such a hard time understanding today's circumstances in the context of eternity.

Our asks are usually prescriptive and superficial. We are collecting straw so we can hastily protect ourselves from the circumstances around us. It feels simple, easy. And it seems to work. We have a structure to protect us - quick, easy, comfortable.

But when the real storms come, the torrential temptations like pride, wealth, or tragedy, the structure we've created for ourselves cannot stand.

The Lord knows better than we do what is best for us. He does not withhold blessing to punish us. He does not delay to torture us. He is inviting us into the full breadth of relationship with Himself. The kind of intimacy that transcends storms (and circumstances altogether).

The Lord wants more for us. He wants to provide what we need. In fact, he wants to provide what we truly want; not just the superficial, quick-fix version but the real deep value we are striving after.

The foundation of character only comes when we make choices toward obedience. All of life's circumstances are an invitation to do so.

Ponder Today: Ask God today about His best for you.

JULY 25: JESUS APPLAUDS

"And they brought to Him a paralytic lying on a bed. Seeing their faith, Jesus said to the paralytic, 'Take courage, son; your sins are forgiven.'" – Matthew 9:2

Faith is the substance of things hoped for. The evidence of things unseen. Only in this season of our existence will we be able to exercise faith; in heaven we will know by sight. The angels gather and watch with intrigue, to see how we exercise our faith. Faith is something they can only know by observation, watching the choices we make. The completely baffling prospect of a creature believing without seeing.

It is not just the angels that are watching. Jesus is watching too. The Lord of Hosts looks on like the proud Father He is.

Jesus performed many miracles of which we are told little. But when we are given details, Jesus often applauds the faith of the person being healed. He acknowledges that they came to him with a sense of belief, reaching for the hem of his garment, pleading from the roadside, or lowering a friend through a hole in the roof.

These people are healed through the miraculous power of Jesus. And as Jesus operates, He celebrates the amazing reality that these people are participating in the working of his power. They are active recipients of His grace.

When we exercise faith, we are living out the Kingdom of God. We are doing our part. The angels watch with fascination. And just as He did when He was on earth, Jesus Himself watches, and applauds.

Ponder Today: Heaven is watching your choices on the edge of their seat, waiting to stand in ovation.

JULY 26: CHOOSING A FATHER

"For you have not received a spirit of slavery leading to fear again, but you have received a spirit of adoption as sons by which we cry out, 'Abba! Father!'" – Romans 8:15

The whole of Romans 8 talks about the choice we have to make. A choice between flesh and spirit. We stand in the gap, being pulled toward both forces. We are the referee who decides the winner of this cosmic battle within our soul.

One of the hard things about choosing the spirit is trusting in God. So much of what He asks of us is counter-intuitive: lose our life to find it, rejoice in suffering, etc. His commands start to sound burdensome to us. We start to think we should just be able to do it our own way.

In verse 15, Paul counters this perspective with the truth. God is not a task-master; He is our father. Choosing the way of the spirit puts shackles on our flesh. It dims the parts of us that are not compatible with the Kingdom of God. If we are not careful, we start to feel as though that is a problem. But God knows what is best for us. He calls us, not as an oppressor, but as a Father. He wants what is best for us.

God is not about rules for the sake of making you follow rules. He is about enhancing our freedom through a proper understanding of boundaries and consequences.

Our choice is about trusting our Father to have our best interest in mind. It is about submitting to His authority and uniting to His purpose. The flesh looks to bind us. The spirit looks to set us free.

Ponder Today: The key to the shackles that bind us are our own choices.

JULY 27: TRUTH AND EMOTION

"The Lord's bond-servant must not be quarrelsome, but be kind to all, able to teach, patient when wronged, with gentleness correcting those who are in opposition, if perhaps God may grant them repentance leading to the knowledge of the truth, and they may come to their senses and escape from the snare of the devil, having been held captive by him to do his will."
– 2 Timothy 2:24-26

We love to be correct. It makes us feel as though we have purpose. It is an aspect of our God-given longing for effectiveness. As we align ourselves with the truth, we participate in God's Kingdom and economy.

But there is more to the truth than knowing the correct answer.

When we sense we have the correct knowledge, a jolt of energy runs through us. We feel as though we are winning at life. In other words, our emotions are heightened because something we value (truth, purpose) is being pressed.

2 Timothy tells us that God's people handle truth with grace. They do not adopt positions of intellectual superiority. In humility, they become witnesses to the truth.

Emotions traditionally labeled as positive can be just as destructive as those we label as negative. All emotion is neutral. It is what we do with it that makes the net gain positive or negative. Our flesh wants to use emotion to validate the greatness of ME. The Spirit longs to use emotion to fuel self-awareness, self-governance, and healthy participation in the kingdom of God.

Truth is more complicated than knowledge. It transcends emotion. Although it includes both of these things, it is also bigger than either on its own. It takes patience and grace to acquire the truth.

Ponder Today: Today, be an advocate for truth rather than an obstacle.

JULY 28: NO HOPE

"For we are sojourners before You, and tenants, as all our fathers were; our days on the earth are like a shadow, and there is no hope." – 1 Chronicles 29:15

In the very last words of this verse, we find what appears to be one of the strangest phrases in Scripture: there is no hope. Although we often feel this way about our short time as Earth-tenants, there is clearly more to this phrase than meets the eye.

There are many other plausible translations, such as "there is no abiding", that help inform our understanding. The idea is that we cannot stay. Our days are numbered. All we do is subject to the effects of time. We cannot hope to find our full meaning here, as tenants and sojourners. There is no abiding in the circumstances of this life. They will, inevitably, come to an end. And this end marks a new beginning.

This verse is found in the middle of a prayer offered by King David at the very end of his life. David is acknowledging a reality that is sometimes hard for us to accept - our lives are transitory. David can't stay. He has to go. Like all men, he must die. But this is not a prayer of lament. It is a prayer of rejoicing. By acknowledging the reality of our short time on this Earth, we allow ourselves to experience life to the fullest. The intensity of life's brevity is our invitation to intentionality.

We have the chance to participate in the great dance of life. The story of God and mankind. This brief life is our one and only opportunity to live and come to know God by faith.

Our hope is not in continuing to pay rent on this Earth long after our lease expires. Our hope is in participating in the Kingdom of God during this short and beautiful life. And doing so as a prelude for what is to come.

Ponder Today: There is hope in this world but our hope is not in this world.

JULY 29: ENTERTAINING ANGELS

"Let love of the brethren continue. Do not neglect to show hospitality to strangers, for by this some have entertained angels without knowing it." – Hebrews 13:1

We often think life in the plains is mundane, boring, or uneventful. If we measure our behavior on what gains us the praise of fickle mankind, we can easily overlook things like hospitality, simple acts of kindness.

When, instead, we chose these everyday behaviors, they are neither boring nor meaningless. They delight the angels. They bring heaven into applause.

Chapter 13 of Hebrews begins with an admonition to love one another. It implores hospitality, remembering prisoners, healthy marriage, and stewarding good character. All of these things are fascinating to the heavenly hosts. To watch us exercise a life of faith, trusting in God, taking what is unseen and bringing it into vision.

We may not know it, but the angels are tuned in. They are watching from Heaven. And they are watching from Earth. Our choices are powerful and awe-inspiring. They have an effect (and a reward) in the heavenly realm.

The author of Hebrews reminds us the angels are witnesses on our account. Celebrating our choices the way a soccer fan does when his team scores a goal. Rooting us on in the kindness we show to one another. Amazed by the incredible opportunity we have and astonished when we take advantage of it exactly the way God designed. It is our great opportunity. Let's give the angels something to cheer about.

Ponder Today: Your act of kindness may go unnoticed by the people around you, but it is the cause of rejoicing in heaven.

JULY 30: THE DWELLING

"Finally, brethren, whatever is true, whatever is honorable, whatever is right, whatever is pure, whatever is lovely, whatever is of good repute, if there is any excellence and if anything worthy of praise, dwell on these things." – Philippians 4:8

The things we dwell on get emphasized and repeated. If we focus on being grateful, it has an exponential effect on our lives - we find more and more to be thankful for. If we focus on how others are wronging us, we pile more and more evidence to support that view of our surroundings.

The things we choose to dwell on are important. They determine patterns and develop perspectives that shape the way we feel, think, and behave. If we dwell on good things, we are establishing patterns of goodness. If we choose bad things, we are opening ourselves up to a blackhole of negativity.

This is not to suggest we should not acknowledge pain, that we need to pretend negative things are all rainbows and sunshine. Pretending reality is not real is not the same as dwelling on what is good. Neither is it healthy or helpful.

Dwelling on what is good is not about ignoring the challenging aspects of reality. It is about acknowledging them, but not setting up camp there, and receiving them in the greater context of reality. It is about naming and weighing the trials, consequences, and disappointments we face as a means to an end, an opportunity to continue to pursue (and see) the presence of God in all things.

A commitment to dwell on what is good is a commitment to trust God and keep our focus on the purpose of His Kingdom. When we do that, all circumstances are an opportunity. All struggles are temporary. And all of our life is a resource to reflect the goodness of God.

Ponder Today: We cannot always help what happens to us but we can decide where to place our focus.

JULY 31: GODLY SORROW

"Godly sorrow brings repentance that leads to salvation and leaves no regret, but worldly sorrow brings death. See what this godly sorrow has produced in you: what earnestness, what eagerness to clear yourselves, what indignation, what alarm, what longing, what concern, what readiness to see justice done." – 2 Corinthians 7:10-11

In Paul's second letter to the church in Corinth, something Paul had written previously caused the church sorrow. Paul says he regretted it at first. His goal wasn't to cause hurt. But after reconsidering and observing where the sorrow has led, he no longer regrets the "godly sorrow" because of the fruit it produced.

Life in the valleys is challenging. Sorrow and suffering are realities we have to acknowledge. Pain is a real thing and we have to bear it with honesty and truth. God only authorizes circumstances we can handle and is always there to help us through.

"Worldly" sorrow brings death; it is an end. It kills. Sorrow according to the world's standards leads to nothingness, to oblivion. It is pain for pain's sake.

But "godly" sorrow leads to life. It produces fruit, spurs action, and strengthens character.

The difference between worldly sorrow and godly sorrow is not specific kinds of circumstances, it is what we make of it. What we allow it to show us. What it makes us earnest for. What kind of alarm it brings.

Valleys are a reality in our lives. We have to go through them. It would be a shame to waste the valleys of our lives. Valleys are an opportunity for growth, development, and productivity. The seeds of life are often sown in the valley, where our eyes are opened to new possibilities.

Like the people of Corinth, we choose what to make of our valleys. Will they usher repentance, eagerness, and longing? Or will they be an end to themselves. If we align with the perspective of God, we allow our sufferings to be a part of the journey rather than the final say.

Ponder Today: The difference between worldly sorrow and godly sorrow is not specific kinds of circumstances, it is what we make of it.

AUGUST 1: PART OF THE MIRACLE

"Nearby stood six stone water jars, the kind used by the Jews for ceremonial washing, each holding from twenty to thirty gallons. Jesus said to the servants, 'Fill the jars with water'; so they filled them to the brim. Then he told them, 'Now draw some out and take it to the master of the banquet.'" – John 2:6-8

Have you ever noticed some of the mundane activities that surround Jesus' miracles? At the wedding in Cana, Jesus asks these servants to fill massive water jars to the brim. Why? He could have filled them as part of the miracle. In the feeding of the five thousand, Jesus sends the disciples out to "go and see" how much food is around. Why doesn't he just do the miracle?

The mundane activities of these servants and the disciples are not a setup, nor are they peripheral background. They are an integral part of the miracle. It helps us understand that these things are happening in the context of normal human living.

It is exciting to read about the miracles of Jesus. But "miracle" just means "something we are not used to seeing." God is always working in incredible ways, what we ought to call miracles.

Consider a firefly or the love between spouses. Science has examined the molecular foundations for our existence and nothing has been solved. Rather, the mystery of how it can all fit together has compounded. God is everywhere holding it all together, actively working.

We often lament the plains of life, the everyday activities like filling water pots. We tend to long for the mountain tops to be rescued from our boredom. This is an attitude that enslaves us to circumstances and robs us of joyful living.

When we choose the perspective that filling a water pot is not a prelude to a miracle but an integral part of the miracle itself, we are beginning to see life as it is. We can embrace the "mundane" as an essential part of the miracle that is the time we've been granted to live on this earth.

Ponder Today: How is God inviting you to be part of the miracle of life today?

AUGUST 2: HUMILITY ON THE MOUNTAIN

"You may say to yourself, 'My power and the strength of my hands have produced this wealth for me.' But remember the Lord your God, for it is he who gives you the ability to produce wealth and so confirms his covenant, which he swore to your ancestors, as it is today." – Deuteronomy 8:17-18

The biggest difference between the three terrains of life - valleys, plains, mountains - is not about inherent value. It is about the way we perceive each. We consider ourselves victims when we are in the valley; we hardly consider the mundane; and we consider ourselves victors on the mountain.

There is danger in all three. We blame God, others, etc. when we are in the plains or valleys, but we take all the credit when we find ourselves on the mountain. We did it. We overcame. We succeeded. The subtext here is that God, the world, and the people around us have tried to arrange challenges to keep us from success, but we have found a way to win.

There are many places in Scripture, from Moses' speech in Deuteronomy to Jesus' admonition at The Last Supper, to remember the Lord. How easily we forget. As soon as things are going well, as soon as we gain a resource or feel good, we forget our dependence on God; the necessity of faith.

All of the arenas of life are transitory. You cannot take your wealth with you when you die; it is unsustainable in the long run. Everything we claim to own was once possessed by someone else and will inevitably change hands to another. Our mountains are temporary tools to invite us to Eternal participation. If we do not use them to honor God and reflect his goodness by loving others, we are wasting the opportunity the mountains provide.

Ponder Today: No matter what terrain of life you are on, the key is to remember God.

AUGUST 3: A RICH PERSPECTIVE

"By faith Moses, when he had grown up, refused to be called the son of Pharaoh's daughter, choosing rather to endure ill-treatment with the people of God than to enjoy the passing pleasures of sin, considering the reproach of Christ greater riches than the treasures of Egypt; for he was looking to the reward."
– Hebrews 11: 24-26

Moses, like all of us, sought a reward. He was looking for treasure, for value, to obtain something of significance. To get ahead. To win. But Moses learned how to find treasure that lasts. To win a victory that never fades.

The faith of Moses was to trust that the riches of God are greater than the riches of man. The "treasures of Egypt" were enormous. Egypt was the wealthiest civilization of that era. But the Bible says Moses considered the "reproach of Christ" to be superior to those riches.

That was a radical perspective then, and it still is today.

The beauty of this perspective is that the rewards from following Christ are real. They are true and lasting. The "treasures of Egypt" Moses forsook are all gone. They were either taken by grave robbers, or are on display in a museum. But Moses is enjoying the treasure he sought.

The rewards of our flesh are fleeting. They don't last, and they don't fulfill. They are incomplete.

God desires to give us the fullness of His treasure. The true riches of life and of the Kingdom of God. God is a giving God, longing to share with us His riches.

But to have our hands open to receive God's treasure, we must first release the treasures of this world. If our hands are full, we have no room to receive.

The key to receiving the treasures of God's kingdom is a change in perspective. To consider what the world ignores as a clear path to the greatest of treasures. The view of Christ, the shame of the world, is greater riches than anything we can gain in this life.

Ponder Today: Few things can transform our attitude more than reimagining what it means to be rich.

AUGUST 4: WHISPERS

"Although the Lord gives you the bread of adversity and the water of affliction, your teachers will be hidden no more; with your own eyes you will see them. Whether you turn to the right or to the left, your ears will hear a voice behind you, saying, 'This is the way; walk in it.'" – Isaiah 30:20-21

At the end of the day, each of us is responsible for the choices we make. We decide to walk "to the right or to the left". As far as our own heart and our own character, we are the referee. We determine what is allowed and what isn't. What to consider and what to abolish. What to follow and which to ignore.

There are many voices vying for our attention. They long to influence us, to help guide our decisions. God Himself sends us many "voices". Teachers (leaders and mentors) whispering in our ears. The (paradoxical) spiritual nourishment of affliction and adversity. Our own eyes. While Satan attempts to pervert, interrupt, or mimic these voices, there is no doubt they continue to speak to us, to call us into obedience.

By learning how to listen, we hone an important decision-making tool: discernment. We tune our ears to the helpful voices and tune out (or disregard) the others. We decide what matters. We learn how to filter the truth from a bombardment of noise.

The whispers are after us. Each is showing us a way. Calling us into his Kingdom. Inviting us to be faithful, obedient, hearers (and doers) of God's Word. That is the way that leads to our greatest fulfillment.

Ponder Today: What are the voices in your life that whisper of The Kingdom of God?

AUGUST 5: TRUTH AS FOUNDATION

"Lord, who may dwell in your sacred tent? Who may live on your holy mountain? The one whose walk is blameless, who does what is righteous, who speaks the truth from their heart." – Psalm 15:1-2

This Psalm taps into a deep human aspiration. The greatest fulfillment a human being can gain stems from an intimate relationship with God. To dwell in God's "sacred tent" as a family member. To live on His "holy mountain" as a constructive citizen that participates in His Kingdom.

To reach this blessed state requires us to proclaim truth. And to walk blameless in our obedience to God.

The truth we are to proclaim is from the heart. Which means the path to walking in intimate fellowship with God begins by altering our perspective toward what is true. To see the world through God's eyes. To embrace reality as it is.

When we see reality as it is, we will recognize sin's false substitutes as frauds. Sin promises everything and delivers nothing. Seeing reality as it is cascades outward from a heart of truth. It leads to a blameless walk. It leads to righteous living.

Paul pictured righteousness as a well-functioning body where each body part sees itself for what it is, and serves its proper role for the body's benefit. Paul makes clear that the body only has one head, and that is Christ.

Walking in righteousness is to serve with our gifts, stewarding the opportunities we have. Righteous living begins with recognizing our capabilities as gifts, and our circumstances as opportunities. If we commit to the truth and proclaim it with courage, even when it is not popular, we walk a journey that enters the sacred presence of God.

Ponder Today: Without an honest commitment to the truth, even when we don't like it, we are on shaky and unstable foundation.

AUGUST 6: THE MIGHTIEST MUSCLE

"I know what it is to be in need, and I know what it is to have plenty. I have learned the secret of being content in any and every situation, whether well fed or hungry, whether living in plenty or in want. I can do all this through him who gives me strength."
– Philippians 4:12-13

The great strength in each of us is not physical or mental. It is spiritual. Our faith is the measure of our muscle. We are given a supernatural gift, an ability to change the world through service, to love and to worship. God grants us His strength. And it matters infinitely more than any other consideration vying for our attention.

Circumstances may shower us with abundance. We may encounter riches and fame. They may overwhelm us with grief. We may encounter tragic sorrow and burdening frustration.

Faith transcends all circumstances. It allows us to find meaning and seize opportunity in every situation and every season. And to be content. Circumstances are not just problems to be solved or spoils to be enjoyed. They are invitations.

Everything we go through invites us to exercise the mightiest of human attributes - faith. They dare us to believe; implore us to have the courage to take action; lift us to be able to perceive truly.

The irony of contentment is that we have to let go of it to reach it. We have to lean on our faith rather than our own understanding. We have to seek God in humility rather than control the circumstance to our own end.

It is a challenge to handle and difficult to steward. Just like any superpower would be.

Ponder Today: The measure of our strength is in whom we place our trust.

AUGUST 7: THE FLOWER OF GRASS

"You have been born again not of seed which is perishable but imperishable, that is, through the living and enduring word of God. For, "All flesh is like grass, And all its glory like the flower of grass. The grass withers, And the flower falls off, But the word of the Lord endures forever." – 1 Peter 1:24-25

When we consider our lives are just a short two-minute adventure, we can react in one of two ways. We can either do everything we can to cling to each passing moment. Or, we can make the most of each moment as a kinetic part of The Story of God and the celebration of his Kingdom.

Too often, we hitch our wagons to what is perishable. We try to make it last. To control how it begins, ends and feels along the way. Only to find our circumstances are like the "flower of grass". It withers and falls away.

C.S. Lewis once remarked on the absurdity of many who spend their lives looking forward to reaching a certain age, only to spend the rest of their lives attempting to cling to the illusion of remaining that age (we can't wait to "grow up" and then we obsessively reminisce about "the glory years").

Each season of life passes to another, and has its own rewards and challenges. When we encounter this inevitable reality, we quickly try to find the next thing to hitch our wagon to. The next perishable thing must be THE thing, we suppose. We are obsessed with more, slaves to our circumstances, because we are trying so hard to stretch what is meant to be a usable resource to an eternal comfort item.

The passage of time is put into perspective by contemplating that which transcends time: the word of God.

Ironically, by shifting our perspective to trusting the enduring Word of God, we find that perishable things can be used for imperishable ends. Our effort and skills can be wasted on investing in the temporal. Or they can be full of purpose as tools for the advancement of God's Eternal Kingdom.

Ponder Today: Perishable things can be used for imperishable means ends

AUGUST 8: CREATURES OF HEAVEN AND EARTH

"You alone are the Lord. You have made the heavens, The heaven of heavens with all their host, The earth and all that is on it, The seas and all that is in them. You give life to all of them And the heavenly host bows down before You" – Nehemiah 9:6

Everything we encounter is a by-product of the work of the Sovereign Lord. The earth, the heavens. Angels, animals, and mankind. It is all a reflection of The One True God.

Throughout Scripture, there are stories of angels appearing to mankind to help us along our way. We often revere angels and look at them in awe. As we should, they are majestic creatures designed by The God of The Universe.

So are you.

Angels play an incredible and awe-inspiring part in the narrative of God. And so do human beings. We have the unique opportunity to trust God through faith, something even the angels can't do. Alongside all other things created by God, humans and angels reflect something about who God is; they are different manifestations of The Truth - evidence of the great and glorious King.

Imagine two celebrities who are in different fields (say an actor and an athlete). Both have admired one another from afar. Both think the other is amazing at what they do.

This is our relationship with the angels. To be awed, for sure. Just about every Biblical character that encounters an angel is floored. It makes one wonder what the experience is like for the angel. Are they nervous to appear before man and help him on his way? Are they excited to be a part of what God is doing? Are they awed by the faith of the fallible humans they come in contact with?

Just like the angels, we were created uniquely to reflect the glory of God. We do not create God's Glory, we simply bear witness to it. Our superpower is faith, the ability to make choices to trust God even when we cannot see, feel, or understand. A pretty astonishing feat. Yet another reason to bow down before the Creator of all things.

Ponder Today: Angels likely revere us as much as we revere them

AUGUST 9: SOW AND REAP

"Do not be deceived, God is not mocked; for whatever a man sows, this he will also reap. For the one who sows to his own flesh will from the flesh reap corruption, but the one who sows to the Spirit will from the Spirit reap eternal life." – Galatians 6:7-8

We all have a choice to make. Whom will we trust? Whom will we serve? Who (or what) will we worship?

And the choice we make has consequences, not only in this life but in the life to come. If we choose to trust in the Lord, we will not be saved from trials but we will be given the resources to overcome them - to rise above the circumstances of this world through a transcendent trust in God's infinite goodness.

Joshua made this choice when he said, "As for me and my house, we will serve the Lord" (Joshua 24:14-15). Ruth made this commitment by proclaiming to Naomi "your God will be my God and your people my people" (Ruth 1:6).

Each day, we are given the opportunity to make the same choice. Choosing is the most effective way humans sow. And what we sow determines what we will reap. What we choose concerning whom we trust leads to a harvest of either destruction or plenty.

The powers of darkness are vying for our attention. And not all of their pleas are vile (at least not in the superficial sense) - some are appealing to our sinful nature. But their pleas are appalling in the heavenly realms, where truth and righteousness are the order of the day.

Each of us serve as the referee in our own lives. The choice is our responsibility.

You are the only one who can settle the matter of flesh and spirit within your own soul. Whom will you trust? What consequences will you reap.

Ponder Today: Choices can be difficult. We may feel tempted to pawn them off by blaming others or making excuses, but in the end we cannot avoid making them and addressing the resulting consequence.

AUGUST 10: CASTING ANXIETY

"Humble yourselves, therefore, under God's mighty hand, that he may lift you up in due time. Cast all your anxiety on him because he cares for you. Be alert and of sober mind. Your enemy the devil prowls around like a roaring lion looking for someone to devour." – 1 Peter 5:6-8

Our society is locked in a great struggle with anxiety. The Bible tells us how to deal with anxiety. We are instructed to "cast" our anxiety onto God.

There is plenty to be anxious about. Satan and the powers of darkness are prowling around like lions, looking for a chance to steal, kill, and destroy the life within us. One of his preferred tactics is to point to circumstances we cannot control or understand.

This verse doesn't tell us to deny this reality. In fact, it tells us to be alert and sober. To see the reality for what it is. Life is filled with peril. We are often put down, ignored, passed over, and abused. We are taken advantage of and taken for granted. We don't get the recognition we think we deserve. All sources of anxiety.

The answer to anxiety is the same no matter the source: humble ourselves under God's mighty hand. Cast our anxieties upon Him. Trust He cares for us, and will lift us up in due time. His time. We sometimes try to avoid anxiety by hiding from reality. Or perhaps we try to control it by seeking control over uncontrollable circumstances. Both are futile.

Anxiety is not pain. The pain will likely remain. But there is no need to remain anxious. God is in control. He desires our best. He will see that all things are put to right. It is hard to wait for His time, we prefer things to be done on our time. But God will decide what is "due time." If we believe this, our reasons for worry diminish greatly.

Ponder Today: Control is not the solution to anxiety.

AUGUST 11: ELEVATE

"Then he took a cup, and when he had given thanks, he gave it to them, and they all drank from it." – Mark 14:23

Such a simple action - picking up a cup, titling it back, and taking a sip. You've done it a thousand times. It is a part of every day, a necessary motion for the mundane activity of drinking. Mundane, but vitally important.

Jesus and His Kingdom help transform the mundane activities of our every day. The sacraments are an example of this. Baptism is a magnification of the practice of washing. Communion a transformed celebration of the mundane practice of eating a meal.

Jesus embraced the mundane and made it clear to us - the plains are an arena of life and they have a place in the Kingdom of God. Sacraments like baptism and communion invite us to see washing and eating differently. They invite us to remember the Eternal within the mundane.

Jesus built pictures of eternal truths into the most basic elements of our daily lives—and this should lead us to worship.

The plains are an opportunity. By taking our everyday activities, our routines, our boredom and our "uneventful" moments or seasons, pressing them through a perspective of faith and opportunity, we can follow Jesus' example and start to find the extraordinary value of the ordinary.

Ponder Today: How do your ordinary, everyday activities invite you into gratitude and worship?

AUGUST 12: THE FOUNDATION OF REWARD

"For no one can lay any foundation other than the one already laid, which is Jesus Christ. If anyone builds on this foundation using gold, silver, costly stones, wood, hay or straw, their work will be shown for what it is, because the Day will bring it to light. It will be revealed with fire, and the fire will test the quality of each person's work. If what has been built survives, the builder will receive a reward." – 1 Corinthians 3:11-14

It seems some people in the church of Corinth wanted to follow Paul and others found him lacking and wanted to follow Apollos. Paul weighs in, but does not really defend himself. He shrugs off both praise and criticism and encourages them to follow Christ.

Why? Because the foundation of our faith is none other than Jesus Christ. Paul had a role, as did Apollos. That role was to build upon the foundation that is Jesus.

Paul admonishes all followers of Jesus to choose the perspective that we are all called to build upon that foundation. Paul was not so concerned about how he was being judged by people. How he might be compared with Apollos. He was concerned about how he would be judged by Jesus in "the Day" of judgement. The Day when all the works of believers are judged, to see what rewards will be given.

Paul asks the believers in Corinth to shift their perspective from worrying about what human "tribe" to belong to, and start focusing on how they are building. In the process, he exhorts us as well.

If, through active obedience, we build with materials that last, God rewards us with the gifts of His Kingdom.

Adopting this perspective, Paul advocates placing everything we do into an eternal perspective. We can listen to others to gain insight and wisdom, but at the end of "the Day", the only opinion that will really matter will be that of Jesus Christ, the true foundation upon which we are building.

Ponder Today: God is the only firm foundation.

AUGUST 13: SHOW IT

"Who is wise and understanding among you? Let them show it by their good life, by deeds done in the humility that comes from wisdom." – James 3:13

Life demands a list of questions be answered. Whom will you serve? What will you do?

The way to really know someone is by watching their actions. It is in our deeds that we reveal what we have learned, whether we have the wisdom, humility and understanding to lead what James calls a "good life".

With our choices, we reveal how we are to answer the great questions of life. Our decisions are our way of "picking a side". Wisdom or folly?

When we display deeds that are the result of humility and wisdom, we are showing off "the good life". We reveal to others the understanding behind our choices.

The Bible tells us there is a narrow way to the good life, and few find it. When we make good choices, we bear witness to the way, the path to the good life.

Most of what we encounter in our daily existence is beyond our ability to control. Circumstances, the actions and opinions of others. Sometimes it seems so chaotic and off base it can be discouraging.

But here is this verse that tells us there is a good life available to us regardless of any of those things outside our control. It is there for us to choose. No one can keep us from it. It is there for us if we gain the understanding to know it, and the wisdom to choose it.

Ponder Today: How do your actions affect the life you lead?

AUGUST 14: THE DETESTERS

"There are those who hate the one who upholds justice in court and detest the one who tells the truth." – Amos 5:10

It is bad enough when we deny the truth in our own lives. But denying the truth leads to an even darker place. It leads to hatred of those who tell the truth. Rather than be chastised and repent, we double down on believing lies and hate those who expose them.

This verse was written during the period of the Kings, over 2500 years ago, and it is as true today as ever. When people deny what is true, it leads to hatred for those willing to speak the truth.

That means there will likely be a price for speaking the truth. Jesus certainly paid a price. His natural allies, the Bible-believing Pharisees, joined forces with the Romans and Sadducees in order to silence His truth-telling. Rather than repent, they hated him to the point of participating in His murder.

As Christians, we are of course called to proclaim the truth, as our Savior proclaimed the truth. We must not allow those who hate us for speaking the truth to keep us from proclaiming it. We are called to be salt and light, and play a visible role in proclaiming truth.

Before we can do that, we have to make sure we are not detesting the truth ourselves. To ensure we have not substituted truth for happy emotion or fulfilled fleshly desires.

To live a life based on truth, we must first have the humility to receive it, to listen to God and learn to tune into his voice. Then we need the courage to proclaim it when the world around us hates us and desires to silence our voice.

We are told we gain great rewards when we suffer the sufferings of Jesus. Many of His sufferings stemmed from His unrelenting commitment to live and speak the truth.

Ponder Today: Speak the truth boldly, but be sure you are speaking the truth.

AUGUST 15: BUTTERFLY

"For through the law I died to the law so that I might live for God. I have been crucified with Christ and I no longer live, but Christ lives in me. The life I now live in the body, I live by faith in the Son of God, who loved me and gave himself for me."
– Galatians 2:19-20

The law of God is shared with mankind to set up a standard of righteousness. A standard, we see time and time again, no one can truly live up to.

It is hard for us to admit, but there are some things in life we cannot control. There are some puzzles we cannot solve, some mysteries we cannot understand. All of our effort and our reasoning leaves us short.

We are like caterpillars trying so hard to fly.

The only way to achieve flight is to spend some time in a cocoon. Some time waiting, being transformed by forces beyond your control. A cocoon might seem like imprisonment; it might seem like it is holding you back. But it is the path to redemption, the road to resurrection.

We must die to live. We have to lay down our arrogant approaches to life and trust in what God has for us. It is the only way to take flight.

Is today your day to fly? Perhaps you have been in the cocoon and God is ready to send you into orbit. Perhaps you have been trying to fly as a caterpillar and it is the day to lay down your efforts and trust what God has to say.

Ponder Today: Your superpower has lain dormant too long. It will cost you something, but it is time to submit to the God of transformation.

AUGUST 16: MORE PRECIOUS

"They are more precious than gold, than much pure gold; they are sweeter than honey, than honey from the honeycomb. By them your servant is warned; in keeping them there is great reward." – Psalm 19:10-11

Psalm 19 speaks of God's law, statutes, commandments and judgments. These are not words we typically associate with the sweetness of honey. Correction, reproof, instruction: these are all words we typically associate with a bitter taste. But sweetness is exactly how the Psalmist describes God's direction.

Why? God's words warn us how to avoid harm. Not only that, God's direction and instruction shows us how to live constructively. It brings us the greatest of rewards.

There is a strange reality about humans - we very often do not know what we actually want. We may think we know. We might think that a few more dollars in the bank account or a few more followers on Instagram will meet a desire of our heart. But "more" is an unachievable destination. Sometimes we have specific goals we believe will bring us happiness. But all too often, those who receive the very things they were so sure they wanted discover it only leads to emptiness.

We live in a world that chases gold and honey, but doesn't realize the infinite supply of something vastly superior to either. God's word provides in abundance and is readily available for us to interact with.

The word of God is more precious than gold and sweeter than honey. It leads us on paths to the fulfillment of our deepest desires.

Ponder Today: What is it you really want? As we dwell on God's word, and follow God's directions, we will find the true riches of life in His Kingdom.

AUGUST 17: STRANGERS

"All these died in faith, without receiving the promises, but having seen them and having welcomed them from a distance, and having confessed that they were strangers and exiles on the earth." – Hebrews 11:13

One of the hardest things about life on earth (for a believer) is that it is not our true home. We are called to lives of delayed gratification. What we see does not satisfy. What we yearn for is the whisper of a promise.

This is hard. We want everything NOW! We want our rewards in full. We are tired of waiting.

But the promises of Eternity are not meant to be limitations. They are meant to set us free. After all, in the greater scheme of things, our time on this planet is just a blip in the radar. We are sojourners/strangers/visitors in this land. Home is on the horizon.

God's design is not that we receive our reward in full in this life. But neither is it that we waste this life. Our decisions here have an Eternal impact. The brevity of this life is a call to action, not an excuse for complacency. Our full reward is later; the experience of promises fulfilled (in a final sort of way) comes on the other side of death. When we welcome these truths "from a distance", it paradoxically brings us closer to them, showing us glimpses of what is to come (and allowing us to be content with that).

While we are here, like the great heroes of Christianity, we are called to be witnesses, to live a life of faith. To put ourselves in alignment with our eternal journey and use this life as an amazing and unique opportunity to serve, love, explore, and share the Kingdom of God.

Ponder Today: Much of life in The Kingdom of God is an exercise in delayed gratification.

AUGUST 18: UNBELIEF

"...if you can do anything, take pity on us and help us." "'If you can'?" said Jesus. "Everything is possible for one who believes." Immediately the boy's father exclaimed, "I do believe; help me overcome my unbelief!" – Mark 9:22-24

This fascinating utterance in Mark 9 comes from a man who is asking Jesus to heal his child. He has faith in Jesus but he also asks Jesus to help him have faith.

Faith is the great opportunity of human existence and the fascination of angels. We exercise this power by trusting in God. Sometimes we think of faith as a one-and-done proposition. You have it or you don't. In some ways that is correct. But faith also manifests in many ways. And the swirl of our circumstances, our emotions, and the challenges of our discernment make faith a choice we have to make every instance, over and over again.

It is like a son who trusts his dad. He might love his father and think the world of him. He might blindly jump off the couch into his father's arms and follow him all around town. But if the pair go bungee jumping together and the dad says, "it'll be alright", the son is going to struggle with trusting him.

Every opportunity, every instance, every circumstance tests our faith. It puts before us a choice. Do we believe? Do we really and truly believe, no matter what? Even when we do not understand or our life is at stake.

Even if our faith is there, well established, we have to choose it. We have to trust it, to lean on it, to live it out faithfully. And Jesus is the great author and finisher of our faith. Our helper. Our support. Our God. The One in whom we can trust.

Ponder Today: Faith is a lifetime work-in-progress.

AUGUST 19: ALL TERRAIN

"The Spirit Himself testifies with our spirit that we are children of God, and if children, heirs also, heirs of God and fellow heirs with Christ, if indeed we suffer with Him so that we may also be glorified with Him. For I consider that the sufferings of this present time are not worthy to be compared with the glory that is to be revealed to us." – Romans 8:16-18

When we are called to relationship with God, it is not all ease and comfort. We are called into relationship with Him, to share in who He is and the Kingdom He has established.

This means we share all facets of experience and all kinds of circumstances with our heavenly Father. We share in his sufferings. We share in his glory. As members of his family, we encounter the struggles and the triumphs he encounters.

This can be an uncomfortable truth. We don't want to share in suffering. We want to avoid that and skip to the best part. But relationship with God is not about the perks; it is about the relationship.

The Valleys are undesirable and pain should not be pursued. But when it arrives, it is an opportunity to lean into our Divine parent. To listen to his advice on how to respond. To be covered by his voice telling us it is ok and that He is right next to us.

We are the family of God. Meant to pursue better circumstances. But even more than that, meant to share in all the terrains of life.

Ponder Today: Relationship with God is available and the primary consideration throughout all of life's diverse circumstances.

AUGUST 20: HUMAN CONSISTENCY

"In everything, set them an example by doing what is good. In your teaching, show integrity, seriousness and soundness of speech that cannot be condemned, so that those who oppose you may be ashamed because they have nothing bad to say about us."
– Titus 2:7-8

When we think about how we are doing as a human being, as a disciple of Jesus, it is tempting and easy for us to think of our best moments. Or our worst. When we think about the example we set for others, we are likely thinking of the highlights, the big moments "on stage", the times when it was clear something important was going on.

But the big moments don't happen in a vacuum. And the way we act in the big moments is partially a manifestation of who we are and how we live day by day.

Even more important, the "small" decisions we make - the way we treat strangers in innocuous situations, the way we respond to our spouse, the way we move and live on a consistent basis, is all vitally important. Most of the examples we set will be the result of behavior we are largely unaware of, subconscious action born out of the patterns and consistency of our everyday behavior.

We cannot wait for a "big" moment to suddenly show who we are. We have to show it in the "small moments". Those daily decisions, the actions of each moment, reveal where we have placed our hope and whom we serve.

Ponder Today: Without consistently good small moments, we will not be capable of consistently big moments.

AUGUST 21: EMPTY STOREHOUSE

"Then he said, 'This is what I'll do. I will tear down my barns and build bigger ones, and there I will store my surplus grain. And I'll say to myself, "You have plenty of grain laid up for many years. Take life easy; eat, drink and be merry."' But God said to him, 'You fool! This very night your life will be demanded from you. Then who will get what you have prepared for yourself?' This is how it will be with whoever stores up things for themselves but is not rich toward God." – Luke 12:18-21

The riches of God are eternal. The superficial treasures of this world are temporary. They will fade. They will fall short. They will let us down.

Too often, we focus on gathering and hoarding the wealth of this world. We want a collection of frivolous joys, hoping we can rely on their memories when things get tough. We imagine a fulfilling life is just one elusive adventure away, one change in circumstance, just one more tax bracket bump. If we can only get there, then we could kick up our heels, relax and live happily ever after.

But trials and difficult circumstances are going to come. The only thing more certain is death. In both instances, our hoarding won't help us. In fact, it will hurt us. If we appear before God with wasted resources to our name, it will be toward our shame rather than our credit.

Although the amplified voices of this world make it seem hoarding is the only way, it is not the sole option. The riches of God look a lot like the riches of man. The difference is they are resources to worship Him and to care for one another rather than to save for self-preservation and self-aggrandizement. God is the King of riches. He has given us all things richly to enjoy, according to 1 Timothy 6:17. He invites us to gain treasures that will not rust or spoil by seeking to live in harmony with the principles of His kingdom. All the treasures of this earth are transitionary. They are passing through our hands, on their way to somewhere else. God invites us to store lasting treasures that will never fade.

Ponder Today: If we appear before God with wasted resources to our name, it will be toward our shame rather than our credit.

AUGUST 22: EVERLASTING TRUTH

"The Law and the Prophets were proclaimed until John. Since that time, the good news of the kingdom of God is being preached, and everyone is forcing their way into it. It is easier for heaven and earth to disappear than for the least stroke of a pen to drop out of the Law." – Luke 16:16-17

Jesus said that He came not to abolish the law, but to fulfill it. Christians can sometimes be dismissive of The Old Testament. But the story of God is intentional from beginning to end.

The great value of The Old Testament is the truth it establishes. The truth of who God is. The truth about the world He created. The truth about people and how they fit within God's system.

The reason Luke makes it clear the law is not something that merely fades away but is fulfilled by Jesus is because he wants people to know that the truth is still the divine barometer. The Old Testament law lets us know what truth is and what it takes to live in communion with the truth.

The sad reality is that none of us are able to do it. The standard of truth is set and we all fall short. In this way, The Old Testament gives us the great gift of showing us how much we need Jesus. On our own, we inevitably betray the truth. With faith in God, we have the opportunity to participate in the truth. It is not an abolishment or a loophole or a work around. Jesus is the fulfillment of the law. The truth.

And this reality, in a way, sets us free. It gives us hope in the possible (Jesus) rather than the impossible (our own ability to interpret and uphold the truth). It changes our source of power, our source of hope, and the way we engage with reality.

Ponder Today: Truth has been set and consistent since the beginning of time. It is woven into the fabric of creation.

AUGUST 23: TARGET

"So we make it our goal to please him, whether we are at home in the body or away from it. For we must all appear before the judgment seat of Christ, so that each of us may receive what is due us for the things done while in the body, whether good or bad." – 2 Corinthians 5:9-10

It is a well-known phenomenon that humans see what they are looking for. We have a bunch of different names for it - confirmation bias, echo chamber, etc. What we are aiming toward is the most important factor for determining our behavior (we go where we are gazing), our perspective (we see the horizon we've turned toward), and our hope (by choosing a target, we are choosing a mission we believe in).

Throughout Scripture, the target of our lives is pretty clear. We are to aim for the pleasure of Christ. The joy of the Lord. His affirmation. He does not need us but He wants us. He wants to delight in what we do. He accepts us no matter who or what we are trying to please. But it breaks his heart when we take advantage of his acceptance and aim our efforts elsewhere.

Both within our days and at the end of our days on earth, God will judge our efforts. Where were we aimed and what did we do? Did we waste time with the wrong targets or did we cast our eye on Him?

Every day we make the foundational choice: where will we aim? What is our target? What is the motivation, the inspiration, the purpose that leads and guides us?

Ponder Today: The target we choose will be the measure of success and the coal in the fire that keeps us moving.

AUGUST 24: DEPENDENT POWER

"The Lord is my strength and my defense; he has become my salvation. He is my God, and I will praise him, my father's God, and I will exalt him." – Exodus 15:2

We humans live in this strange juxtaposition where we are strong and mighty creatures, capable of important decisions and life-giving action. We are superheroes in the created world. We have power even the angels lack. Yet, it is not to our own credit or for our own good. It is for the good of God's Kingdom, of others, and also to ourselves.

So we are mighty beings in the created realm, but the true value of our strength is lost when separated from the source. It becomes messy and ugly, ruined and perverted; a cause of pain rather than joy.

God is the source of our strength. This is both comforting and frustrating. It is difficult because it is outside our control and requires a sense of mystery and trust. But it is comforting and freeing in the sense that it takes the ultimate weight off of our shoulders. Only God is truly in control. We can do our best and are commanded to steward what the Lord gives us, but He is the arbiter of truth and goodness. He is the source of power.

The incredible thing about today is that God is loaning you, his child, some of that power. Power to love and to serve. Power to trust and to perceive. Power to believe.

Ponder Today: God is the source of our strength. When we try to do it alone, we detach from that which makes us capable in the first place.

AUGUST 25: LIONS AND LIMITS

"The lions may roar and growl, yet the teeth of the great lions are broken." – Job 4:10

Job's friend Eliphaz does not get everything right in the Book of Job. But as he talks with his friend and tries to figure out what is going on in Job's life, he makes an interesting observation. He points out just how frail and perishable life can be.

When we approach God, we are often thinking about our current feelings or circumstances. We are zeroed in on our setting for today and we want God to help. We want our negative feelings to go away and our circumstances to change. We want more understanding spouses and more patient bosses. We want a raise and a car and a satisfying vacation.

We want to be healthy lions that growl and roar. We want to eradicate negativity and feel perfectly good all of the time. But we are perishable creatures living in a decaying world. When one circumstance is "fixed", we are soon to discover new challenges and new discontent. When our negative feelings subside, they are only at peace until another expectation is unmet or a value is threatened. We will continue to struggle with feeling and with circumstances beyond our control.

Like Job, even if we do everything right, life is still a challenge, a mystery. God wants us to see past the limits of feeling and circumstance and trust in him. It is the only way to eternity, an invitation to participate in something that transcends the temporal while still living in a temporal reality. It is the gift of God and the challenge of today.

Ponder Today: Life is a mystery. And that fact is an invitation to place our trust in God. he only other choice is despair.

AUGUST 26: CHOICES TO BE MADE

"Do not boast about tomorrow, for you do not know what a day may bring." – Proverbs 27:1

No matter how long we live, life on this earth is brief. And if we are not careful, there are multiple ways to get stuck in the brevity. It freezes us, sinking us into an overwhelmed apathy. It can also frighten us, so that we are constantly looking for the day it all ends.

One of the advantages to a brief, 2-minute ride on this planet is that it invites us to appreciate today. We cannot control or predict tomorrow. We cannot change the past. What we can do is focus on the here and now. We can make choices today that celebrate life and make the most of our journey.

The time is short but the opportunities are immense. The chance to know God by faith. The invitation to serve and care for one another. The calling to reflect Christ and His Kingdom.

Circumstances and emotions are so fickle, they change so rapidly. And they are impossible to control, perfectly predict, or fully avoid.

What we can control is our choices in this moment, on this day. We can decide to adopt a perspective of gratitude. We can choose joy and hope and forgiveness. We can love one another and listen for God's voice. Tomorrow is a myriad of choices we cannot get to yet. Today is a myriad of choices ready to be made.

Ponder Today: We get ourselves lost when we try to control what cannot be controlled. Focus on your choices today.

AUGUST 27: FAITH ARRIVES

"Consequently, faith comes from hearing the message, and the message is heard through the word about Christ." – Romans 10:17

The only way to increase our faith is through hearing and believing the message of Christ.

We cannot gain faith through met expectations, specific circumstances, or any other temporal measure. Humans waste a lot of time trying to grow their faith by manipulating circumstances. We try to prove our faith by controlling the world around us.

That is not how faith works.

We gain faith by listening. Faith is not a proof; it is a trust. We trust God by tuning our hearts to hear His voice. By learning from what He has to say to us - through Scripture, our community, nature, etc. Faith is trusting in God. It is not leaning on our own understanding.

The message of Scripture is that Christ is worthy of our trust. He is God and nobody else is God. As such, He is all that is worthy of our faith.

When we listen to the voice of God, we open ourselves to more faith. We expose ourselves to the source of faith - the author and perfecter. It is how faith arrives, how it proves its worth, and how we grow in it.

There is nothing more pressing for our day than listening to God. As we open our ears to hear what he has to say, what is clear in His Scriptures and what is blaring through the natural world, we unclog our perspective and allow faith the opportunity to grow, increase, and bear fruit.

Ponder Today: We waste a lot of time trying to grow faith by manipulating circumstances.

AUGUST 28: HE PROSPERS

"Blessed is the one who does not walk in step with the wicked or stand in the way that sinners take or sit in the company of mockers, but whose delight is in the law of the Lord, and who meditates on his law day and night. That person is like a tree planted by streams of water, which yields its fruit in season and whose leaf does not wither - whatever they do prospers."
– Psalm 1:1-3

There are a lot of voices in this world trying to tell us what it means to succeed. What does being rich look like and how do we get it?

Psalm 1 implores us to hear the word of God, to find joy and trust in it, to walk in it and with it, and to do what it commands.

When we follow God's guidance, we are like a tree firmly embedded in the earth near a source of nourishment. The seasons may change around us, but the steadfastness of our position will surely bear fruit.

We are so impatient, uprooting ourselves and trying all sorts of ways to succeed, to be happy, to enjoy a meaningful life. We try fame and validation, money and power. But none of it works. These are not the true source of prosperity.

God promises us all the riches we can handle. But the true currency of The Kingdom of God is relationship. Starting with our relationship with God and including the way we care for one another, there is nothing richer than being with one another in unity of purpose.

Ponder Today: The Bible says that we prosper by listening to God and courageously doing what he asks of us.

AUGUST 29: CONFIRM AND ESTABLISH

"Be of sober spirit, be on the alert. Your adversary, the devil, prowls around like a roaring lion, seeking someone to devour. But resist him, firm in your faith, knowing that the same experiences of suffering are being accomplished by your brethren who are in the world. After you have suffered for a little while, the God of all grace, who called you to His eternal glory in Christ, will Himself perfect, confirm, strengthen and establish you." – 1 Peter 5:8-10

Suffering is a universal human experience. It is an inevitable terrain of life, an experience we cannot fully ignore or avoid.

The Bible confirms over and over again that our suffering is a season that will one day end. The hope of Christ is not just the light at the end of the tunnel. It is the light in the tunnel. Meanwhile, it is the process by which Christ will "perfect, confirm, strengthen, and establish" His people.

Suffering is a tool in God's hand. It helps us develop the character of a faithful witness, to establish trust in a God greater than our circumstances, and to bond us in intimacy with Him and with one another.

The biggest temptation we face in suffering is to allow Satan permission to devour us. We often respond to suffering by inflicting more suffering upon ourselves or others. Pain is a circumstance that God uses to develop us, to teach us, and empower us to steward wisely. When we treat it or approach it as anything else, we will often magnify pain unnecessarily. We do this by trying to deny our hurt or by trying to avoid it. But the only way to heal faster is to face our sorrow with courage.

Satan is looking to devour believers. He is looking to take our pain and use it as a catalyst for self-destruction. God is looking to teach us through our pain, to confirm and establish us. The choice of how to treat our pain and to whom we surrender its power is up to each of us.

Ponder Today: Pain is a circumstance that God uses to develop us, to teach us, and empower us to steward wisely.

AUGUST 30: ALL THE WHILE

"He who keeps the commandment keeps his soul, But he who is careless of conduct will die." – Proverbs 19:16

There are a lot of ways we die. Death is the absence of life. And that can come in a physical, literal sense or in a spiritual sense. Loss of life is just one way we cease to be.

One of the great epidemics of death in the modern world is apathy. We are complacent, obsessed with our phones and our instant gratification; addicted to television and beverages. We have made an idol out of numbing ourselves.

Many people are waiting around day in and day out for something to wake them from their stupor. We want more out of life. We are looking at circumstances - the next dating relationship, an online purchase, our team winning the championship, etc. - hoping this will catapult us out of our funk and into elicit joy.

All the while, we are missing the opportunity of every day. We are careless in how we steward our own conduct, in what we do and say, how we treat one another, and our relationship with God.

Listening to God, caring for one another, and keeping God's commands may not seem flashy and exciting. It is a daily discipline. The plains of life. We would rather have the passion of the mountains and we wait around for it rather than living our day with care.

When apathy sets in, it can be really hard to get out of. Complacency is a quicksand that can steal the joy out of living. It robs us of a true perspective - that every day is an adventure, an opportunity to know God by faith and to love one another.

Ponder Today: Apathy is the most dangerous threat to vibrant living.

AUGUST 31: SANCTIFY

"My prayer is not that you take them out of the world but that you protect them from the evil one. They are not of the world, even as I am not of it. Sanctify them by the truth; your word is truth." – John 17:15-17

The word "sanctify" means "to make holy". It is the Greek word hagiazo, the same word used in the Lord's Prayer when it says Hallowed be Thy Name. It suggests being separated from sin, growing and learning in such a way that we lean further into the Spirit and further away from the flesh.

This passage in John tells us that the vision of The Gospel is not for us to be removed from the world, but to be sanctified while we live in it. The earth is just a context, a setting. The mission is to learn to be more holy and less subservient to Satan and the flesh.

How do we do this? There is only one way. The truth. Truth found in nature, in the Scriptures, and in our own hearts.

We are becoming a society more and more allergic to the truth. We don't always like how it makes us feel or what it asks us to do. It is easier to adopt false narratives, to put on masks, to assimilate into the temporal and superficial promises of a jagged reality.

Truth is an acquired taste. It is sometimes hard to hear. It will challenge and convict us. It won't rescue us from difficult circumstances (at least not by preventing them). The truth costs us. It is also the only thing that sets us free. The only way to be sanctified.

Ponder Today: Is your sanctification more important to you than your comfort?

SEPTEMBER 1: THE COSMIC QUESTION

"I have not coveted anyone's silver or gold or clothing. You yourselves know that these hands of mine have supplied my own needs and the needs of my companions. In everything I did, I showed you that by this kind of hard work we must help the weak, remembering the words the Lord Jesus himself said: 'It is more blessed to give than to receive.'" – Acts 20:33-35

The last phrase of this passage is so powerful and so familiar, we often miss the incredible message in it. "It is more blessed to give than to receive". This suggests we receive a greater blessing by giving. There is greater value (for us) in serving than in hoarding. And so, in essence, the verse is saying we receive (true riches) more by giving than we do by receiving (earthly riches). This is a profound truth: giving and serving are not just beneficial to others, they benefit the giver as well.

We too often seek mountaintop experiences, worldly riches, and temporary emotional relief because we believe it is what will do us the most good. Human beings always act in the manner they perceive to be in their best interest.

What Paul is defending here is his stance in the cosmic question: what is really in my best interest? Is it the silver and gold that belongs to others? Or is it helping the weak and remembering Jesus? Is it coveting others through the lens of comparison and envy? Or is it working hard to steward what is rightly ours? Is it obsessing over our fleshly desires? Or is it seeing the value of our needs and the needs of others as equally important and mutually beneficial?

We have to decide every day what we believe is in our best interest. What does it take to be blessed? The riches of this world or the promises of the Kingdom of God? Stewarding our gifts and opportunities to serve and provide? Or hoarding our treasures to brag and validate? How we answer these questions will determine the way we live, love, and serve.

Ponder Today: What we really believe is best for us is the thing we will chase.

The following is a 6-day series on the life of Noah:

SEPTEMBER 2: DAY ONE - BUILD AN ARK

"Thus Noah did; according to all that God had commanded him, so he did." – Genesis 6:22

God asks Noah to take action, to do something specific. Basically, He is saying, "You are righteous in a corrupt world, so here is what I want you to do…

"I want you to build an ark. Make it just like this."

God gives the instruction and the blueprint. And Noah does according to all that God commanded him. As he was told, so he did.

We are not so different. We are believers, living in a corrupt world, seeking intimacy with God. And he has given us something to do. We've got our marching orders just like Noah.

God has commanded us to build an ark. God gives us something to do. An ark to build.

Our ark is the life we live. Our ark is living a life that exhibits the resurrection power of Jesus. Our blueprint is the commands of Jesus.

That is what will save us from the negative consequences of sin. And like Noah, when we walk in the resurrection power of Jesus, we gain great reward.

As God commands us to act, He gives us the specifications - the dimensions and limitations of a well-lived life.

What is the condition of your ark? Have you followed the specifications? Will it stand when the weather turns sour? Noah is provided in numerous places in the Bible as an example of obedience. Let's build our ark just the way Jesus told us to.

Ponder Today: We are all called to be an ark-builder. Decision by decision, to construct a life in obedience to the Lord.

SEPTEMBER 3: DAY 2 - GOD IS GOD

"But without faith it is impossible to please Him, for he who comes to God must believe that He is, and that He is a rewarder of those who diligently seek Him." – Hebrews 11:5-6

Noah is one of the prominent members of the "Hall of Faith" in chapter 11 of the book of Hebrews. Noah is our example because he pleased God by doing all God asked of him.

Hebrews 11 wants us to follow the example of these heroes of faith, like Noah. But it tells us that we cannot please God without first acknowledging that God is truly God. We must believe that "He is."

We are invited to believe God is really GOD. Not a genie in a bottle we can conjure up when we need help. Not an innocuous Santa that hands out goodies. But a Consuming Fire – and an ever-present help in the time of need. The Sovereign Creator of All – who became the Servant of All. The very Definition of Love.

We do not define GOD. GOD defines us. And if we want to have Award-Winning Hebrews 11 Faith, we have to submit to God as He is, not as we would make Him.

If we don't believe that God is GOD, then it won't make sense to diligently seek Him. It will make a lot more sense to diligently seek our own way. If we don't see God as GOD, we are inclined to have the attitude of "That might be ok for others, but I know what is best for me." God knows and seeks our best and, if we want to be let in on the answers, we need to seek His voice.

Wisdom and reward begin with this: an acknowledgment of God. If we are going to build an ark based on his specifications, we have to start by trusting in Him as the Creator, Designer, and Sustainer of the Universe. To acknowledge that if we build an ark according to His specifications, it will turn out for our best.

Ponder Today: Board by board, nail by nail, day by day, you are building an ark unto the Lord.

SEPTEMBER 4: DAY 3 - LOVE WELL

"By faith Noah, when warned about things not yet seen, in holy fear built an ark..." – Hebrews 11:7

The Hall of Faith is full of great ark-builders. Like us, these people are called to erect an ark of faithful obedience, a life of service. And a life of love - one key specification to build your ark is to love well.

But love is not as simple as just being nice. Noah is not renowned for his politeness, his upbeat and positive attitude. Real love is doing what's in the best interest of others. Someone who needs an intervention might not appreciate it in the moment. Or perhaps ever. But it is love nonetheless.

Noah intervened to confront the wickedness around him by building an ark. In doing so he offered them an intervention – a better way.

Scripture provides a blueprint for the self-interest of each human being. When we live according to that blueprint, we are building an ark with our lives. We are accepting the invitation to live a better way.

God's perspective, revealed to us through His holy word, lets us know what is best for each of us. Which informs us how to live well. How to truly love.

It takes real courage to love well. It isn't always applauded when we pursue true love and invest in God's perspective of what it means to care for one another. To pursue not only our best interest, but the interest of others.

Noah trusted God and showed people a way to be delivered from death. But it wasn't popular. Almost everyone declined. But Noah pleased God. And that is why his life was a great success.

Ponder Today: The foundation to any truly great life is loving well.

SEPTEMBER 5: DAY 4 - A COMPLETE MAN

"Noah was a just man, perfect in his time." – Genesis 6:9

The word "perfect" here can be confusing. Noah is not being referred to as flawless, in the way we normally consider perfection. It is not that he is devoid of faults, absent of sin.

"Perfect" is translated in the Greek OT with the word telios. "Telios" might be better translated as "complete".

Telios shows up as the word "finisher" in Hebrews 12:2 - "[Jesus] is the author and finisher of our faith".

The idea is that Noah was a complete person. He was just. He was righteous. Noah walked with God; he tried his best, believing God and doing as God commanded. Making his decisions in accordance with God's way. Noah was "complete" in terms of the kind of life God calls us to.

When Noah built the ark just as God asked him, according to the instructions God gave, Noah illustrates to us what being "complete" looks like. It looks like following God's ways without any shortcuts. Without any "I think I know better".

It is comforting we do not have to be perfect, in the modern sense of the word. We are, however, called to complete our ark. To make it seaworthy. To continue working on it until our lives are finished. To seek to do all God asks of us. No more, no less.

Jesus authored our faith. Which means He originated it. He completed our faith, rounding it out. He nailed every sin to the cross and paved our way into heaven. To be a child of God requires simple faith.

To please God requires that we believe He is, and that He is a rewarder of those who diligently seek Him. To have the commitment to "telios". To complete what God has given us to do.

Our opportunity is to complete our ark through righteous living in the power of Jesus' resurrection.

Ponder Today: Sometimes our pursuit of perfection poisons our pursuit of completeness.

SEPTEMBER 6: DAY 5 - A LONG HORIZON

"In the six hundredth year of Noah's life, in the second month, on the seventeenth day of the month, on the same day all the fountains of the great deep burst open, and the floodgates of the sky were opened." – Genesis 7:11

One of the most important lessons we can glean from the life of Noah is the horizon of our faith.

God asks us, like Noah, to move our reward horizon far off, including beyond our lifetime. He did not let Noah know exactly what it would look like after the waters receded. He did tell him one of His promises was going to take a hundred and twenty years. That's a long time to trust.

God asks us to trust Him for our entire life. And beyond. We ought to build our ark with an eye toward Eternity. To please God, we must believe that He is and that He is a rewarder of those who diligently seek him (Heb 11:6).

The rewards we seek will not be fully realized during our lifetime on this Earth. Our faithfulness will see its true victory in Heaven. And that requires a lot of faith on our part. It is challenging to live in this world according to promises that extend beyond this world.

This is the thing that fascinates the angels. That we would be able to extend our trust beyond the horizon of what we can see. That we might put our hope in something we cannot understand.

The horizons of our reward are in direct proportion to their greatness. There is so much in store for those who are faithful to God. God wants us to believe that His rewards will be worth it.

Ponder Today: It is challenging to live in this world according to promises that extend beyond this world.

SEPTEMBER 7: DAY 6 - DILIGENCE

"But without faith it is impossible to please Him, for he who comes to God must believe that He is, and that He is a rewarder of those who diligently seek Him." – Hebrews 11:5-6

Award-winning Faith requires us to believe God rewards those who diligently seek Him. To believe in God's benevolence. That He wants to reward us.

To please God requires that we believe the benefit to us will be worth the trouble of diligently seeking His ways.

Building our ark takes an entire lifetime, however long that is. And it will be uphill much of the way. It requires that we look beyond the horizon of anything we can see and touch to know "it will be worth it all".

The only way we will remain steadfast, diligent, and committed to the practice of building our lives according to God's blueprint is if we trust that his way is best, that it will work to our greatest benefit. Like Noah, who spent a century building an ark precisely as God asked.

In reality, no one does anything unless they believe it will be of personal benefit. Even when we sacrifice, we expect a future benefit. Like deferring spending to invest in retirement. Trusting God is the best kind of investment. It has a guaranteed return.

Ark building is hard work. Our labors and our pains will be quickly abandoned unless we believe that God's promise will make it worth our while. The Apostle Paul says that what God will do for those who love Him is beyond our capacity to comprehend.

But Noah's life provides an illustration to contemplate. His diligence in following God's blueprint allowed him to escape destruction as it fell all around him. And his obedience became a blessing to every human descendant on earth.

That is a lot of reward. And an excellent inspiration to diligently seek to follow the path God has laid out for us.

Ponder Today: Faithfulness is not just worth it in the end. It is the best path for the present.

This concludes our 6-day series on the life of Noah.

SEPTEMBER 8: YOURS AND NOT YOURS

"The secret things belong to the Lord our God, but the things revealed belong to us and to our children forever, that we may follow all the words of this law." – Deuteronomy 29:29

Sometimes we try very hard to make the decisions that are not ours to make. We want to control the circumstances around us. We want to mandate the actions and attitudes of others. On some level, what we really want is to be God.

The first sin in The Garden was man wanting to take God's place, to steward the mysteries. To know the secret things. To be in charge. To be sovereign.

Only God is God.

We are minor characters in the cosmic story. But we are minor characters with a major impact. Our choices matter. They matter for us and for those around us. For the lives we are living and the legacy we leave the generations after us. Our choices are important for today and for Eternity.

The key is to let go of the choices that do not belong to us and focus on how to steward the ones that do. One of the tragic side-effects of trying to control what only God can control is that we overlook what choices are available to us. We underestimate the weight they carry. We ignore them or take them for granted.

The covenant God makes with the Old Testament fathers is two-way: for them to make choices with what God has granted them stewardship over and to trust God with everything else. The same applies to all of us today.

Ponder Today: It is a great relief in one's life when he can truly discern what is his to steward and what he needs to let go.

SEPTEMBER 9: POWER TO WITNESS

"'He said to them: 'It is not for you to know the times or dates the Father has set by his own authority. But you will receive power when the Holy Spirit comes on you; and you will be my witnesses in Jerusalem, and in all Judea and Samaria, and to the ends of the earth.'" – Acts 1:7-8

The Holy Spirit is the power supply within us. It gives us our strength. It empowers our faith. It allows us to make choices in alignment with who God is and what He wants for our lives.

A lot of perversions and false teachings have erupted that claim the Holy Spirit is the source of power to achieve our fleshly desires. We can have worldly wealth and avoid suffering if we just tap into this supernatural source of strength.

But the Bible is clear that The Holy Spirit is not a tool to achieve our lusts. It is the source by which we are empowered to love others, thereby testifying to the world the truth of The Gospel.

The main difference between the power of superheroes and the power of super villains is the manner in which they use their strength. Is it to help others or for personal material gain?

The power of The Holy Spirit allows us to live meaningful lives. To make wise choices. To experience the riches of intimacy with God and to love others. We most effectively testify to God's goodness by living a life of wise stewardship.

Ponder Today: The great power of the Holy Spirit is to aid in daily discernment.

SEPTEMBER 10: SOLID FOOD

"Anyone who lives on milk, being still an infant, is not acquainted with the teaching about righteousness. But solid food is for the mature, who by constant use have trained themselves to distinguish good from evil." – Matthew 5:13-14

When we are first getting to know God, it makes sense for us to consume spiritual milk - to learn the basics of wisdom and discernment, love and forgiveness. To allow ourselves to be trained toward righteousness.

It can feel pretty good. We see growth and change. We see fruit. And a big reason for this is the milk stage of our spiritual development is about learning how the world works. Like the honeymoon phase, we are falling in love, full of passion and excitement.

But we are meant for more. We are meant for the kind of faith that hurts. The kind that costs us something, that requires courage, and pushes us to discover what is truly in our best interest.

These solid foods can be an acquired taste. We start to experience the exceptions to how the world works. We are confronted with the mysteries and our inability to control.

Our reaction is often to want to go back to the milk. To stop progressing and linger where it is more comfortable and less confusing. We want the Vending Machine rather than relationship; the quick quip rather than the complicated relationship.

In the end, this settling robs us of the truest beauty The Kingdom of God has to offer. The intimacy that develops through conflict. The binding that happens through confusion. The unity of diversity. Only through engaging these challenges will we experience the fullness of the Kingdom of Heaven.

Ponder Today: Perhaps you have been settling for milk for too long. What is the next step toward solid food?

SEPTEMBER 11: EVERLASTING

"Why do you complain, Jacob? Why do you say, Israel, 'My way is hidden from the Lord; my cause is disregarded by my God'? Do you not know? Have you not heard? The Lord is the everlasting God, the Creator of the ends of the earth. He will not grow tired or weary, and his understanding no one can fathom."
– Isaiah 40:27-28

Our memories are short. Our vision is limited. When difficult circumstances arrive, we tend to feel as if they have always been there and they always will be. We do not think "things are this way for now"; we just think "things are this way".

Difficult circumstances are not only temporary, they are complex. The way we feel about them is just part of the truth. There is more going on than we are aware of.

Even when trials come knocking, there are opportunities. Even when tragedy strikes, there is appreciation to be found. When we lean toward gratitude, we position ourselves to remember who God is.

We sometimes focus so closely on our circumstances, we forget the bigger picture of who God is. We forget that He is everlasting. Worthy of our trust. And our hope. We too often take our eyes off Him and zero in on what is going on around us.

And we often project our confusion onto Him. We accuse him of being inept or disinterested. He seems tired. Perhaps He has run out of energy. Perhaps He is not going to follow through.

God is not circumstantial. He is not bound to Time or any other human limitations. He is God. Today, tomorrow, and forevermore. He will not grow weary. His understanding is beyond our comprehension. No matter what we are experiencing, these are the reasons to trust in Him.

Ponder Today: When we don't have answers to our questions, that is a reason to lean into trusting God not an excuse to flee from Him.

SEPTEMBER 12: FOR NOW

"Dear friends, now we are children of God, and what we will be has not yet been made known. But we know that when Christ appears, we shall be like him, for we shall see him as he is. All who have this hope in him purify themselves, just as he is pure."
– 1 John 3:2-3

Today is another day of your life. It is fast and furious and full of opportunity.

There is a part of the human spirit that longs for what is to be. And this is rightly so because our ultimate hope, our full redemption is a future experience. To see Christ as He is, in all His fullness, is too tempting a desire to hold at bay. We long for that day. We trust in it and set our hearts toward it.

But that day is not today. We can hope and imagine and anticipate what is to come. We should. But we should ALSO make the most of today. As imperfect as it is, it is not devoid of meaning. Far from it. It is not absent of thrill or purpose.

Today, we are children of God. Learning and growing. Progressing and trusting. We are getting to experience the wild adventure ride of life for a short season. An opportunity for faith - the one thing we won't be able to do in Heaven. An opportunity to make choices, to enjoy the life God has blessed us with and to steward the gifts bestowed on us.

Like any great roller coaster, the thrill comes with some trepidation. We can't have one without the other. The joy of this life is a unique experience. And the loops of circumstance, the speed of the track, and the uncertainty of the next turn are all uncomfortable. But we get to choose whether the discomfort takes away from the adventure or adds to it.

Ponder Today: What can you do to better appreciate the opportunity of life today?

SEPTEMBER 13: PEACE IN BELIEVING

"Now may the God of hope fill you with all joy and peace in believing, so that you will abound in hope by the power of the Holy Spirit." – Romans 15:13

We seek peace through a variety of methods. We try to avoid pain, to control or predict circumstances. We try to make the "right" choices about what job to take or even where to go for dinner. We entrust our peace to our season of life, our emotions, and our circumstance.

But the only true source of peace comes through believing. Through trust. It is a paradox. An oxymoron. We gain by letting go. We experience peace through trust.

The same could be said for our pathways to joy and hope.

Our unique opportunity in this life is to live by faith, to place our trust in God. Belief. Hope. They are all suggesting the same thing: a life of faith. It is the key to succeeding in this world.

We cannot find peace through manipulating or controlling circumstances (or other people), through certainty and the removal of discomfort, nor through the avoidance of pain or the numbness of complacency.

The only way to experience this life for all it is worth is through believing. Where will you place your hope today? In whom will you trust.

Ponder Today: Trust is the key to peace, hope, and joy in this life. Place yours carefully.

SEPTEMBER 14: PRECIOUS TREASURE

"There is precious treasure and oil in the dwelling of the wise, but a foolish man swallows it up." – Proverbs 21:20

The concept of treasure, riches, and wealth have intrigued, fascinated, and allured people for ages. We talk in the modern world of a "status symbol". Material riches, worldly success, feels to us a measure of status. A way of validating who we are and what we do.

We seek both acceptance and approval from the world's standard definition of success.

When the Bible speaks of treasure, it is as much how we use it as what we have. Materials are a means to an end, the resources to help us gain the true treasure. Success comes through wisdom. We win at life by making meaningful choices not by hoarding dollar bills.

The foolish man swallows worldly possessions. He internalizes it and refuses to allow anyone near it. This does not just prevent others from being blessed, it prevents the hoarder from being blessed.

All of the things God has given us are tools to draw us into relationship with him, to empower us to reflect his essence within us and to care for one another. When we pursue resources as an end rather than a means, we have turned to idolatry. The true riches, the precious treasure, in The Kingdom of God is fellowship with the King of the Universe.

Ponder Today: It is not what we have but what we do with it that makes a treasure precious.

SEPTEMBER 15: VALLEY

"But in everything commending ourselves as servants of God, in much endurance, in afflictions, in hardships, in distresses, in beatings, in imprisonments, in tumults, in labors, in sleeplessness, in hunger, in purity, in knowledge, in patience, in kindness, in the Holy Spirit, in genuine love, in the word of truth, in the power of God; by the weapons of righteousness for the right hand and the left, by glory and dishonor, by evil report and good report; regarded as deceivers and yet true." – 2 Corinthians 6:4-8

Our calling in life is to love one another and commit to the truth. This is not always a popular decision. It is not always understood.

Truth transcends all of our circumstances. Even when our seasons and settings are difficult, the truth remains. Many people fall away from walking in faith when they realize the cost.

There is a cost, but Paul considered it an investment. At the end of his life he comments on his suffering, saying "I know whom I have believed and am persuaded that He is able to keep what I have committed to Him until that Day." Paul considered his suffering like a heavenly savings account in God's bank, that would be there on the day of judgment.

It takes courage and vision to suffer with purpose. It takes an eternal perspective. One that sees difficult circumstances as opportunities to make an eternal investment. It looks like foolishness to the world. We might bear the brunt of an "evil report."

Nothing others do changes God's instruction how best to seek our own self-interest. Speaking and living the truth, in grace, is the example Jesus gave us to follow.

So, do not let circumstances or opinion derail your commitment to the truth of the gospel. No matter your circumstances, pursue righteousness. Love. The "cost" is an eternal investment, one with a guaranteed return.

Ponder Today: We cannot control the consequences of our choices but we can control our commitment to the standard by which we make those choices.

SEPTEMBER 16: TEST AND APPROVE

"Do not conform to the pattern of this world, but be transformed by the renewing of your mind. Then you will be able to test and approve what God's will is - his good, pleasing and perfect will." – Romans 12:2

Most of life will be spent on the plains. Although the mountains are most exciting and the valleys most devastating, the plains are the most prevalent.

In order to make the most out of life, we have to figure out how to live through the mundane with excellence. How do we steward boredom and the everyday opportunities that might not make our lifetime highlight reel?

The way we steward the plains is the most indicative measure for the character we are developing.

Accepting the value of the plains does not mean resigning ourselves to apathy. Scripture says that one of the most powerful ways to express our faith is by avoiding the world's call to complacency.

And so, the plains are an opportunity. This particular arena of life presents us with a choice: apathy or integrity. Will we melt into the mundane, giving our hearts to the flesh and the sleepy numbness of complacency? Or will we see each day, each moment as a chance to know God by faith, to love and care for one another, and participate in the Kingdom of Heaven?

All arenas of life are valuable. The plains invite us into consistency, discernment, and renewed patterns. The plains are a fertile testing ground, a place where we can pursue God's approval by stewarding well the choices before us.

Ponder Today: The difference between intention and apathy is an individual's choice.

SEPTEMBER 17: MONEY AS MASTER

"No one can serve two masters; for either he will hate the one and love the other, or he will be devoted to one and despise the other. You cannot serve God and wealth." – Matthew 6:24

There is nothing wrong with having wealth. Money is not the enemy. Worldly success itself is not the adversary.

Whether you are wealthy or not, the real danger is what is often translated in this verse as "the love of money". In other words, wealth is a problem if it becomes your master. If it serves The Gospel, wealth can be a positive resource. It is the posture of our hearts not the possession of our materials that is at fault when things go awry.

This is often used as an excuse for wealthy people to hoard their riches and swear it is not the master they serve. This is one of the challenges of material success. You have to constantly check which master you are serving.

One great way to measure this is to ask yourself what your money serves. What does it work to do? Some answers might be: to make more money or to help others or to make myself feel powerful or to worship God. Be honest, not about what you wish you use it for but how you actually use it. What is the reality?

The good news is that today is a new day. You have the ability to decide today whom you will serve. You can direct your wealth toward the riches of the Kingdom. There is no better master.

Ponder Today: Follow the trail of your resources and it will lead to your master.

SEPTEMBER 18: WALKING IN THE TRUTH

"For I was very glad when brethren came and testified to your truth, that is, how you are walking in truth. I have no greater joy than this, to hear of my children walking in the truth."
– 3 John 1:3-4

Although we often associate the word "truth" with "how I really feel", it is much more accurate to describe it as "how things really are".

When we focus on our emotions, we let them dictate reality. Our minds create narratives that match, validate, and reinforce the way we feel about things. How we wish they were rather than how they are.

Walking in the truth means we are exploring reality. We are seeking to discover what is real and what is a by-product of our inaccurate perceptions.

Elsewhere, Scripture says the truth "sets us free". Living in a false reality might seem better than facing the discomfort of the truth. But in the end it leads to confusion, apathy, and destruction.

Current reality is an acquired taste, but it is our friend.

In modern society, you might hear the phrase, "perception is reality". It is a dangerous idea, suggesting that how we see things is more important than how they are, that we should not waste time trying to walk in the truth but should resign ourselves to walking in the illusion. Playing the game rather than living the reality.

John has warned his audience about this and is delighted they have chosen the better way. Likewise, we have the opportunity to commit to the truth. In humility, to seek what is real and what is right.

Ponder Today: Being blunt about how you feel is not the same thing as speaking the truth.

SEPTEMBER 19: A WAY OUT

"No temptation has overtaken you but such as is common to man; and God is faithful, who will not allow you to be tempted beyond what you are able, but with the temptation will provide the way of escape also, so that you will be able to endure it. Therefore, my beloved, flee from idolatry." – 1 Corinthians 10:13-14

Because we are a people focused on circumstances, we often read this verse with the idea it is saying God will get us out of any circumstance we find ourselves in. That He will provide a way to change, control, or overcome our setting in favor of a better one.

But these verses are about overcoming internal temptation. And the way we overcome the temptations of our flesh is through the power of choice. Not a change in venue. Not a more comfortable circumstance. Always through a choice.

No matter what our situation, we always have a choice. We have the ability to decide whom we are going to serve and what action we are going to take. It may not rescue us from our circumstances, but it will rescue us from the temptation to use our circumstance as an excuse to ruin our character.

Choice is our way out. That is why Paul follows up this famous verse about what we can bear by imploring us to flee from idolatry. Depending on an external power that is not God is idolatry. God has bestowed on us the role of the referee in matters of our own character. We need look nowhere else. The way out is within us. Through the power God has granted each of us, we can make choices that avoid temptation and idolatry. Choices that honor him and serve one another.

Ponder Today: The only way we overcome both trial and temptation is through the power of choice.

SEPTEMBER 20: ABOUND

"Each of you should give what you have decided in your heart to give, not reluctantly or under compulsion, for God loves a cheerful giver. And God is able to bless you abundantly, so that in all things at all times, having all that you need, you will abound in every good work." – 2 Corinthians 9:7-8

We often see this verse used in sermons on tithing, suggesting that if you give your money (cheerfully), God will bless you abundantly by making sure you continue to thrive financially.

While that certainly might be one application of this passage, it falls short of the central message Paul is trying to communicate. In fact, a few verses down (12), he clarifies that "giving" is not just about serving others, but also about worshipping God - giving our trust and affection.

The point Paul is trying to make is that you are abundantly blessed in a lot of different ways. Physical resources, intellect and ability, time and the opportunity to make choices. And that all of these things are given to you so that you might abound in every good work.

We are blessed to serve, equipped to love. Not just because God wants us to care for others but because caring for others is also in our own self-interest.

Faith, trust in God, empowers us to be superheroes in this world. To use the variety of opportunities we have been given to serve, love, and worship. In the movies, superpowers do not make a superhero. Villains have power too. What makes them heroic is what they do with those gifts. Do they serve, love, protect or do they steal, kill, destroy?

Our choice is the greatest power we hold, the most abundant gift we have been given. What we choose to do with it today determines where we abide, whom we serve, and whether or not we live a life of abundance.

Ponder Today: What does your power serve? Where do your choices abide?

SEPTEMBER 21: COSMETICS

"Your beauty should not come from outward adornment, such as elaborate hairstyles and the wearing of gold jewelry or fine clothes. Rather, it should be that of your inner self, the unfading beauty of a gentle and quiet spirit, which is of great worth in God's sight." – 1 Peter 3:3-4

When we approach God, we are often coming with cosmetics on our mind. Help me to look better in the eyes of my fellow man. Help me to feel better. Help ease the weight of my circumstances.

In essence, we are asking that things be easier. We want a setting makeover, a paint job to slap over our challenging circumstances and relationships. We want things to appear better, convinced if they appear better, they will actually be better.

We seek outward adornment for our inner selves. Hairstyles, jewelry, fine clothes. These are all meant to avoid dealing with the reality of how we look. And it carries into other arenas of our life. We want this for our society - just put some jewelry on this issue. Maybe if this confrontation had a new hairdo, we could convince ourselves it wasn't really necessary to address the core issue at all.

We think the great value of circumstantial cosmetics is that it makes things easier. The truth is cosmetics covers the truth. It silences inner strength and covers true beauty. It keeps us from making the difficult choices that reveal who we are and whom we trust. It keeps us from ourselves more than it prevents pain.

Ponder Today: One of the devil's most seductive tricks is to tell you that how you appear is more important than who you are.

SEPTEMBER 22: A GRAND CHOICE

"Woe to him who says to wood, 'Come to life!' Or to lifeless stone, 'Wake up!' Can it give guidance? It is covered with gold and silver; there is no breath in it." – Habakkuk 2:19

One of the three things humans control is the choice of whom or what to trust. Where we place our faith. On what we decide to depend.

We must either trust in God or place our trust in something, or someone, else who is wholly undependable. It is a great gift that we are given this choice. It is a major distinction that, for now, separates us from the angels, for they see God.

At one time in history it was common for people to place their dependence in gods of gilded wood. We think of this as archaic. But this ancient practice was really a means to trust in self. The basic formulation was "This idol will give me what I want when I want it, it is a power I can manipulate and control."

We can trust money as a means to depend on ourselves. Sometimes we place our faith in our own illusions, such as the illusion that we actually know and can control the approval of others.

Although it is difficult to trust a God we cannot see, it is by far the most rational choice. The alternative is to trust something, or someone, observably undependable, like a piece of driftwood fashioned into an image.

It takes way more faith to believe that creation fashioned itself than to believe it was designed by a marvelous Creator. Even so, we are drawn to embrace illusions of control. To trust in a purposeless material props up the mirage that we are master rather than servant.

However, at some point mirages vanish. Illusions are revealed. And we are left with the reality that "It was, at the end of the day, just a piece of wood, not a god." Although we cannot see God, his handiwork is everywhere, if we choose to see it. Our opportunity to trust God is foundational to making other choices that lead to life and fulfillment according to our design.

Ponder Today: The question of who to trust should not be about what you can manipulate to your own ends.

SEPTEMBER 23: A LINE OF CHOICES

"But seek first his kingdom and his righteousness, and all these things will be given to you as well." – Matthew 6:33

You have a lot of choices to make today. Research shows that we make thousands and thousands of decisions every single day.

Our choices have consequences. They lead to effects we feel in our own lives and in the lives of others. They also set up the next choice we have to make. And the ones after that. It is easy to see how patterns develop and habits form within the thousands of choices we make each day.

Yet each decision is powerful enough to chart a new course. Or to reinforce a good one. To lead to positive effects - the riches of the kingdom. And to put us on the doorstep of more good choices.

Joshua proclaimed that he and his house will serve the Lord. Moses put before the people of Israel the choice of life and death. Each day, we begin with a choice. Whom will we serve? To which Kingdom shall we align?

The choice we make sets up the choices to follow. It sets the course of our day.

Let's be intentional about beginning this day with the Lord. Choose Him. Commit to His righteousness and His Kingdom. And see where the day leads.

Ponder Today: Our choices have an exponential effect on one another. Yet each one is powerful enough to alter our course entirely.

SEPTEMBER 24: REMNANT

"But I will leave within you the meek and humble. The remnant of Israel will trust in the name of the Lord." – Zephaniah 3:12

Throughout its pages, the Bible speaks about or infers that God retains "a remnant". The remnant are those who pass through the gauntlet of circumstances with their faith intact. Those who do not lose heart or surrender their courage to continue to walk in truth and grace.

The command Jesus gave us to be the "salt" of the world is a call to live as a remnant. When salt is applied, it only needs to be a small amount in order to have its designed effect. That's also the job of a remnant. When it retains its character, it preserves all it surrounds.

We tend to think of being salt when we walk through life's valleys. But the greatest opportunity to serve as a salty remnant is on life's plains, simply because that is where most of life occurs.

The plains contain a vast array of experiences. A myriad of opportunities. Every single one of them brimming with it opportunity as well as peril. But this is a perspective we must choose. The plains do not impose it upon us. If we aren't intentional about seeing life on the plains as an opportunity to be salt, they can become a hypnotic routine. Like monotonous white stripes on an endless straight road.

There are no meaningless choices. Each and every day, the decisions we make have an impact on who we are, whom we trust, and where we aim our worship.

Living life on the plains as salt, as a member of the remnant is transformative. But it requires adopting a perspective that what the world considers menial, like taking the trouble to deliver a cup of cool water to a person in need, is actually something that is great in God's economy.

Today is an opportunity to live a remnant lifestyle. Those who trust God with small things will receive the riches of his kingdom.

Ponder Today: The Remnant are those who survive the gauntlet of circumstances with their faith increased.

SEPTEMBER 25: MEASURING ABUNDANCE

"Then he said to them, 'Watch out! Be on your guard against all kinds of greed; life does not consist in an abundance of possessions.'"– Luke 12:15

It is hard for us to accept the idea that abundant life is not measured by the possessions we accumulate or the number of dollars in our net worth. Much of the world's strategy is to convince us that the only way to make our lives, or the lives of our families, better is to have more money. To get more things.

This perspective leads us to greed and unhappiness. "More" is an unobtainable objective that guarantees frustration and emptiness. Jesus is warning us against the perspective that abundance is an issue of material rather than spiritual gain. He warns us to "be on guard against all kinds of greed" because the opportunities for greed abound.

Jesus also tells us the greatest life opportunity with respect to material possessions is to give them all up for His kingdom. We can do this by transferring ownership to Him; it is His already. By recognizing we are stewards rather than owners, we can enjoy the bounty of God's grace without worry. It is all a matter of perspective, the way we view our sense of responsibility, ownership, and opportunity for stewardship.

If you have a material possession that you don't enjoy, get rid of it. God has given us richly all things to enjoy, and placed us as His stewards. We can hold all we possess with an open hand, and gain full enjoyment of His blessings each day.

Ponder Today: We can experience abundance in poverty, and we can experience misery while rich.

SEPTEMBER 26: PARTICIPATING IN MYSTERY

"I want to know Christ—yes, to know the power of his resurrection and participation in his sufferings, becoming like him in his death, and so, somehow, attaining to the resurrection from the dead." – Philippians 3:10-11

Our life on this planet is brief. We are, as the Scripture says, "a mist that appears for a little while and then vanishes".

To be fair, we pack a lot into these brief little lives. Joy and sorrow, and everything in between. The whole thing is an adventure. A thrill. A roller coaster of ups and downs. Perhaps the most defining characteristic of our brief existence is mystery. We do not know what will happen next. We are not sure how to interpret or understand things. We are not God.

This mystery leads many to fear. It can lead to a crippling complacency much like someone scared of roller coasters who closes their eyes and grips the safety bar with white-knuckled terror, just waiting for it to be over.

Not the best way to enjoy a "thrill ride" and not the best way to enjoy the brief life you've been given.

The point of our brief existence is to point us to God. To invite us into participating in the beauty of His Kingdom. The mysterious beauty. To trust in him no matter what turns and dips await us. To believe in the one who made the roller coaster, the track, and each person invited onto the ride.

Life is mysterious. We experience deaths and resurrections in many forms. May we do it all clinging to Christ and make the most of the brief time we have.

Ponder Today: The mystery of existence can either terrorize us or inspire us.

SEPTEMBER 27: HEAVENLY TREASURES

"Do not store up for yourselves treasures on earth, where moths and vermin destroy, and where thieves break in and steal. But store up for yourselves treasures in heaven, where moths and vermin do not destroy, and where thieves do not break in and steal. For where your treasure is, there your heart will be also." – Matthew 6:19-21

Heaven is certainly a real location. But it is not a place we expect to visit in this life. However, this verse says it is a place our hearts can dwell even while we remain on the earth. How can that be?

We house our hearts in heaven when we spend our money on the things of heaven. When we spend generously to serve others. Jesus makes clear in this verse from the Sermon on the Mount that this is highly advisable.

But the principle is broader. It says we can tell where our heart is at any point by reviewing our actual expenditures. Our heart follows our spending.

Did you pick up the check to show off that you could? Or out of generosity? One places our heart in heaven, the other at the mercy of opinion.

It is wise to occasionally check our investment accounts and adjust based on how we see the market developing. It is even wiser to check our bank statement and assess where we have invested our heart.

Jesus tells us that heaven is a place where God's will is done. It is also a place we can house our hearts and treasures while still living on earth. He is in a real sense inviting us into the perspective and riches of Heaven now, as well as the future. When we invest our heart in heaven, we also transfer our financial assets to a heavenly "safety deposit box". It will still be there when we arrive.

Ponder Today: Heaven as geography is only the tip of the iceberg. Heaven as perspective is the key to existence now and forevermore.

SEPTEMBER 28: WHO DOES NOT LIE

"Paul, a servant of God and an apostle of Jesus Christ to further the faith of God's elect and their knowledge of the truth that leads to godliness - in the hope of eternal life, which God, who does not lie, promised before the beginning of time." – Titus 1:1-2

Throughout Scripture, a commitment to pursue truth is a significant marker for God's people. It is one of the ten commandments in Exodus and part of the armor of God in Ephesians. Honesty, integrity, prophesying reality, and seeing things as they are important indicators of one's commitment to Christ and His Ways.

We acknowledge that sometimes "the truth hurts". It is an acquired taste. The truth is not just the reality we want to hear, but reality as it is.

Truth is confusing only because we are not God. We serve the truth. So much of the journey of the faithful is about pursuing and upholding truth because it is so easy for us to lose sight of what is true, real, and right.

The first couple of verses in the book of Titus aim to further the knowledge of truth within the faithful. This is the path to godliness because God Himself is The Truth. The same things that make the truth so challenging and sometimes unflattering are the reasons to celebrate. Truth is not just a practice to bring us closer to God. Truth is part of the character of God. He who does not lie. Who makes and fulfills promises. Who names things as they are. Who sees the fullness of reality that often eludes the rest of us.

We follow the truth because it leads to God. And because it is God. Jesus said I AM the truth. He promises that pursuing Him is the only way to find, perceive, accept, and choose what is true.

Ponder Today: Truth and God are one.

SEPTEMBER 29: MOSES, THE FAITH SUPERHERO

"By faith Moses, when he had grown up, refused to be known as the son of Pharaoh's daughter. He chose to be mistreated along with the people of God rather than to enjoy the fleeting pleasures of sin. He regarded disgrace for the sake of Christ as of greater value than the treasures of Egypt, because he was looking ahead to his reward." – Hebrews 11:25-26

We often think of superheroes in terms of what they can do. But one of the great markers of our superheroes is what they refuse to do. Luke Skywalker refuses to give in to the dark side. Batman refuses to ignore injustice. Heroes separate themselves from villains because they refuse to use their strengths solely for their own gain at the cost of others.

Moses is regarded as one of the great heroes of the faith. He had his flaws and his setbacks. But he refused earthly riches, and instead chose to serve God. He chose to be mistreated with God's people over a comfortable and profitable association with Pharaoh.

Why would Moses refuse such things? Because "He was looking ahead to his reward." Moses was making an eternal investment that would last. He chose the permanence of heavenly treasures rather than the "fleeting pleasures of sin." He had the eyes of faith to see beyond this life.

Moses had readily available to him the riches of this world, the promises of the flesh. He refused them. He knew they would not last. They were "fleeting."

Moses is a faith superhero because he placed his trust in God for a reward he could not see. He sought treasure in heaven. At great cost to himself, in service of others, and in faith that the rewards of righteousness outweigh the fleeting promises of the flesh.

Each day we must choose whom we trust. What do we believe? What reward will we seek, and what reward will we refuse? It is an exercise of the most heroic resource available to us - our faith. God commanded Moses, He also commands us to follow Him.

Ponder Today: Heroes are marked both by what they do and what they refuse to do.

SEPTEMBER 30: SETTLE

"The Reubenites and Gadites, who had very large herds and flocks, saw that the lands of Jazer and Gilead were suitable for livestock. So they came to Moses and Eleazar the priest and to the leaders of the community, and said... 'the land the Lord subdued before the people of Israel—are suitable for livestock, and your servants have livestock. If we have found favor in your eyes,' they said, 'let this land be given to your servants as our possession. Do not make us cross the Jordan.'" – Numbers 32:1-2, 4-5

We have a lot of Reuben and Gad in our daily perspectives. Like these tribes of Israel, we have been wandering through the wilderness of life. We are confused and thirsty. We have also seen God show up in amazing ways. The Gadites were there every day when manna appeared on the desert ground. The Reubenites were around when the Red Sea parted. But these things are hard to remember when we are in the desert. It is much easier to focus on the negative.

We have also received the promises of God. For Gad and Reuben, this was a land "flowing with milk and honey". For us, it is a kingdom, The Kingdom of Heaven, which Jesus told us was coming and, in fact, had come!

Maybe the promises are too crazy to believe. Maybe they are too enigmatic for us to make sense of. And so, like these two tribes of Israel, we settle for something less.

We see how things could be just the way we want them to be. And we ask God for that. We don't need his mysterious promises that might come with a catch - unknown dangers. We will settle for what makes sense to us, what we can control and comprehend. This is far enough.

God calls us to faithfulness. He calls us to The Promised Land and then He both empowers and equips us to fight courageously for it. The lesser part of our makeup does not want something so complicated, so challenging. We want something easy, simple. Something, honestly, that requires a little less faith, a little more trust in ourselves than in something beyond our capacity to control.

Don't settle for a watered-down version of life. There is more. God has promised a new perspective, a better place. If we settle for our own agenda, we run the risk of disqualifying ourselves from all God has in store.

Ponder Today: To "settle" does not mean to accept what you don't want in lieu of what you do. It means to accept what your flesh desires in lieu of what God desires for you.

OCTOBER 1: WANT AND PLENTY

"I know what it is to be in need, and I know what it is to have plenty. I have learned the secret of being content in any and every situation, whether well fed or hungry, whether living in plenty or in want. I can do all this through him who gives me strength."
– Philippians 4:12-13

Our circumstances ebb and flow like the tide. In one day and out the next. Seasons of joy and sorrow. Want and plenty.

And while life's circumstances are transitioning between up and down, settling into long seasons of waiting or what we might determine to be a forgetful holding pattern, both God's eternal kingdom and our call to participate in it continue.

When we allow ourselves to become slaves to our circumstances, we commit to an inconsistent, unpredictable, and sometimes stalled carousel of events and seasons.

The secret to faithfulness is this: to remain faithful. Through the eternal consistency of Jesus' eternal self, we can find the contentment that feels otherwise elusive, slippery, and sometimes overlooked.

When we rest in Christ's strength, we can do all things. We can succeed. We can suffer. We can wait. We can comprehend and obey; we can question and learn, we cannot know (or not be able to control) and trust.

The key to dealing with our circumstances is transcending them. Christ can do all. Christ is all. In every terrain of life, God's power beckons us to put our faith in him.

Ponder Today: God's presence is a constant source of hope throughout all of life's circumstances.

OCTOBER 2: STOCKPILE

"The wise store up choice food and olive oil, but fools gulp theirs down. Whoever pursues righteousness and love finds life, righteousness and honor." – Proverbs 20:20-21

All that has found its way into our possession is transitory. It came from somewhere and will go somewhere else. While we have it, we do not own it (in an eternal sense). We are only borrowing. And as we are in this season of borrowing, it is our responsibility to figure out how to steward what we have.

We often think we can stockpile our gifts and be even more safe, comfortable, or in control. Our cupboards are altars. Our bank accounts are idols. We are putting our trust in them rather than using them to serve the God we trust.

The mountaintops and material possessions are wonderful gifts. They are opportunities, resources for the Kingdom. They are not trophies to trumpet self-worth or collector's items to hoard. They are tools to be used.

And this is not just true for the uber-wealthy. All of us have gifts. All of us have resources and abilities. Being responsible with what we have is a question every person has to answer, a reality we all must face.

Ponder Today: Whom will you serve today with your time, your gifts and talents, your money, your relationships, and your choices?

OCTOBER 3: MORNING GLORY

"The life of mortals is like grass, they flourish like a flower of the field; the wind blows over it and it is gone, and its place remembers it no more. But from everlasting to everlasting the Lord's love is with those who fear him." – Psalm 103:15-17

A morning glory bud bursts forth in the early light of the day, displaying a beautiful flower that stretches toward the sun. The vine and the leaves all lead up to this particular morning when the flower reveals itself.

By lunchtime, the flower has receded. It has come and gone in a matter of hours.

When the Bible talks about glory, it means something's essence being revealed. The glory of the morning glory is a flower that shines forth in radiant beauty for just a couple of hours.

We are cosmic morning glories. Our time from birth to death is brief. And our essence is a representation of the sun, the source of life. We flash into existence for a brief time with a finite number of opportunities to make the most of our time.

Unlike the flowers, we have the ability to choose. Choice is the heart of our essence. And our brief time in the sun is an opportunity to make decisions, to steward an existence one way or the other. We cannot add or decrease God's glory - His essence is always what it is. But through our choices we reveal our own essence, either as a participant in The Kingdom of God or an adversary.

You have budded and bloomed. You are in your prime. Your brief existence is underway, and your choices are before you.

Ponder Today: Like the flowers of the field, we exist for a purpose. An enigmatic, beautiful purpose.

OCTOBER 4: ASK

"If any of you lacks wisdom, you should ask God, who gives generously to all without finding fault, and it will be given to you." – James 1:5

We serve as the referee in our own lives. The arbiter between flesh and spirit, wisdom and foolishness. Our ability to choose is powerful. It is the way we commit to our faith and the way we exercise it. Decision-making determines where we will go and how we will perceive. It is the most important thing about being human.

Scripture is clear: we are not left to our own devices when it comes to decision-making. The challenges, obstacles, and options can be overwhelming.

The key to good decision making is listening to God. Reaching out in faithful obedience to interact with the Lord of the universe. Hear what He was to say and use it as the guidepost by which to make choices.

James says all we need to attain wisdom is a willing and inquisitive heart. It also says we will not be given wisdom if we ask with wrong motives - to spend what we get on our own fleshly desires.

But if we truly trust that God is the source of wisdom and approach Him with humble and eager ears, He will grant us wisdom. He will guide our decision-making. He will help us find a way.

There are thousands of choices in front of you today. What will you choose? How will you determine your choices?

Ponder Today: Begin today by asking for wisdom and you will set yourself up for a day of wise and righteous choices.

OCTOBER 5: RICHLY BLESSED

"A faithful person will be richly blessed, but one eager to get rich will not go unpunished." – Proverbs 28:20

When Scripture talks about wealth, prosperity, and success, it is defining those things by a different standard than the world. Riches are spiritual not superficial. Success is not about what you possess but how you steward.

As we navigate the challenges of defining success differently than the world does, the Lord promises us the vast richness of His presence. He promises to be with us. To interact with us. To engage in relationship with us.

Life is full of challenges, trials, and complicated scenarios. God's guidance is simple: "trust in me".

Faithfulness is about staying consistently committed to Christ in the midst of a carousel of circumstances. It is about tethering our souls to the eternal truth of God's goodness rather than revolving, temporary, and superficial circumstances.

When we do this, remaining faithful to God, we find the true riches of Christ's Kingdom, which happen to be the things for which we were created and therefore the things we want most. Peace. Joy. Perspective. Intimacy. These are the richest blessings available to us and they are available this very day.

Whom will you serve? To whom will you remain faithful? The answer will determine how richly you experience this short but meaningful life.

Ponder Today: The true value of your life is your faithfulness not your bank account.

The following is a 7-day series on The Sermon on the Mount:

OCTOBER 6: DAY 1 - HIS OWN AUTHORITY

"Now when Jesus saw the crowds, he went up on a mountainside and sat down. His disciples came to him, and he began to teach them...When Jesus had finished saying these things, the crowds were amazed at his teaching, because he taught as one who had authority, and not as their teachers of the law."
– Matthew 5:1-2; 7:28-29

Considered one of Jesus' earliest and most quintessential collection of teachings, The Sermon on the Mount includes The Lord's Prayer, The Beatitudes, and a host of other familiar sayings and parables.

But the most important part of The Sermon on The Mount is not what is being said but Who is saying it. We take this for granted today, but Matthew notes that the first reaction to this set of teachings was an amazement that Jesus was saying these things on His Own Authority.

Whenever the scribes taught, they appealed to the highest authority they could to substantiate the truth of what they said. Rabbi's would often provide lengthy rabbinic genealogies to support what they taught. Throughout this sermon Jesus appeals to the Highest authority there was – Himself. Every single time (fourteen total) He said "But I say to you...", it was a theological thunderclap. This is God made flesh, divinity in human form.

Jesus enters the scene as a type of Moses. He was a Second Moses like He was a Second Adam. He is teaching on a mountain, just like Moses got the tablets on Mount Sinai. But Moses was an intermediary between God and man while Jesus was both a human intermediary as well as God Himself. Instead of writing on a tablet of stone, He writes His word in our hearts.

As you consider the teachings of The Sermon on The Mount, do not forget the incredible claim Jesus is making concerning His own authority. If it is true in this sermon, it is true in our lives. He is not just the messenger behind these teachings. He is the author. The Authority who humbled Himself and became a man so we might know what is true.

Ponder Today: Jesus is the ultimate authority over all things

OCTOBER 7: DAY 2 - BLESSED BY MERCY

"Blessed are those who hunger and thirst for righteousness, for they will be filled. Blessed are the merciful, for they will be shown mercy." – Matthew 5:6-7

The Greek word translated "Blessed" is Makarios. Makarios describes a complete fulfillment in life. It is an enduring condition rather than a fleeting happiness.

As Jesus launches into The Beatitudes to tell us how to be "blessed" (Makarios), it is important for us to know that He is using a literary device called a chiasm - wherein the most important elements are found in the middle. These verses (6 and 7) are the center of the Beatitudes and the main message of the chiasm: Blessed (Makarios) are those who hunger and thirst for righteousness. Blessed (Makarios) are the merciful. Jesus is establishing HIs Kingdom on a foundation of both righteousness and mercy. They are two sides of the Kingdom coin.

The righteousness that Jesus describes is a social harmony, like a championship team. A "right way" that is chosen rather than imposed. "Righteousness" can also be translated "justice".

We tend to desire justice for others and mercy for ourselves. But in Jesus' kingdom platform, when someone is merciful, they enter into blessing (makarios) because they too shall receive mercy (from the King). Mercy is a compliment to rather than a substitute for righteousness. Righteousness (harmony) comes about because we are merciful and seek to lead others to follow God's ways, for their own benefit.

The social harmony His Kingdom provides is unlike anything the world offers. It is the byproduct of truth and grace. We don't compromise standards. The standards are for the benefit of the community. Righteousness is a focus on God and mercy a focus on others. Offense is a focus on self.

The kingdoms of the earth focus on dominion and control over others. Those who inhabit the Kingdom of Heaven find the good life through serving one another in love.

Ponder Today: Justice and mercy are not two separate options. They are two sides of the same coin.

OCTOBER 8: DAY 3 - THE SPIRIT AND THE LETTER

"Do not think that I have come to abolish the Law or the Prophets; I have not come to abolish them but to fulfill them. For truly I tell you, until heaven and earth disappear, not the smallest letter, not the least stroke of a pen, will by any means disappear from the Law until everything is accomplished" – Matthew 5:17-18

In the Sermon on the Mount Jesus tells His disciples that seeking righteousness with mercy is the core essence of His Kingdom. He further instructs His disciples that they must surpass the righteousness of the scribes and Pharisees in order to live up to Kingdom standards.

The Pharisees were meticulous rule-followers. But Kingdom righteousness flows from a heart of mercy toward others.

It is anger with a brother that is the root violation of righteousness (social harmony). Murder is the effect. Anger is the cause. Jesus shows this to be true in the way we perceive adultery, taking oaths (making promises), divorce, and our ideas of justice/judging one another.

Righteousness is primarily about our inner perspective (spirit of the law) rather than what we do when we know we are being watched, our outward actions (letter of the law).

Being hyper-focused on the letter of the law (like the Pharisees) misses the deep truth about the way our motivations and perspective shape our attitude, and ultimately our actions toward others.

Jesus wasn't trying to measure up to His disciples' expectations. In fact, they were astonished at the authority with which He taught. Jesus was seeking to pull them to a higher plane of living, so they could be blessed (Makarios, fulfilled in life).

If we want to seek the fulfillment Jesus promises by mercifully seeking His Kingdom and His righteousness, a good starting point is to shift our self-talk from "What do they think of me" to "How can I pull those around me towards a more fruitful life?"

This is the fulfillment of the law and the prophets. The law Jesus came to embody and fulfill. A law of love, the inner workings of the heart.

Ponder Today: Justice must work internally before it has a chance to apply externally.

OCTOBER 9: DAY 4 - HEAVENLY REWARD

"Do not store up for yourselves treasures on earth, where moths and vermin destroy, and where thieves break in and steal. But store up for yourselves treasures in heaven, where moths and vermin do not destroy, and where thieves do not break in and steal. For where your treasure is, there your heart will be also."
– Matthew 6:19-21

When it comes right down to it, humans are willing to do things for one reason: we perceive it to be in our self-interest. We will willingly (sometime eagerly) endure hardship or defer pleasure so that we can obtain good rewards. This is actually very Biblical. God created and designed us to seek and pursue our own benefit. Jesus acknowledges this reality in setting the standard by which we should love others "as we love ourselves." However, our perspective about what is truly in our self-interest is often skewed.

Jesus clarifies exactly what is in our best interest - the rewards of His Kingdom. Jesus encourages His disciples to seek the best (truest) rewards. Treasures that will endure. Nothing on earth can match the rewards of our Father in Heaven.

In His Sermon on the Mount, Jesus presents this as a binary choice. We can either seek a reward from our Father who is in heaven or we can seek reward in the world's systems and the approval of man. We can't do both, we must pick one or the other. We can't serve God and money.

Matthew 6 talks about how we give, how we pray, and how we fast. Just three examples of the way we encounter this choice: do we fast or pray to impress others and receive the reward of their approval or to seek God and trust His reward in His time?

Our hearts always follow where we invest our treasure. The extent to which our finances are investing in family, neighbors, and the various communities in which we reside are a clue to where our heart is focused.

If we rely upon earthly riches, we are certain to not only lose our treasure, we also fill our heart with the things of a world that will one day be no more. By choosing the treasures of heaven, we elect to pursue real and lasting reward. That is how our true self-interest is best served.

Ponder Today: The rewards you pursue reveal the source of your trust.

OCTOBER 10: DAY 5 - TWO MASTERS

"No one can serve two masters. Either you will hate the one and love the other, or you will be devoted to the one and despise the other. You cannot serve both God and money." – Matthew 6:24

Jesus has said much in The Sermon on the Mount about how His disciples can thrive in His Kingdom. He has taught it is in our best interest to pursue His righteousness and rewards rather than the empty promises of the world. He emphasizes that serving God is a heart condition - not just an external to-do list.

Here Jesus emphasizes the binary nature of our most fundamental choices: who we serve. We like the idea of getting God's reward. But we often think we can do that by making our devotional life merely one of the things we do. Perhaps we compartmentalize our Sunday self, keeping him a safe distance from our Friday night self. In doing this we seek to harvest the best of both worlds. Meanwhile we also maintain a Monday self; looking out for Number One in the dog-eat-dog business world.

Jesus is clear we can't have it both ways. The rewards of Kingdom living are not available if we only pursue it during some segment of our lives. Kingdom living is being devoted to seeking God's righteousness in a manner that is merciful toward others in all aspects of our lives.

We cannot truly serve God and material prosperity. If wealth is our master, we will be devoted to its insatiable demands. We will be consumed by the pursuit of the unachievable goal of "more". We will seek and find the treasures of the world, which moth and rust will destroy.

If Jesus is our master, He must necessarily transform all other selves. Our work self must serve Him and His Kingdom. Our social self too. Each of these selves is a necessary participant in seeking His kingdom and His righteousness.

There may be two (or more) masters barking out commands, but the servant can only choose to follow one of them. The heart will follow the one it loves. Which master will we choose? The world promises everything and delivers nothing. Jesus asks us to lay our lives down for others and promises we gain all in return.

Ponder Today: We cannot compartmentalize our faith, either it will permeate to all areas of our life or disappear under their weight.

OCTOBER 11: DAY 6 - SIDE-STREETS

"But seek first his kingdom and his righteousness, and all these things will be given to you as well." – Matthew 6:33

It is difficult to fathom, but the divine Jesus was actually human. So He can identify with the daily difficulties of his followers. He knows the disciples to whom He addresses the Sermon on the Mount have dally concerns – getting clothed, fed and housed. And He knows those things tend to create worry. Anxiety. Angst.

Jesus makes a provocative statement: "Seek God's kingdom first, and all the other things you are concerned about will be added".

Since Kingdom righteousness is a condition of the heart, it really begins with gaining a proper perspective. God made us and has our best interest at heart. He gave us the gift of making choices, the power and knowledge to make good decisions. He gave us a "narrow gate" through which we can find the fulfillment for which our heart yearns.

If we seek, we will find. If we knock, the door of opportunity will be opened to us. God is our good Father and he desires what is best for us. Keeping our focus on him is the only way to righteousness.

One aspect seems apparent, if we seek Jesus' kingdom and His righteousness as our first priority, it will most certainly affect our perspective on life's daily necessities. Worry about what we do not have can be replaced with gratitude for what we do have.

Kingdom living is a more productive way of living. Living in integrity, serving others, setting aside addictions to pleasure and fame all naturally lead to having more capacity to meet our daily needs.

The Sermon on the Mount is much more than a spiritual guide. It is an imminently practical means to meet our deepest longings. But the route to get there will not be as broad, obvious, and instantly-gratifying as sin, which is why not many find it.

Ponder Today: The Sermon on the Mount is much more than a spiritual guide. It is an imminently practical means to meet our deepest longings.

OCTOBER 12: DAY 7 - THE GOLDEN RULE

"So in everything, do to others what you would have them do to you, for this sums up the Law and the Prophets." – Matthew 7:12

As Jesus begins to close the Sermon on The Mount, he sums up his teaching (and indeed "all the Law and The Prophets") by setting forth what has come to be known as The Golden Rule.

Jesus assumes (rightly, of course) everyone wants to be treated with fairness, kindness, and mercy. Since righteousness is social harmony, it makes sense that the key to achieving it is to treat others as you desire to be treated. It is quite practical. Any group that expends all its resources on activities that create mutual benefit is going to be amazingly successful.

Jesus acknowledges the reality that we as humans pursue self-interest. That is presumed in His admonition. But also presumed is the reality that we often mis-perceive our own self-interest. Selfishness is self-destructive. Righteousness is about serving God in community, treating other humans as we would like to be treated, no matter their station.

Jesus concludes The Sermon on the Mount with a warning: don't let false teachers distract you from God's Kingdom. Follow the voice of the True Master. Seek His Kingdom. Pursue righteousness. Love and serve one another as co-laborers in Christ. And unite under Jesus who has spoken all of these things From His Own Authority. The false teachers are out to distract you, to feed the dangerously insatiable desires of the flesh. To be self-focused rather than others-focused.

The sum of the entire Bible is to treat others as we desire to be treated. Nested within this advice for living is the key to finding true success. Jesus called choosing this perspective a narrow gate, a path that is sometimes hard to see. It requires effort to see but guarantees success if followed. Not success we can demand, but success we can trust will be ours in due time.

Ponder Today: Unity in heart and spirit, toward oneself and toward others, is the great command of Scripture.

This concludes our 7-day series on The Sermon on the Mount.

OCTOBER 13: TRUSTWORTHY

"The Lord detests lying lips, but he delights in people who are trustworthy." – Proverbs 12:22

When God created the world, there was a thread of truth woven through all the elements of creation. People and animals. Vegetation and seas. Ideas and language. All of it is a careful tapestry woven together by the God of all goodness and truth.

For this reason, all of creation feels adverse consequences when it denies the truth. We try to operate outside of reality. We try to ignore the pattern, the foundation of the universe.

When we speak truthfully, we cooperate with God's ordered world. We participate in Eternity. We align ourselves with who God is and what He is about.

The truth can sometimes be challenging. We might prefer something that is more comfortable or simpler according to our individual agenda.

But the truth is its own reward. It is always wiser and better to align with the thread of all existence, the God of all things, than to fight against it.

Pursuing the truth faithfully comes with its own set of consequences. It may hurt. People may not like it. You may not particularly enjoy it. But the cost of ignoring the truth is much greater than the cost of aligning with it.

In the end, God's delight is a prize too great for the wise to ignore. There is no greater prize. There is no greater joy.

Today, let us search for the truth with humility. Let us find it and align with it with vehement courage. To the delight of the Lord.

Ponder Today: Truth is woven into the fabric of every element of creation.

OCTOBER 14: SOAR

"He gives strength to the weary and increases the power of the weak. Even youths grow tired and weary, and young men stumble and fall; but those who hope in the Lord will renew their strength. They will soar on wings like eagles; they will run and not grow weary, they will walk and not be faint." – Isaiah 40:29-31

In every superhero movie, there is the one scene where the hero comes into his/her own. It usually entails the hero walking or standing in a striking pose with their chest puffed out (and maybe a cape billowing in the wind). We love superhero movies precisely for this moment. It makes us feel as if we might be strong, capable.

Just like the superheroes in those movies, our moments of triumph, our strength, does not come out of a vacuum. It comes through challenge, learning, overcoming obstacles and remaining faithful to the cause.

God is the source of strength for faith superheroes like you. He knows you are weary. He knows you are tired. But He renews strength by the promise of His presence, with which we can participate in incredible things.

If you are down today, tired and worn thin, look up to Jesus, the source of your strength. Be renewed by His presence. There are mountains to climb today, distances to walk, air in which to soar.

Ponder Today: Jesus is the motivation, the goal, and the source of both hope and perseverance.

OCTOBER 15: A TALE OF TWO CHOICES

"To You, O Lord, I lift up my soul. O my God, in You I trust, Do not let me be ashamed. Do not let my enemies exult over me. Indeed, none of those who wait for You will be ashamed; Those who deal treacherously without cause will be ashamed." – Psalm 25:1-3

When it comes to matters of character, we have a choice between two options. There are a lot of ways to explain it. Flesh and spirit. Wisdom and foolishness. Our choice reveals in which option we have placed our trust.

In most situations, the choice of flesh is one preoccupied with instant gratification: what feels good now. And choices of the spirit are based on delayed gratification: trust and hope.

We find it difficult to face mystery, uncertainty. To grapple with the reality that we are not God and we are not in control. To trust something other than our own base desires.

And in the midst of this difficulty, we make treacherous choices. Decisions that abandon truth and try to gain a delusion of control by fulfilling our most immediate superficial desire.

It is hard to wait. It is difficult to trust in the Lord. Faith is a challenging proposition, absurd to the world and the flesh within us.

God promises that those who choose the spirit win in the end. That the delayed gratification is true and lasting while our addiction with instant gratification is insatiable and meaningless. God will not embarrass us in the end by withholding the fullness of his blessing forever. Enigmatically, the waiting is even part of the blessing.

Ponder Today: With all of its manifestations and permutations, all of your choices are really a decision between flesh and spirit. Which will you choose today?

OCTOBER 16: IN ORDER TO SEE

"Jesus said to her, 'Did I not say to you that if you believe, you will see the glory of God?'" – John 11:40

Faith is a filter that allows us to see the world as it truly is. It is like when you are getting your eyes checked and they put the machine on a variety of settings and then ask you to read the letters on the chart.

To see the glory of God is to see things as they are. We often think that revealing God's glory means our circumstances are going to change. It is hard for us to deal with struggle and our inability to understand. Which is exactly why faith is required of us.

Faith does not change our circumstances, it changes the way we perceive our circumstances. Faith brings clarity to life and all of its experiences.

Since "glory" really means "the essence of something", it makes sense that the more faith we have the more clearly we perceive God's glory. The gift of faith is like a new eyeglass prescription. It allows us to see things for what they are worth.

Faith invites us to see all of our experiences and circumstances as an opportunity to make wise choices. It helps us to see God for all He is worth. And to see that glory reflected in all the arenas we find ourselves in.

Ponder Today: Faith does not change our circumstances, it changes the way we perceive our circumstances.

OCTOBER 17: PATIENCE

"Be still before the Lord and wait patiently for him; do not fret when people succeed in their ways, when they carry out their wicked schemes. Refrain from anger and turn from wrath; do not fret—it leads only to evil. For those who are evil will be destroyed but those who hope in the Lord will inherit the land."
– Psalm 37:7-9

When it comes right down to it, suffering is an act of patience (and patience an act of suffering). One of the fruits of the spirit, patience is a vital piece to the well-lived life. This virtue, by its nature, necessitates some element of discomfort.

It is hard for us to suffer, to wait and hope for a redemption to come, even in the best of circumstances. Faith is an exercise in delayed gratification. And that hurts. It costs us something. Especially as we see others make the ever-enticing choice of instant gratification and, from our side of the fence, the results seem much better than the challenge and trust required in waiting.

We want to act in anger, instantly. We want our rewards, now. We want all of life to make sense, to be comfortable, and to have a greater sense of control.

Too often, our lives are a flurry of activity as we try to avoid the silence of waiting. We try to sidestep the stillness of faith by taking matters into our own hands.

Hope comes at a price. Patience costs us the temptation right in front of us. But the Lord promises redemption. He promises His delayed-gratification rewards are greater, fuller, and more true than those instant-gratification superficialities we long for. There is pain in patience. But there is also a prize. Not just future rewards, but a life of more noble character, wisdom, and trust.

Ponder Today: Patience requires a certain kind of pain that only be redeemed in time.

OCTOBER 18: THE VIRTUOUS LIFE

"Therefore, as God's chosen people, holy and dearly loved, clothe yourselves with compassion, kindness, humility, gentleness and patience. Bear with each other and forgive one another if any of you has a grievance against someone. Forgive as the Lord forgave you. And over all these virtues put on love, which binds them all together in perfect unity." – Colossians 3:12-14

No matter our circumstances, our net worth, or the degree of fame and human recognition we achieve, the key to a successful life is a life of virtue. Instead of bills and likes, properties and awards, we are called to compassion, kindness, gentleness, and patience.

Love is what binds all these things together. In order to apply love, forgiveness is required. And not just any forgiveness. But the same kind of forgiveness Jesus gave us. Jesus forgave "while we were yet sinners." We are, therefore, called to forgive preemptively. Even if the other person has not forgiven. This is what it looks like to behave as "chosen people" who are "holy and dearly loved."

This is successful living.

The world has its own concept of successful living - a concept that is pretty much the opposite of what Paul admonishes. It elevates superficial gains and surface-level affirmations.

Too often we adopt the world's ways. When we speak of wanting a "better life" for our children, we too often speak of material gain rather than stellar character. We have succumbed to believing we can manipulate our way to happiness through material circumstances.

As God's chosen people, we are called to a better way. A path more true. A path of virtue.

The virtue of every day comes through the hard work of abundant obedience to Christ. The life that is truly life. Which, in the end, is more thrilling and more rewarding than superficial one-off moments. Love binds all the virtues in perfect unity. God dearly loves us and desires our best, and living in this unity of virtue is a life of true success.

Ponder Today: Virtue is the key to a successful life.

OCTOBER 19: LOSING HEART

"Therefore we do not lose heart. Though outwardly we are wasting away, yet inwardly we are being renewed day by day. For our light and momentary troubles are achieving for us an eternal glory that far outweighs them all. So we fix our eyes not on what is seen, but on what is unseen, since what is seen is temporary, but what is unseen is eternal." – 2 Corinthians 4:16-18

The choices we make affect the people around us. They inform our experiences and shape our character. Sometimes the far-reaching effects of our decisions do not reveal themselves until much later, and sometimes not at all.

It can be wearisome. Life is a puzzle we do not have the answer to - only God does. Our choices can affect things but they cannot solve everything. Mysteries abound. The struggle continues.

Paul encourages us here that the glory of eternity outweighs our momentary struggles and confusion. If we stay steadfast, continue to make wise decisions, and focus on what we can steward (letting go of what we can't), God will reward us with relationship and perspective.

If we try to train our perspective on "figuring out" the world and solving all of its issues, we will grow steadily weary. If we fix our eyes on Christ, we align ourselves with the deepest truth possible. And doing so actually aids our efforts to try to make the world a better place.

In the end, God is in control and we are not. Submitting to this reality allows us to make the best choices possible today and every day.

Ponder Today: Life is a puzzle we do not have the answer to.

OCTOBER 20: ALREADY ATTAINED

"I press on toward the goal to win the prize for which God has called me heavenward in Christ Jesus. All of us, then, who are mature should take such a view of things. And if on some point you think differently, that too God will make clear to you. Only let us live up to what we have already attained." – Philippians 3:14-16

The journey of life on this earth is over in the blink of an eye. It is short and sweet. A brief wisp in the long story of Eternity.

God has given us an acceptance that spans eternity. His grace leads us from everlasting to everlasting. Life on earth is one short frame in a long reel. God is the director, producer, and true star in the cosmic story. The story of Heaven.

Our prize is to participate in this story. To play our part well. To cast a view heavenward and engage in fellowship with Christ Jesus.

When we view our lives in light of Eternity, we take on a spiritual maturity that unlocks many of the riches of God's Kingdom.

Our immaturity comes when we lose sight of this perspective. We try to control our circumstances and convert the temporal, superficial experience of this life into an idol we can worship, manipulate, and control.

We try to work toward the heaven we have rebranded in our own image rather than out of God's true eternal kingdom. Through God's acceptance, we have already attained access to His Kingdom. Heaven is now, as well as later. Our brief life on this earth is, at best, a celebration of Eternity to come.

Ponder Today: Pray that God may transform your perspective into a "mature view".

OCTOBER 21: ENTRUSTED

"He who is faithful in a very little thing is faithful also in much; and he who is unrighteous in a very little thing is unrighteous also in much. Therefore if you have not been faithful in the use of unrighteous wealth, who will entrust the true riches to you?"
– Luke 16:10-11

Everything we come across is an opportunity. The situations and circumstances we encounter. The wealth and possessions we accumulate. The gifts and talents we discover. The knowledge we gain. The wisdom bestowed upon us.

We spend so much time trying to attain More. We imagine our struggles are a result of lacking quantity. If only we had more money, a better job, a different relationship. If only we lived in a city with more to do (or less to do). We waste so much time fantasizing about what we don't have. What we do have is being hoarded on a shelf, ignored and unused, lacking in gratitude and mobility.

Scripture says we have all we need for righteousness. The good life is not about what you have or how much you have. It is about what you do with the opportunities in front of you.

When we are faithful with opportunities, there is a compounding effect on our lives. It leads to more opportunity. This does not necessarily mean more wealth, more stuff, or perfect circumstances. It means we are entrusted with opportunities to teach and influence others, to serve and care, to engage in meaningful relationships.

The true riches of the Kingdom are not the things we have but the opportunity to steward those things to celebrate Christ and His Kingdom.

Ponder Today: All we have been granted is an invitation to faithfulness.

OCTOBER 22: REALITY

"From the least to the greatest, all are greedy for gain, prophets and priests alike, all practice deceit. They dress the wound of my people as though it were not serious. 'Peace, peace,' they say, when there is no peace." – Jeremiah 6:13-14

We are all wired to pursue our own self-interest. When we recognize that serving others, listening to God, and chasing after righteousness is actually the best thing we can do for ourselves, it transforms how we live.

All too often, we are deceived and led astray by the empty promises of this world and the lustful desires of the flesh. We start to believe (wrongly) that certain things are in our best interest.

Greed can lead to a compounding problem. The more we don't get what we think we want, the more we try to fight, manipulate, and control both our circumstances and the people around us to correct what we feel is off course. Unchecked, this leads to delusion. We start to deny reality. We call false things true and sick things well.

One of the great gifts of fellowship with God is that it helps us to see things as they are. Refusing to acknowledge reality is a confusing shackle we sometimes find ourselves in, not sure how to escape.

Trusting God helps alleviate our fear of circumstances because we know we can trust Him no matter what the circumstances entail. We do not have to be so worried about acknowledging the truth of how things are because we lean on a God who works all things for good.

A perspective that acknowledges reality takes courage and faithfulness. It is in our best interest to do so.

Ponder Today: Manipulating others does not just harm them, but you as well. Serving others does not just benefit them, but you as well.

OCTOBER 23: POINT OF VIEW

"So from now on we regard no one from a worldly point of view. Though we once regarded Christ in this way, we do so no longer." – 2 Corinthians 5:16

When Paul encounters Christ on the road to Damascus, he can no longer hold to his former lifestyle. He trusts God and His promises. He puts his faith in Jesus and is obedient/submissive to God's direction in his life, even to the point of death.

As Paul discovers the truth of Jesus and His gospel, he informs the Corinthians - he is obliged to share it with others.

Paul, like many of us, used to view religion from a worldly point of view. God was something he could use to achieve his own agenda and pursue his own end. It is a temptation many of us are familiar with.

Paul's encounter with Christ humbled him, showed him the truth, and introduced him to what he describes as the "fear" of the Lord (2 Cor. 5:11). To revere and honor Him, to recognize Him as judge, and to accept the truth that His agenda is better than our own.

When we view God and others from a worldly point of view, it sows derision and divisiveness among us. When we adopt God's point of view, we see the opportunity for unity, synergy, and truth within all of us.

Ponder Today: It is more than possible to use all of the Christian lingo but pursue faith from a worldly point of view rather than the vision of the gospel.

OCTOBER 24: DEED AND TRUTH

"Little children, let us not love with word or with tongue, but in deed and truth." – 1 John 3:18

The gulf between word and deed can be significant. We claim to love something. We say we trust one thing or another. It takes little to no effort to declare that something is important to us.

There is nothing more revealing about our true beliefs and our real priorities than observing what we actually do. Saying is easy. That doesn't mean it is not important. It is hugely important. Yet, if we don't follow through, if our actions don't match what we say, the words are little more than a vapor in the wind.

There is a reason doing is connected to truth in this verse. When we are inconsistent, our lack of action neutralizes our speaking. This verse admonishes us to do what we say and say what we do. If they don't work in harmony, if one eclipses the other, both are ineffective.

Love is mainly about action. It is a doing. Love is serving the best interest of others. It is acting toward our own best interest, the truest manifestation of who we are.

This requires adopting God's perspective. Acknowledging truth is an acquired taste for all of us. But while seeing what's really true might be uncomfortable, nothing is better for us.

We can see in truth and speak in truth only when we love in truth. And love is putting faith into action. Nothing says more about what we believe, what we love, and what we value than what we do. John implores us to be consistent (and true) as we translate our words into action; for this is the true nature of love.

Ponder Today: If what we say does not match what we do, it undermines the validity of both.

OCTOBER 25: A GROUP OF INDIVIDUALS

"Speaking the truth in love, we are to grow up in all aspects into Him who is the head, even Christ, from whom the whole body, being fitted and held together by what every joint supplies, according to the proper working of each individual part, causes the growth of the body for the building up of itself in love." – Ephesians 4:15-16

The Bible has multiple references to the people of God as "The Body". Each of us is a part of that body – a leg or arm or earlobe. We each have our part to play.

Imagine if your body was made up of antagonistic parts. If our leg and eye were at war with one another, it would neutralize our ability to be effective.

Life is a team sport. And to be effective, we need to know our role, play our part well, and rely on our teammates to perform their functions.

Many of us accept this analogy but then wrestle to be the head - the part of the body that tells everyone else what to do. But that's the one job the Bible makes clear is already filled. Jesus is the head. The only thing that keeps each appendage from making an idol of itself is their dependency and submission to the head.

The truth keeps us in alignment. The Head keeps us connected. It keeps us properly focused. It reminds us that we are in this together and that there is a purpose we can only achieve within community.

Ponder Today: We are a part of the Body of Christ and Jesus is the Head of the Body.

OCTOBER 26: BE CONTENT

"Not that I speak from want, for I have learned to be content in whatever circumstances I am." – Philippians 4:11

It would be difficult to imagine someone who experienced more striving than the Apostle Paul. He relentlessly traveled to spread the gospel and plant churches. He risked the elements and endured persecution. And he never asked for financial support for himself. How could he persevere through all this difficulty?

The answer is quite paradoxical: he learned to endure by learning to be content.

This does not mean he was complacent. He constantly advocated, planned, and initiated. What Paul did not do was demand particular results. He did not idolize a specific circumstance, which allowed him to discover peace in all circumstances. The apostle to the Gentiles did not place "work conditions" on God.

The great theologian Francis Schaeffer had an interesting definition of true spirituality that echoes this aspect of Paul's life. Schaeffer postulated that true spirituality is continuing to strive no matter the circumstances. Fighting the battles we find ourselves in. Waiting with courage and patience. Stewarding with wisdom and humility.

The greater sense we have of our calling, the more readily we can see circumstances as merely the water in which we swim. Circumstances should not define us. Nor should they define success or failure. Circumstances are merely the field we play on, the arena in which we perform. Paul admonishes us that whether we are performing before thousands in Carnegie Hall or on a street corner, we should be content to be faithful with where God has placed us, and to faithfully do the job he has set before us.

Ponder Today: The key to abundance is the perspective we choose.

OCTOBER 27: RADICAL ACCEPTANCE

"Therefore, accept one another, just as Christ also accepted us to the glory of God." – Romans 15:7

Scripture teaches that we are fully accepted in Christ. He has called us His. Yet, it also beckons us, in response to this acceptance, to pursue a life of approval.

We tend to struggle with differentiating between approval and acceptance. We worry that if God does not approve of a particular choice or character trait, our acceptance will disappear as well. Thankfully that is not the case. We are fully and completely accepted by God's grace.

Likewise, we are called to accept one another, just as we are accepted by God. That means there is no place for condemnation. We are commanded to meet people where they are. Does that mean we must approve everything others do? Not at all. But we are to accept them unconditionally, just as Christ accepted us.

We often think we are glorifying God when we try to fix people. But this verse tells us that we glorify God when we accept one another with the same radical grace with which we are accepted in Christ.

We then have a foundation to walk in righteousness, as Jesus has called us. When we accept others with the radical acceptance we have received, we acknowledge the glory God.

Ponder Today: We need to learn to receive the difference between acceptance and approval AND be able to give it as well.

OCTOBER 28: A BETTER PLACE

"But as it is, they desire a better country, that is, a heavenly one. Therefore God is not ashamed to be called their God; for He has prepared a city for them." – Hebrews 11:16

Life on Earth is an adventure, a brief ride through the ebbs and flows of what it means to be human. But adventures are not ends unto themselves. Any good adventure is born of desire. A desire for something greater than what we currently possess. What propels us to fully enjoy our earthly adventure is the desire to arrive at a heavenly city.

Ironically, desiring to relocate to a heavenly country is an essential part of enjoying our stay on this earth. It is part of what makes this life exciting. This brief journey is a preparation to fully enjoy what awaits.

If modern technology is any indication, we seem to be a people longing for immediate gratification. We live in an age that relentlessly reduces waiting. So perhaps it is more challenging than ever to accept the delayed realities of God's promise: a heavenly city prepared as a great reward for those who seek and follow God.

But we can also choose the perspective that this challenge makes the adventure even greater. The best way to navigate the tension is through faith.

This verse comes from Hebrews 11, which is often called the "Hall of Faith." Many faith superheroes are cited. Some, like Samson, squandered much of their lives, but ended well. Some experienced amazing mountaintops of success, being agents of God's miraculous works. Others experienced the valleys of martyrdom.

What they held in common was an eye toward a greater prize. They pursued their adventure with great gusto, exercising the obedience of faith, knowing God is faithful to fulfill His promise. The promise that the end of the adventure is a city God has prepared.

Ponder Today: The reality that life on earth is imperfect either propels our journey toward Heaven or freezes us from it. The choice is ours.

OCTOBER 29: THE INEVITABILITY OF TRUST

"Some trust in chariots and some in horses, But we will trust in the name of the Lord, our God." – Psalm 20:7

Trust is the starting point for every human activity. Human beings cannot escape trusting. We must trust something or someone in order to function. We can't take our car onto the highway without trusting other drivers. We can't board a plane without trusting an airline's employees.

Trust is necessary because we are finite. Our sphere of comprehension is tiny. Faith is required because there is so much beyond our capacity. So, one of the most important choices in our lives becomes who (or what) we trust.

The world offers us all sorts of things to trust. The equivalent of "chariots and horses" in our age is governments and politicians. Pop culture offers a different menu of options in which to trust - the allure of fame and celebrity; Consumer ads; the affirmation of our peers; happiness through purchase and accumulation.

Life's circumstances are much like the earth's movement. They relentlessly swirl around us, but we can remain "still" when we exercise faith in what is real and true. When we place our trust in stable things we become more stable ourselves.

As one of the three things we can control, whom or what we trust is a powerful catalyst for the kind of life we live and the type of influence we wield. It ought to be something we do with great intentionality.

Ponder Today: When we place our trust in stable things we become more stable ourselves.

OCTOBER 30: IN HIS HANDS

"...and in Your hand is power and might; and it lies in Your hand to make great and to strengthen everyone. Now therefore, our God, we thank You, and praise Your glorious name."
– 1 Chronicles 29:12-13

We use our hands for all sorts of things. The point of a finger, to guide or to condemn. A grip to welcome, hold or wield. A touch to comfort or to tend.

The Lord's Hands work in the same way. By a diversity of means, the gifts and beauty of the Lord are passed and handled, carried and cared for, by the Hands of God.

He holds in His Hand the secret mysteries of creation. He holds the meaning of life. He carries blessing and glory in his palms.

Sin and idolatry come when we try to take things that properly belong in God's hands "into our own hands". Perhaps we don't trust what the Lord is doing. Where He is guiding or what He is holding.

We sometimes try to make circumstances serve us. We seek control. We desire what properly belongs in God's hands to be in our own. By clutching what is not ours we sacrifice our greatest blessing.

Through the Hands of the Lord, we have access to all good things. If we let go our own compulsion to take God's place, we are free to receive what He offers, what He provides. When we live in thanksgiving and praise for what comes to us from God's Hands, we gain nothing less than strength and glory. The fingerprints that created the universe will show up in our daily lives.

Ponder Today: God seeks to serve us, will we allow it?

OCTOBER 31: THE AVENGER

"Never take your own revenge, beloved, but leave room for the wrath of God, for it is written, 'Vengeance is Mine, I will repay,' says the Lord." – Romans 12:19

An avenger is one who acts out revenge. The practical application to the concept of vengeance. It is the one who takes the responsibility for punishing wrongdoers by inflicting harm on those wrongdoers.

God is righteous. We are made in His image, which means we have a desire for things to be right. Problem is, we often get mixed up as to whose job it is to make things right.

When we try to serve as the avenger, it simply doesn't work. We are prone to confuse true righteousness with our own selfish ambition or our inaccurate perspective. Justice is not really served when we react to evil in pride. The key to real justice is recognition of the proper authority.

As hard as it is, we must leave it to Him. Trusting God requires that we trust Him to be our avenger. The Lord says "I will repay". Leaving wrath to Him to avenge in His time and in His way is simply trusting God will do what He says.

By setting aside our need for personal vengeance, we strengthen our character. We trust God by taking Him at His word. And we love others by slowing the rampant cycle of pain in our world.

When we react, we are actually ceding control to our agitator. We are now focusing on the priority of the agitator, rather than of our own mission. By not reacting (turning the other cheek) we allow time for emotions to calm; time to refocus our mission, how to pursue the best for others.

When we allow God His proper place as Avenger, we not only recognize reality, we lean into practicality. We avoid ceding control to those who seek harm.

What will God's vengeance look like? God will decide. It might look like Him dying in our place. Or theirs. It might look like grace and love and forgiveness. And that should be a cause of rejoicing.

Ponder Today: We are too biased and imperfect to hand out vengeance without overstepping our bounds.

NOVEMBER 1: SELF-EVALUATION

"Why are you downcast, O my soul? Why so disturbed within me? Put your hope in God, for I will yet praise him, my Savior and my God." – Psalm 42:11

The Psalmist here is exercising one of the most fundamental of human exercises - self talk. He is asking himself questions to try to help discover a true perspective.

What is critical about this self talk is it does not assume an answer. It is not a rhetorical question. The Psalmist is trying to slow himself down, to evaluate what he is thinking and why.

Often our self talk goes unnoticed and unchecked. When this happens, we tend to reinforce our patterned perspectives, often developed by the false narrative and world-centered narratives that can dominate our mind. We choose a perspective, whether we realize it or not.

To engage in intentional self talk is to give oneself the best chance possible to discern the truth. To challenge oneself. To examine all angles, or at least as many as can be discerned.

The emotions this Psalmist faces - downcast, disturbed - could take the lead and try to reinforce themselves, manipulating any chances of a different perspective in their own image. Instead, he allows himself to examine. Why am I downcast?

In the end, he concludes that his hope is in God and he will choose a perspective of praise. Whatever circumstances caused him to be downcast haven't gone away. Whatever caused him to be disturbed has continued on. What has changed is his own perspective; his willingness to choose to live above his circumstances.

We cannot get there without a little self-evaluation. A chat with ourselves to help discover what we are feeling, what we are thinking, what is our perspective, and what is true.

Ponder Today: God's strength gives us the power to discern our own lives, to see our need for change, and to take steps toward betterment.

NOVEMBER 2: CASTING NETS

"When He had finished teaching them, He said to Simon, 'Put out into the deep water and let down your nets for a catch.'" – Luke 5:4

Throughout the gospels, we see a common trajectory. Various characters in diverse circumstances all encounter Jesus and are sent out to serve others.

The disciples in Luke 5 have been listening to Jesus. They have been exposed to the truth about who He is. It is an intoxicating place to be. Peter, in another passage, will ask to build three shelters for Jesus, Moses, and Elijah at the Mount of Transfiguration.

We long for these mountains, the place where we can go and sit at the feet of Jesus, to consume His peace and His love, to be comforted by His presence.

But that is only the first half of the trajectory. Jesus told the disciples He will send them out to "fish for people". He asks them to cast their nets into the deep water for a huge haul.

Our mountaintop experiences are not just about our own joy. They are equipping stations, checkpoints along the journey. We are taught so we might teach. We are served so we might serve. And we are loved so that we might love. We are caught so we might help catch.

We are not simply consumers of God's love, we are participants in it. If we obsess over the mountains, we will miss out on what God is calling us into. If we refuse to cast our nets, to descend the mountains and serve others, we are shirking our calling and all but wasting the experience of the mountaintops.

Ponder Today: We are called to serve. Mountaintops are not the finish line. They are catalysts along the journey.

NOVEMBER 3: PERSEVERANCE AND DISCERNMENT

"Whoever sows to please their flesh, from the flesh will reap destruction; whoever sows to please the Spirit, from the Spirit will reap eternal life. Let us not become weary in doing good, for at the proper time we will reap a harvest if we do not give up."
– Galatians 6:8-9

Perseverance is one of the most necessary components for vibrant living. We are too easily knocked off course.

In some ways, we are all persevering. We go to work every day (even if we hate it) to collect a paycheck, buy groceries and pay rent. We are committed to staying alive, so we persist in staying warm, eating and drinking.

The heart of our perseverance problem is not our willingness to endure, it is our ability to commit to the things worth enduring for. We have a discernment problem.

God is calling us into a life of truth, a life of accurate perspective that drives our thoughts and behaviors. He is inviting us to persevere through all kinds of circumstances by clinging to His promises and His truth.

If we persevere with the wrong end in mind, our sowing leads to destruction. But the sowing that leads to destruction often feels like the path of least resistance.

Conversely, sowing to the Spirit usually doesn't feel good. It includes things like giving up on bitterness and refusing to react to criticism. It gets tiring, doing good.

The key to proper perseverance is choosing a proper perspective; by faith, committing to the truth and pursuing it through all of life's arenas and circumstances. Perseverance begins with discernment, evaluating what is real and right and true. Believing unseen promises as though they are visible.

It continues with the commitment to keep going.

Ponder Today: Perseverance is all about commitment. It is the artery from what we sow to what we reap.

NOVEMBER 4: THE WILL OF GOD

"This is the will of God: your sanctification" – 1 Thessalonians 4:3

We tend to focus on "God's will" with respect to circumstances, in large part because circumstances press in upon us daily. We want to know if we are doing the "right" things, if our struggling circumstances mean we are outside God's will.

The Bible states in plain language what God's will is. It says so right here in 1 Thessalonians (and it lets you know it is saying so).

The specific thing that is the will of God is our "sanctification." This word means to be set apart to God's service. What that means is that whatever we choose to do circumstantially is not the key to following God's will. It is not a certain job or a specific relationship. God's will is not a circumstance. It is the complicated process of sanctification, which means being "set apart" to God's service.

It is not what we do or where we live, but how we do what we do that matters. Regardless of where we dwell or what we choose to do with our time, God's will for our lives is that we live a life of obedience. And no geography, no circumstance will provide it by magic. Neither will any circumstance disqualify us from pursuing it.

God's will is not for us to do, but for us to be. To be faithful disciples. To see the lessons and the opportunities in each struggle. To follow his ways through all the arenas of life.

Ponder Today: God's will is not about what happens. It is about what we are in the midst in what happens.

NOVEMBER 5: TUNE OUR HEARTS

"Make your ear attentive to wisdom, Incline your heart to understanding" – Proverbs 2:2

Every human claims to be an advocate for truth. We do not like being misled. We demand honesty.

Unless the truth hurts.

Then we prefer to redefine truth, and make it in our own image. Instead of inclining our heart to understand what is actually true, we substitute a false data point or perspective and call it "true".

But deep down, we know better. There is something in us that thirsts for truth. Something that nags at our souls. When we tell a lie to preserve our self-image, our soul grieves that a part of us has died.

Truth is like a tuning fork that harmonizes us with the heart of God. Like an instrument, we are in constant need of fine-tuning. If our ear isn't adjusted to the truth, it is hard to tell if we are making music or noise. If we will incline our hearts to seek and understand his ways, He will forge us into an instrument of infinite skill, created for His divine purpose.

Truth can hurt. It can expose. It can make us "look bad." Our value for truth often goes out the window when it comes in conflict with our value for being approved by others. But this is living life as an out-of-tune instrument. Sour notes are painful to listen to. The truth tunes us to be played by our Master with perfection. And our calling as human beings is to live in harmony with Him.

Ponder Today: How we feel about things is not the measure of a God-centered life. Neither is what others think of us. Our willingness to pursue truth is the measure of our alignment with Him.

NOVEMBER 6: LEVEL UP

"Therefore leaving the elementary teaching about the Christ, let us press on to maturity, not laying again a foundation of repentance from dead works and of faith toward God" – Hebrews 6:1

When playing a video game, we are striving to "level up". The irony is that reaching the next level propels us into harder challenges. Those harder challenges and additional promises of leveling up are rewarding because we are getting closer to the end, the goal. And a primary goal of this life is to walk in faith toward God.

The world offers myriads of false substitutes for us to follow. Alternatives to believe in. But God desires for us to grow. To mature. And maturity requires us to live by faith in Jesus. To walk in the Spirit.

God gives us a way to "level up." God promises that we can have all the gold we desire, all the prizes and rewards we can handle. All we have to do is listen to Him and act in obedience to His direction. This doesn't mean God is a genie. Far from it. Genies listen to their master. In order to live in faith toward God, we must listen to Him.

God is a kind and giving God, who desires our best. He has designed for us to gain his bounty by listening to His word. To learn to walk the path of life by believing His way is the best way for us. To gain the "gold" of wealth in this life by faith. To "level up" to greater faith, moving on from things that are elementary.

The treasure of life awaits at the end of our "game". As we "level up", we increase our faith toward God. Our ability to listen and follow. This is the path of maturity, and ultimately of victory.

Ponder Today: With each leveling up, the challenges grow more difficult, not less.

NOVEMBER 7: THE PROVIDER

"I know how to get along with humble means, and I also know how to live in prosperity; in any and every circumstance I have learned the secret of being filled and going hungry, both of having abundance and suffering need. I can do all things through Him who strengthens me." – Philippians 4:12-13

It is easy for us to compartmentalize the seasons of life. It makes it simpler to cipher what is fun and what is hard and what is in between. The plains can seem boring. What is "in between" becomes a kind of apathy. A complacency that undermines the value of daily living.

God provides in mysterious ways. Within every moment, He provides all that we need for life and for righteousness. His goodness is in abundance. It is even in sorrow. As strange as it sounds, His provision can be found even among the most "boring" of circumstances.

After all, boredom is a matter of perspective. If we are bored, it is no one's fault but our own. Boredom is an inability or unwillingness to see and celebrate God's provision. The Israelites got bored in the desert. Bored with manna. Bored waiting on Moses to come down from the mountain. Because of this they missed God's blessing and incurred God's wrath.

In all that we are and all that we face, God has already provided. The question is whether we have eyes to see. The Apostle Paul learned to be content no matter the circumstance. That means he learned to adopt a perspective that he was being blessed no matter his surroundings. He didn't learn this through radical independence, but radical dependence. "I can do all things through Christ who strengthens me" applies to every situation, even the routines of daily life.

Ponder Today: Boredom is a matter of perspective.

NOVEMBER 8: THE OUTLET

"I was with you in weakness and in fear and in much trembling, and my message and my preaching were not in persuasive words of wisdom, but in demonstration of the Spirit and of power, so that your faith would not rest on the wisdom of men, but on the power of God." – 1 Corinthians 2:3-5

Our spiritual life is like those wall outlets with two plug-in options. Two sources of power. Either choice will provide electricity. But only ono will work for a given appliance.

There is a similar choice in the spiritual realm. Two sorts of power. One is the foolishness of this world. When we plug our hope into the "wisdom" of mankind, we seek financial wealth or political position. These things provide a kind of power. It is power that provides an illusion of control. Worldly power lasts for a short time, then goes dead.

Our other alternative is to choose to plug our faith into the power of God. This is like plugging in to an electrical grid that will never fail. There are no black outs in God's economy.

Most of us tend to toggle between the two outlets. We rely on an earthly perspective until we get in trouble, then scramble to change outlets. We tend to avoid living in the reality that we are weak, frail, and uncertain. Our ability to comprehend is very small. Our ability to alter the circumstances around us is very slight. But we tend to prefer to live an illusion that says otherwise. Our own fragility is a hard pill to swallow.

Although Paul had a commission directly from Jesus, he realized his weakness. He embraced his weakness, stating that in his weakness he was made strong by the power of God. Paul was able to choose a true perspective that recognized spiritual realities in a physical world.

Ponder Today: Plugging into the correct outlet won't necessarily change our circumstances. Tapping into the power of God gives us the power to navigate all of life's circumstances.

NOVEMBER 9: SAVE THE PSUCHE

"Therefore, putting aside all filthiness and all that remains of wickedness, in humility receive the word implanted, which is able to save your souls." – James 1:21

The word translated "souls" in this verse is the Greek word "psuche." Psuche is where we get the English word psyche and is translated half the time "life" and half the time "soul". They are the same thing in the Bible.

The word translated "save" is the Greek word "sozo." It is sometimes translated "heal" or "make whole". This is because "sozo" means "something is delivered from something." The context tells us what is being delivered from what. If a sick person is delivered from illness, they are "sozo" or "saved" from sickness. Which is why the translators might render "sozo" "healed" or "made whole."

So how do we save ("sozo") our lives ("psuche") from wickedness and filthiness? We save our "lives" (or "psuche") from wickedness and filthiness by putting it aside. A bit of a paradox. Why does the Bible tell us to "put aside our wickedness?" Why not "avoid" or "steer clear from?"

The preceding verses in James 1 tell us. The reason we are told to put aside wickedness is because the wickedness is within us. In our flesh. Our old nature is still with us. That is what tempts us. It will dominate if we don't set it aside.

Being able to listen to people requires us to set aside self for a moment so we can see as they see. This skill translates to hearing what the Bible teaches. Listening to the Spirit. And this word, implanted, "saves our psuche" from the adverse consequences of following the desires of the flesh.

Ponder Today: The Word, not just heard but implanted, has the power to save us from ourselves, and thereby save our lives.

NOVEMBER 10: THE SHAPE OF MOUNTAINS

"...strengthened with all power, according to His glorious might, for the attaining of all steadfastness and patience; joyously giving thanks to the Father, who has qualified us to share in the inheritance of the saints in Light." – Colossians 1:11-12

The thrill of climbing a mountain is enticing. It is a beautiful view. A challenge and an accomplishment.

Mountaintops are a beautiful arena of life. From there, we can see long distances. We can be awed by the big picture as well as the intricacies. We can enjoy the vast panorama of possibilities.

When we use a mountain as a metaphor, we usually think of the summit as the finish line. But it isn't, really. The end of the mountain is not the top of it. Nobody climbing a high mountain finishes a successful journey on the summit.

There are no cities on the peaks of the world's highest mountains. It is not meant to be a permanent destination.

We are fortunate to encounter experiences that awe and inspire us. These spiritual highs are like physical mountains; a successful journey ends when we descend. The sights from the mountaintop can serve to inspire us and to bring us joy and hope. But the practical application of what we gain from the mountaintop occurs in the valleys and on the plains.

If our reaction to coming down from the mountain is disappointment, we need a shift in perspective. The opportunities of learning and transformational growth require a variety of terrains. Humans can't live on high mountains, we can only visit for a short time or they become deadly. But the snow collected on the high mountains bring rivers of life to the valleys and plains.

When we choose a true perspective about life's spiritual mountaintops, they too provide rivers of life-giving refreshment for our everyday lives.

Ponder Today: The summit is only the halfway point of traversing a mountain.

NOVEMBER 11: TRUE LOVE

"Love is patient, love is kind and is not jealous; love does not brag and is not arrogant, does not act unbecomingly; it does not seek its own, is not provoked, does not take into account a wrong suffered, does not rejoice in unrighteousness, but rejoices with the truth; bears all things, believes all things, hopes all things, endures all things." – 1 Corinthians 13:4-7

A lot is said about true love. The world longs for affection. We long to adore and to be adored. But true love is not really about emotion.

The Apostle Paul tells us that true love is patient. That means making a choice to continue to engage when circumstances are irritating. Love is kind. That means choosing to treat someone as we want to be treated.

True love is a choice. Taking action. True Love is making decisions that benefit others, choices that often bring additional difficulty.

True love will likely cause pain. But it is worth it. It is worth it because love is what brings meaning to all we do. Anything we do that is outside of love doesn't matter. It doesn't last. It is fleeting. All we do out of true love brings lasting benefit.

We cannot exercise true love with an inward focus. Of course, the great paradox is that we experience true life by dying to self. When we set aside selfish desires in order to love truly, that is when we are most fulfilled.

Let's take inventory of our actions. What choices are we making to love? Are our interactions with our children or grandchildren for their best interest or for our own prestige? Are we seeking the best for our spouse or appeasing them to minimize discomfort? Are we avoiding awkwardness with friends or taking actions to elevate their wellbeing?

Love is about not just what we choose to do but why we choose to do it.

Ponder Today: The only way to participate in true love is to contribute choices to its cause. To intentionally live it out.

NOVEMBER 12: SILOS

"The God who made the world and everything in it is the Lord of heaven and earth. He doesn't live in shrines made by human hands." – Acts 17:24

One of the ironic pitfalls of the spiritual life comes from our attempts to compartmentalize our journey. We take good concepts like a "quiet time" or a "discipline" and turn them into spiritual silos. Instead of using these good things to launch our spiritual journey onto the plains of life, we isolate our spiritual lives. We read our devotional in the morning. Check. Then we can go about our day and live as the world lives.

Spiritual disciplines are designed to usher us toward a life of godliness. The point of preparing our heart with devotional thought is not to contain God. It is to unleash the power of God.

If we turn devotional moments into a brief monastery visit, we are missing the point. And missing the opportunity.

We are not called to contemplate a life of faith. We are called to walk a life of faith. We are called to journey and steward and choose. Faithfulness is a lifestyle. Not a practice we do as one of many things in our schedule, but a way of life that transcends our entire calendar.

The point of devotional activities is to prepare for the walk. To make certain we know where we are going, and have what we need for the journey. Devotional activities should be an integral part of life, no matter what terrain we happen to be traversing.

If our disciplines are not informing our daily decisions, we are leaving much on the table. We have given Him some of our time. But He invites more. He asks for it all. And He promises our reward will be the full experience of life.

Ponder Today: Faithfulness is a lifestyle. Not a practice we do as one of many things in our schedule, but a way of life that transcends our entire calendar.

NOVEMBER 13: THE GREATEST TREASURE

"That night God appeared to Solomon and said to him, 'Ask for whatever you want me to give you.' Solomon answered God, 'You have shown great kindness to David my father and have made me king in his place. Now, Lord God, let your promise to my father David be confirmed, for you have made me king over a people who are as numerous as the dust of the earth. Give me wisdom and knowledge, that I may lead this people, for who is able to govern this great people of yours?'" – 2 Chronicles 1:7-10

Solomon has an unbelievable opportunity laid before him. The God of the universe has granted him one request. No limits or conditions.

The discerning son of David decides what he wants most in the world is a true perspective. He asks for wisdom and discernment so that he might better assess right and wrong, truth and lie, good and bad.

There is no greater treasure in the kingdom of God than wisdom. No greater reward. Nothing more useful or beneficial to the disciple.

God grants Solomon wisdom and continues to place his favor on the king.

God is ready to impart wisdom, share discernment, and distribute perspective. He is knocking, desiring to sit down and share his vast understanding. It is for us to seek. To pursue. To listen.

We cannot get wisdom on our own; it must come from God. We cannot gain discernment out of our own strength; we must choose to trust God for it.

Ponder Today: There is no greater treasure than the wisdom of God. If we are willing to seek, then we will find.

NOVEMBER 14: STEADFAST RESISTANCE

"Be sober, be vigilant; because your adversary the devil walks about like a roaring lion, seeking whom he may devour. Resist him, steadfast in the faith, knowing that the same sufferings are experienced by your brotherhood in the world." – 1 Peter 5:8-9

The Bible commands us to "resist" the devil. It does not say for how long. It just says to resist.

It does not say in what capacity. It just says to resist. It does not tell us what It will look like when the roaring lion "flees". It just tells us to resist until he does.

This verse gives us two complementary ways to resist. First is to be steadfast in the faith. The main thing the devil wants is to get us to trust in something besides God. Perhaps self. Perhaps money or power. Perhaps pleasures. Trusting in the fulfillment of appetites leads to addiction. Addiction devours our lives.

Trusting in the wrong thing is the seed of our own destruction. It is one way we can be "devoured."

The other way this verse tells us to resist the devil is to realize and know that this is our common lot. The same sufferings are experienced by believers all over the world. We are not alone. The devil opposes, and seeks to destroy, all of humanity - believers in particular.

That means life is a team sport. Resisting the devil is something we are meant to do together. We are most vulnerable when we are alone. Living by faith is something we are meant to do in community. We are to resist together.

Resistance is active, not passive. If we keep resisting, we are promised victory. But the time and manner of the victory is not up to us. When we adopt this perspective, it makes perfect sense to resist, no matter what.

Ponder Today: Resist the devil out there (forces of darkness in this world) and the devil inside (the flesh).

This following is a 5-day series on The Lord's Prayer:

NOVEMBER 15: DAY 1 - THE REWARD OF PRAYER

"But when you pray, go into your room, close the door and pray to your Father, who is unseen. Then your Father, who sees what is done in secret, will reward you." – Matthew 6:6

The Lord's Prayer is one of the most well-known and consistently practiced passages of Scripture. Throughout the world, for the past two thousand years, people have followed Jesus' model of how we ought to pray, reciting The Lord's Prayer in cathedrals and homes.

Prayer is an essential aspect of relationship with God. It is our communication conduit with The Divine. Like so many things meant for good, we often repurpose prayer in our own image. We use it as an opportunity to list our demands before God, missing the part of communication that involves listening. Or we pray loudly in the presence of others, for their benefit rather than for God's - turning prayer into a performance.

This is what Jesus is speaking to when, during The Sermon on The Mount, He addresses the issue of prayer. He tells us how to pray and what to pray. And most importantly, He tells us why to pray: prayer leads to our great benefit.

We often overlook the promise of reward leading into The Lord's Prayer. God is saying that if we pray properly, we will receive a benefit, a treasure. A reward.

What is the reward? It is multi-faceted. The reward of prayer includes intimacy with God. But if we see what's there, the Lord's Prayer also brings us into intimacy with our family and friends. The Lord's Prayer reflects a theme of the Sermon on the Mount, that our fellowship and walk with God depends upon how we treat others.

The Lord's Prayer equips us to seek harmony with others. To live with a forgiving spirit. To choose a perspective that leads to a life full of blessings and absent offense. Part of this is quite practical. Forgiveness brings freedom from being controlled by anger or bitterness.

Prayer is not a performance for the benefit of others. It is not an obligation. Prayer is the path to rewarding relationships, both with God as well as with others.

Ponder Today: The rewards of prayer are neither frivolous or superficial.

NOVEMBER 16: DAY 2 - CONSISTENT FORGIVENESS

"And forgive us our debts, as we also have forgiven our debtors." – Matthew 6:12

The Lord's Prayer follows a literary device called a chiasm. In a chiasm, the main point is in the middle of the passage.

The middle of the chiasm is this verse about forgiveness. That is why the very first verse after The Lord's Prayer (v14) says: "For if you forgive other people, your heavenly father will forgive you". It is harkening back to the main/central emphasis of the prayer.

So why is forgiveness the central point of this prayer?

Perhaps it is Jesus' way of saying that intimacy with God begins with taking ownership of our choices. Forgiveness is our own choice. It is required of us as a part of our fellowship and walk with God. It requires putting aside offense and seeking the best for others. To pray the Lord's Prayer rightly requires some self-reflection. For we are asking God to treat us as we treat others.

As we forgive others through the experiences of life, we are promised a similar forgiveness from God. That leads to intimacy. Perhaps that also means our mistakes and flaws are taken care of in this life, and when we stand before the fiery judgment seat of Christ our deeds will have already been burned away through forgiveness.

When we exercise forgiveness and ask God to love and forgive us as we are loving and forgiving our fellow man, we unlock the keys to the kingdom. We start to see reality as it is. We begin to partake of God's great rewards.

Ponder Today: Intimacy with God begins with taking ownership of our choices.

NOVEMBER 17: DAY 3 - THE MERCY PRINCIPLE

"Give us today our daily bread...And lead us not into temptation, but deliver us from the evil one." – Matthew 6:11,13

In The Lord's Prayer, forgiveness is central. Life transformation, as well as intimacy with God, works from the inside out. Until we are transformed through the grace of forgiveness, and adopt a true perspective that accepts we cannot control people or circumstances through anger or bitterness, our views will be tainted and our life experience marred.

The petitions in these verses are mirror images in the Lord's Prayer chiasm. They each speak of dependence. The first is a recognition that we are dependent upon God's mercy and provision for our physical needs - our "daily bread". We often live the illusion that we are self-sufficient. As we contemplate the fragility of our world, we can either despair or trust. Living a daily reality that we are dependent upon the Lord brings security, for the Lord has our best interest at heart.

The mirror verse speaks of spiritual dependence, that we be "delivered from the evil one". Satan is always ready with a tempting lie, a falsity that leads us astray. The Bible tells us he is like a ravenous lion, seeking someone to devour. Our security depends upon trusting God's care.

One of Satan's lies is that a change in circumstance will bring us happiness. Reality is that no matter what our circumstances might be, happiness lies in embracing whatever is with gratitude. The focus of the Lord's Prayer aligns our hearts with the reality of our dependence on God. It brims with the truth of what we cannot control (physical and spiritual security) and what we can (forgiving others).

There are only three things we can control. The central message of forgiveness in the chiasm concerns one of those things - our choices. In the balance of His prayer Jesus expands to the other two things we control - our attitude/perspective and whom we trust. For the things we cannot control, we must choose who to trust. Jesus teaches us to be intentional to actively trust God.

The Lord's Prayer shows us we ought to root our security in trusting God in both physical as well as spiritual dimensions. The Lord's Prayer aligns us with God in multiple ways, including aligning our perspective with what is true. In this manner we are choosing ways that lead to life and fulfillment.

Ponder Today: The heart of idolatry is wanting what we don't need.

NOVEMBER 18: DAY 4 - ON EARTH AND HEAVEN

"Your kingdom come, your will be done, on earth as it is in heaven... for thine is the kingdom." – Matthew 6:10,13

The concentric circles of The Lord's Prayer chiasm continue with an acknowledgement of God's authority.

The fundamental choice for all of us is whether we will accept and trust Jesus as our ultimate authority or rely on something else.

We tend to think of "heaven" mainly as a place where God resides. But this verse notes a key characteristic of heaven, that it is a place where God's will is done. Multiple verses tell us that Satan still has access to heaven for a limited time, but he does not have the power to exert his will in heaven. For heaven is a place where God's will is done. When we take Jesus as our prime authority and do His will, we bring this aspect of heaven down to earth.

It is in obedience to God that we align with reality in the world. One of many reasons to avoid all other gods is because they are not real. Jesus is the way, the truth, and the life. Our reward for accepting and choosing the realities of The Lord's Prayer is to live the reality of the kingdom of heaven while dwelling upon the earth.

The Lord's Prayer is about recognizing and properly acting upon reality. There is an acknowledgement of our part to play in making choices, such as forgiving others, walking in obedience to God as the ultimate authority, and resisting temptation. There is acknowledgment that we will face circumstances beyond our control and must rely on God's help to obtain our daily bread. The Lord's Prayer sets our perspective. God is the ultimate authority and the perfection of heaven rests in the reality that there only God's will is done.

If we embrace these perspectives, it will lead to all the attitudes Jesus tells us in the first part of this most famous of sermons that leads to us being "blessed." The Lord's Prayer leads to a shift in perspective, but leads to the greatest of blessings.

Ponder Today: The Lord's Prayer is about accepting and responding to reality.

NOVEMBER 19: DAY 5 - POWER AND GLORY

"Our Father in heaven, hallowed be your name... (Yours is) the power and glory forever. Amen." – Matthew 6: 9,13

The beginning and the end of The Lord's Prayer are statements as to the very nature of God, His glory. Jesus' glory is in His power, for He alone is God. The creator and sustainer of all.

Glory is the essence of something being observed. God's glory is seen in all He has made. The observable majesty of heavenly bodies speak loudly of the essence of God in His power as a creator. The glory of God is also seen when we walk in obedience, bringing the harmony of righteousness into our sphere. God's glory is even seen when it is contrasted with things that oppose God, as when God's glory was shown through the resistance of Pharaoh.

God's power and glory does not depend upon anything. Everything shows God's glory. God's glory simply is. There is no need to manufacture glory for God. Everything will reflect God's glory in some way. Our choice is whether to reflect God's glory as a fruit-bearing vine, a creation that fulfills its design, or as an obstinate resistor that demonstrates God's righteous discipline.

The Lord's Prayer puts us into a mindset to declare His glory by reflecting His nature. To live according to the parameters of his Kingdom, and to steward our life choices in the arenas we find ourselves.

The Lord's Prayer is an invitation for us to live as the creation God made us to be. It is a pathway, a key to unlock the incredible power of reality. To reveal the truth in us and the world around us. A big part of that power is a true perspective about what is, and the path we can choose to gain the blessings we crave.

Ponder Today: Prayer is an invitation to glory.

This concludes our 5-day series on The Lord's Prayer.

NOVEMBER 20: ACTIVE FAITH

**"Now faith is the assurance of things hoped for, the conviction of things not seen. For by it the men of old gained approval."
– Hebrews 11:1-2**

We often speak of faith in passive terms. If you Google "verses about faith", you'll find most links describe how to maintain a certain kind of hope during times of trouble.

But we are not called to a faith that merely hopes during desperate times. We are called to a living faith during all times. The faith that gains God's approval is active.

This passage introduces what some call the "Hall of Faith." The rest of the chapter provides examples of men and women who acted on God's commands, trusting His promise.

The examples are diverse but action-oriented. Noah was faithful on the job. Rahab changed teams. Each example glistens like rays of sunlight. But sometimes the promise was fulfilled in the next life. Abel was faithful in worship, obeying God's way to sacrifice, and lost his physical life.

The vital thing about faith is what we believe. The key thing to believe is that God is good. Whatever He allows into our lives is our best opportunity, even when it doesn't seem to make sense. If He says "build a boat on dry land", there is a good reason. Even if we don't understand it for years.

No matter where we are, how we are called, or what our circumstances are, we are exhorted to live according to God's commands, trusting his promise that his way is for our best. This is how to please God. The key to crossing the finish line of life victorious.

Ponder Today: Faith is conviction that if we follow God's way, it will yield our best result, whether or not it feels that way.

NOVEMBER 21: DEEP TRUST

"Blessed is the man who trusts in the Lord. And whose trust is the Lord. 'For he will be like a tree planted by the water, that extends its roots by a stream, And will not fear when the heat comes; But its leaves will be green, And it will not be anxious in a year of drought, Nor cease to yield fruit.'" – Jeremiah 17:7-8

Most of us trust without even thinking about it. We trust gravity. We trust oxygen. To a large degree, we live in an oblivion of trust. This is mostly a blessing. If we thought about all of the things we blindly trust, we would do little else.

We can become aware of our trust when it is broken. Some cataclysmic event or sudden breakup. The reality of the danger, the risk we are constantly living in, erupts to the surface, and makes us aware.

Then we have a choice. Knowing the risks can lead to fear that can be either healthy or unhealthy. As we mature, we have an opportunity; awareness of danger can lead to trust in God.

We find fruitfulness not in survival or risk-avoidance, and certainly not in oblivion. We find our most prolific fruitfulness through trusting Him. As we become aware of our earthly surroundings we realize they are like a hot, barren desert. Trusting in God is like a desert tree that sinks its roots down to an endless source of water.

God's provision is not to give us control but to call us to faith. To trust Him. Children trust because they are oblivious. We are called to trust as children, but we are also called to much more. We are called to trust like a desert tree. To sink our roots in what we cannot see, and through our faith abound and be fruitful in a dry and barren world.

Ponder Today: Trust allows us to transcend circumstances.

NOVEMBER 22: BUCKETS

"For all the promises of God in Him are Yes, and in Him Amen, to the glory of God through us." – 2 Corinthians 1:20

No circumstance disqualifies us from hearing (and saying) "Yes" to the kingdom of God.

Humans love to compartmentalize. We wade through our days and load up circumstances into the two buckets of what we call "good" and "bad". We toil through life trying to control the flow of water into the good bucket. In our frazzled efforts, one thing we rarely do is stop to evaluate our perspective on the buckets – what we define as "good" and "bad".

All circumstances are an opportunity. All of them. They are all valuable. Every one is useful. At a minimum, each circumstance is an opportunity to exercise faith, an amazing activity we will only be able to do in this life. No event can be discarded as unimportant. From the mundane to the tragic, everything that happens to us opens an avenue of availability to exercise faith in relationship with God and one another.

God is transcendent over our compartmentalizing. He is there through it all. We might say "no" to God's promises. We attempt to control or compartmentalize on our own terms. But God's promises are always "Yes" anyways. His invitation is there for us to say "Yes" as well. The choice to perceive his truth belongs to us. The choice to participate in "Yes" is ours.

Ponder Today: In God, all we encounter is an opportunity to worship.

NOVEMBER 23: A SUPERHERO'S LAUNCH-PAD

"But the _______, unbelieving, abominable, murderers, sexually immoral, sorcerers, idolaters, and all liars shall have their part in the lake which burns with fire and brimstone, which is the second death." – Revelation 21:8

Do you remember what goes in the blank for this verse from Revelation? Probably not. The list includes murder, idolatry, and liars. The harshest consequences applied to the worst behaviors. What starts the list? What behavior comes first?

The answer might surprise you. The word that goes in the blank is "cowardly."

We don't typically consider cowardice as a trait that belongs in the company with the other things in this list. But if you look at what Revelation asks believers to do, it mostly requires great courage. Which is really consistent with all of Scripture. The heroes of the faith, the stories of Scripture, and the call of the Kingdom are all a demonstration of courage.

One casualty in elevating courage is our natural tendency to value niceness. It takes real courage to be kind. Genuine fortitude to turn the other cheek. But groveling before evil in niceness is not virtuous. Staying silent, remaining uninvolved when we have the power to confront wrong, may feel nice. But it is not in our long-term interest.

It takes real courage to adopt a perspective that is true. To be genuine. To love truly. Which is why God so highly esteems courage. When we adopt this perspective, we establish the foundation to unleash our inner faith superhero, and do amazing things in the Kingdom of God.

Ponder Today: Courage is the gateway to faithfulness, fruitfulness, and hope.

NOVEMBER 24: THE PERFECT MOMENT

"Behold, You desire truth in the innermost being, and in the hidden part You will make me know wisdom." – Psalm 51:6

Have you ever looked over the ocean or experienced the forest in full fall color or had some other experience that caused an exuberance sweep over you? Have you ever exhaled slowly, smiled and thought, "this is perfect"?

Those moments are few and far between. If we live near the ocean it soon becomes routine. Peak color lasts a short time. But when we have the eyes to see, all moments can be spectacular.

Wisdom includes the ability to see every moment as brimming with opportunity, not just when circumstances feel "perfect". Those " feel perfect" circumstances can remind us that every circumstance is "perfect" in the sense of being a great opportunity to live by faith, learn, grow in our walk, be conformed to the image of Christ, and connect with others.

Times of hurt or everyday grind have just as much value as those perfect moments, regardless of what our emotions tell us.

Every moment is a perfect moment. A perfect moment to trust God and walk in His ways. It might be a hard moment or a mundane moment. But it is also a time when we can choose. We can decide to see and worship the True Living God. To live a life of faith in community with The Lord of the Universe.

The perfect moments are to be celebrated. To be basked in for as long as they linger, which usually is very brief. But don't wait for your senses to make your choices. Today is a day of goodness. A day of worship and celebration. Believe it, and choose it.

Ponder Today: In seeking superficial perfection, we miss the true and diverse manifestations of Perfection all around us.

NOVEMBER 25: DIVINE CURRENCY

"For it is not the one who commends himself who is approved, but the one whom the Lord commends." – 2 Corinthians 10:18

God's acceptance is unconditional. Like the love of a good parent. But, also like a good parent, his approval is something we can gain or lose based on how we act and believe. Good parenting never rejects. Never stops loving. But also does not approve that which is destructive to us.

We sometimes make tho mistake of thinking we must gain God's approval in order to be accepted by Him. But that would mean Jesus' sacrifice was not enough. Our acceptance in His sight does not depend one bit upon what we do. The actions we take do not affect our familial relationship with God.

But our God, who loves and accepts us unconditionally, is also a parent that disciplines perfectly. God will always be perfect in pursuing our best interest. Accordingly, God will never approve behavior that is self-destructive. He will only approve that which brings true goodness.

We are prone to choose things that are bad for us. We don't do what is commendable, then commend ourselves. When we do this, we are deceived. Self-approval is not satisfying. God's approval is that for which our hearts truly long.

The treasure of Heaven is God's approval. When we gain that, we gain our heart's desire. Material wealth is just a pale substitute for the true wealth that comes from faithful obedience. He does not give us a yacht to show us His approval. He gives us his approval as our greatest reward. It is not a means to something else. It is the currency itself. Our true treasure.

Ponder Today: God's approval is the greatest joy we can endure.

NOVEMBER 26: SCALES

"A just balance and scales belong to the Lord; All the weights of the bag are His concern." – Proverbs 16:11

Every parent has had their child scream the accusation, "that's not fair!" While responses might vary, many parents may say something like, "Yeah, life's not fair."

The Bible doesn't talk a lot about "fairness". Like from a child, "fair" often just means "I get what I want." It is mired in bias. This view is immature and self-serving, but also naturally come by.

It is an extremely good thing that God is not fair, and that we don't actually get our way. Life is unfair because Jesus took on all our sins for us. We ought to be condemned, but we are forgiven.

Instead of fairness, the Bible talks a lot about justice. God is the arbiter of justice. He is the lawmaker, the attorney, the judge, and the jury. In order to fully meet justice, He paid the price for our sins. He freely gave us a pardon while fully paying the full price Himself.

This can be a source of frustration for us. We like the illusion we are in control. We like to think we have earned what we receive. But when it comes to righteousness in God's sight, we can never measure up. When we are weighed, we are always found wanting.

But thanks be to God that Jesus steps upon the scales along with us. In Him all requirements are met. And we are fully accepted in the eyes of God... because of Jesus. We can't add anything. In Jesus, we have the righteousness of God.

Ponder Today: We have to receive out of God's power so that we can give from God's power.

NOVEMBER 27: PASSION TO PERSEVERE

"Consider it all joy, my brethren, when you encounter various trials, knowing that the testing of your faith produces endurance. And let endurance have its perfect result, so that you may be perfect and complete, lacking in nothing." – James 1:2-4

How can we choose a perspective that says " trials are good because they bring me joy?" That's what this verse commands. The next set of verses provide an answer: because trials produce enduring faith.

The word translated "perfect" can also be rendered "complete". Finished. Continuing to believe God has our best interest at heart, and live in His ways no matter the circumstances is the path to become all God made us to be. This is the way to cross the finish line of life a victor.

A few verses later we are promised that Jesus will award the "crown of life" for all those victors who endure in their faith.

The word translated "endurance" can also be translated "patience." Patience is only possible when our circumstances are annoying. James invites us to choose a perspective that sees opportunity in annoyance.

Faith is a challenging endeavor. There is uncertainty, imperfection, and conviction.

Perseverance is the tool that allows us to transcend the limitations of our own ability and understanding. It allows us to grow, to change, and to see things more truly.

If we want all that life has to offer, and to live life to its fullest, we can choose to view the challenges of life as opportunities to grow our faith.

Ponder Today: Perseverance allows us to transform pain, confusion, and uncertainty into growth.

NOVEMBER 28: A PROPHET'S SUCCESS

"It is the Lord your God you must follow, and him you must revere. Keep his commands and obey him; serve him and hold fast to him." – Deuteronomy 13:4

The first three verses of Deuteronomy 13 warn against believing false prophets. More to the point, they warn against trusting in circumstances. Moses commands that even if a prophet predicts something that comes to pass, that does not immediately mean they are to be trusted.

It is an important teaching for us today. We tend to trust our imperfect perception of circumstances. If something happens we like, we should not assume it is God blessing us. If something happens we don't like, we should not assume it is a punishment. Our feelings about a circumstance should not dictate our belief.

Moses warns us to make choices based on what is true. Our trust, our reverence, belongs not in the manifestation of particular circumstances (finding a spouse, getting rich, etc.) but in The Lord.

If we follow our circumstances, we will follow a false prophet. A promise that happiness lies just beyond a circumstance, like riches or relationship, is idolatry.

If we have the courage to follow the Lord, we will find him faithful and true in all circumstances, including trials. True success is more complicated, more transcendent than our emotions. It only comes through faith, placing our trust in the one true good, The Lord Jesus Christ.

Ponder Today: Are you pursuing the idol of circumstances over the heart of God?

NOVEMBER 29: THE APPEARANCE

"But the Lord said to Samuel, 'Do not look at his appearance or at the height of his stature, because I have rejected him; for God sees not as man sees, for man looks at the outward appearance, but the Lord looks at the heart.'" – 1 Samuel 16:7

During the early days of the nation of Israel, the people came to Samuel and asked to have a king. Samuel was old and his sons were corrupt. Samuel was dejected. But God told him, "They are not rejecting you, they are rejecting Me, that I should reign over them".

They no longer wanted all the cumbersome obligations of being self-governing. They wanted someone else to take responsibility for their well-being. This, God said, was rejecting Him as their King.

Further, the people wanted to be like other nations. They wanted an earthly ruler to guide them and protect them. They put appearances over reality.

The Lord judged the people the way He usually judges sin: He gave them what they asked for.

But God had Samuel first warn the people. He warned that the king would impose tyranny upon them with high taxes and confiscation of their labors and property. Then, He said, "When you cry out, I won't listen, because you got what you demanded." The people said "We don't care, we want a king."

The ensuing debacle of King Saul's reign is a picture of the appearances we strive for versus the truth of what God calls us to. Saul was tall and handsome. He had "the look." But he did not have the substance.

When the people rejected self-governance, they attempted to shift responsibilities that were properly theirs to someone else. With freedom comes great responsibility. When we refuse to take responsibility, we end up in bondage.

We are often offered illusions, the appearance that freedom from responsibility leads to happiness. It is a lie that leads to bondage. When we commit to be self-governing, to walk in the Spirit and its fruit of self-control, we walk with God as our King. We choose reality over appearance, and in doing so, sow into our own souls seeds that God promises will lead to our fulfillment.

Ponder Today: We are all deceived by the fallacy of appearances.

NOVEMBER 30: THE WISE HEARER

"Listen to advice and accept discipline, and at the end you will be counted among the wise." – Proverbs 19:20

The wise man is always learning. The best leaders are continuously seeking growth.

We spend so much of our time trying to justify who we already are. And sometimes our stubbornness gets in the way of who we might become.

How do we learn? How do we grow?

We do so by listening to others. By opening our hearts and minds to the ideas, stories, and experiences of those around us. The Bible talks a lot about the power of listening.

It takes true humility to hear others for what they are worth. It takes curiosity and a real sense of value in the person across from you. We are made for community. We grow through hearing what the people around us have to say, then discerning what to absorb and what to deflect.

Listening to others is the precursor to listening to God. There is a convicting passage in 1 John that challenges, "if they cannot love their brothers and sisters, whom they have seen, how can they love God, whom they have not seen?"

Listening to others is the gateway to hearing God's voice. It takes an added measure of humility, curiosity, and value to internalize what God is saying and let it transform our attitudes and behavior.

Ponder Today: We learn by listening.

DECEMBER 1: KINGDOM CHARACTER

"For the kingdom of God is not a matter of eating and drinking, but of righteousness, peace and joy in the Holy Spirit, because anyone who serves Christ in this way is pleasing to God and receives human approval." – Romans 14:17-18

One of the classic workarounds Christians try to get away with is to make our faith a matter of rules and regulations, what Paul calls "eating and drinking" here. A lot of the reason we struggle with reading Scripture is because we have put up mental blockers to strip it of its life. We read it like a student handbook or the owner's manual for a used car. It is about stingy regulations that inhibit our freedom and are only necessary in times of trouble or turmoil.

But the Kingdom of God is alive. It is active, living and breathing. Through the pages of Scripture, the elements of nature, and the deep longings of your soul. It is a matter of righteousness.

Pursuing the character of the Kingdom is not about following rules, but about being with Jesus. It is about what is wise and foolish for your own sake as well as in consideration for how the world works, how to care for others, and who to trust.

Peace and joy are not orders; they are outcomes. The result of stepping into God's acceptance of us and living out of it. The regulations are not a taskmaster's whip, they are the guideposts to help lead us where we truly want to go, the crossroads between who God has made us to be and who we truly want to be.

Ponder Today: Faith is not about following rules; it is about falling in love.

DECEMBER 2: THE TRUE JUDGE

"The one who eats is not to regard with contempt the one who does not eat, and the one who does not eat is not to judge the one who eats, for God has accepted him. Who are you to judge the servant of another? To his own master he stands or falls; and he will stand, for the Lord is able to make him stand."
– Romans 14:3-4

One of the best ways we can love others is modeling the Divine example of acceptance and approval. In our modern world, the two often blur into one. But they are very different things in Scripture. Acceptance is an unmerited, unconditional state of grace bestowed on us by God. Nothing can strip it away. We are accepted, no matter what we do.

With acceptance as our base coating, we are able to pursue God's approval. His acceptance covers all circumstances, but He is not beholden to approve of the things we do that are not holy and, therefore, not beneficial to us. What is beneficial is something God decides. He is the judge.

With few exceptions (such as false teachers) there is no reason to reject anyone. This passage speaks of the controversy of whether it is morally acceptable for believers to eat meat that has been sacrificed to a pagan idol. Paul's answer: let that be between them and God. God will decide what is beneficial. Their job is to accept people as they are, because that is what God has done.

Approval is different. We should approve only that behavior which is beneficial. We don't want to approve self-destruction. We want to approve what is beneficial and good. But the goal is not to "be right." The goal is their success. That they might "stand." Taking this approach ought to cause our relationships to be enveloped in grace, and centered on seeking the best for others.

We have an amazing opportunity. We can serve instead of seeking to be served. We can grant others the grace of unconditional acceptance, while also exercising the wisdom of approving that which is beneficial. In doing so, we can choose a true perspective that God, not us, is the True Judge of all.

Ponder Today: God's example of the distinction between acceptance and approval is one for us to follow

DECEMBER 3: CLOTHED IN WHITE

"He who overcomes will thus be clothed in white garments; and I will not erase his name from the book of life, and I will confess his name before My Father and before His angels." – Revelation 3:5

The context of Revelation 3 is a message to a church that has become complacent. John is writing to the church in Sardis, famous for its brand but lacking in its spiritual substance. They look impressive but are asleep. Apathetic. The religious world is applauding them, but the God of the Universe is not impressed.

The call on Sardis is a great reminder for each of us. It is easy to coast. To relax and let someone else have what is ours to steward. To become complacent. Jesus calls us to awaken. To come to life. To regain the territory of our choices, our perspective, and our influence.

It is easy to settle for a life that merely looks religious. The appearance of righteousness. Performing for the superficial applause of people. But God sees all. He evaluates the heart. In the end, there is no actual escape from true reality. John talks about these facades as soiled clothing.

We are called to overcome our apathy. To turn the routine into an opportunity rather than an obstacle. We are called to a better perspective, an eternal view. To see what is true through the eyes of faith. This is the breath of life for our circumstances. It awakens us to who God is and what he is doing. More importantly, it tells us the possessions truly worth seeking. In this instance, recognition and praise from the Father.

Activation involves effort. It involves risk. There is an exposure to getting off the couch or out from behind the scenes. It is vulnerable to live your life. But the rewards outweigh the risks. The reward is God's eternal approval.

Ponder Today: Apathy is the refusal to take ownership of one's choices.

This is the first in a 4-day series focused on Advent. The series will be spread throughout the 4 weeks of the Advent season, with one per week, ending on Christmas Day.

DECEMBER 4: DAY 1 - THE HEAVEN-SIDE OF ADVENT

"Therefore, when He comes into the world, He says, 'Sacrifice and offering You have not desired, But a body You have prepared for Me; In whole burnt offerings and sacrifices for sin You have taken no pleasure.' Then I said, 'Behold, I have come (In the scroll of the book it is written of Me) To do Your will, O God.'" – Hebrews 10:5-7

Can you imagine the moment when Jesus left heaven and came to earth to take up lodging in the small and vulnerable body of a baby human? What would He have thought? What would He have said? Would He have given a long and emotional good bye to all He had known for so long? Would a choir of angels sing a song of sorrow or a song of joy?

We actually know one thing Jesus said when He left heaven, because this scripture passage tells us: "Behold I have come to do your will, O God." This is a New Testament quote of Psalm 40:7-8, written roughly a thousand years before Jesus was born.

The primary characteristic of Jesus' Heavenly departure was determination. Determination to follow His Father in full obedience. Jesus left a perfect home, with a perfect relationship, where He served as King of Creation, and came to earth to redeem a fallen race of creatures by taking their failings upon Himself. As 2 Cor 8:9 tells us that although Jesus was rich (in heaven) He became poor (on earth) that we, through His poverty, might also become rich. It is the greatest difference between Jesus and any other claim to divinity - He came down. Not his messenger. He Himself. To restore us to intimacy with God.

Christmas is the season to celebrate the realities of Jesus' sacrifice and the opportunity it affords us. The chance to be reconciled to Him. To be in relationship, in communion, with the Divine. True riches are spiritual in this life. They will become tangible in the next. Jesus came that we might have true riches. The greatest gift imaginable.

Ponder Today: The thing that most separates Christianity from all other major religions is that Jesus Himself came down to earth, mingling intimately the humane with the divine.

DECEMBER 5: KNOWING GOD

"I have heard of You by the hearing of the ear; But now my eye sees You; Therefore I retract" – Job 42:5,6a

Job thought He knew God. He was a faithful servant (God Himself lauded him as so), trusted deeply in God, and cared about His Maker immensely.

Throughout the book of Job, his faithfulness never wavers. But his knowledge does. What he thinks he knows, he soon realizes, is not the full extent of who God is.

When Job realizes he does not know God as well as he thought, it initiates the end of his long trial.

In Chapter 40, verse 4 (two chapters before today's verse), Job confesses "I am vile", which could also be translated, "I am small". Job went from thinking he could win an argument with God to just saying, in essence, you are too big for me. Now that Job understands how vast God is, how unable he is to fully know God, he relents. Job stops trying to question God's ways.

Knowing God means realizing God is so far beyond us. We might not be able to recognize His benevolent intent through all the fog of difficult circumstances. But it is that very thing that makes difficulty so ripe with opportunity. It allows us to see that God is so beautiful, so wonderful, so vast. He transcends our reason and our circumstances. He is in both but contained by neither.

In order to live in the fullness of life, we have to acknowledge that God is God and we are not. We are not equals at a negotiating table. He does not owe us an explanation. He is up to "more than we can ask or imagine" (Ephesians 3:20). The true call in our lives to know God is not about figuring Him out - it is about trusting Him. To believe that He has our best interest at heart, even when that seems impossible to fathom.

Ponder Today: Circumstances are the opportunity for identity to be made known to the glory of God.

DECEMBER 6: SECRET IDENTITY

"His intent was that now, through the church, the manifold wisdom of God should be made known to the rulers and authorities in the heavenly realms." – Ephesians 3:10

One thing we scarcely notice when we watch superhero movies is the fact that they are largely anonymous to the other characters. We are watching the movie from an insider's perspective, a kind of documentarian view, which allows us to see the inner workings from an elevated perch.

But in the world of the superhero, there is a lot the public does not know. A lot they don't acknowledge. And a lot they do not understand.

Like the superheroes of the movie screen, every believer has incredible ability, gifts given by the Holy Spirit. We all have the opportunity to use our gifts and talents in an extraordinary way. There is power within us, waiting to be awakened.

Also like the movies, when we exercise our gifts, it might be invisible to most of those living around us.

Finally, like the movies, there is an enormous audience watching us from an elevated perch and an insider's perspective: principalities and powers in the heavenly places. And when they see us follow Jesus in service and obedience, applying our gifts as unto the Lord, they learn about God.

We have the awesome privilege, and responsibility, to let God's power flow out of us to serve others. It matters in this world, as well as to an "audience" we can't even see.

Ponder Today: Your superpower is not a show for others. It may go unnoticed and underappreciated by the world. They are not its aim.

DECEMBER 7: FULL OF GRACE

"And the Word became flesh, and dwelt among us, and we saw His glory, glory as of the only begotten from the Father, full of grace and truth." – John 1:14

God grants us new birth by His grace (or favor). It is given to us unconditionally. It is not that there is no merit to this grace; it is that the merit is that of Christ. It is unconditional for us because Jesus merited the grace (favor) by becoming a sacrifice on our behalf. In this way, His acceptance of us is unconditional.

Even though we are completely accepted, God does not approve self-destructive behavior. He wants the best for us. He approves obedience to His Way, which is in our best interest. And He grants His favor, or approval, when we make good choices. This is independent of His acceptance.

In the same way, we ought to speak the truth with grace. To accept people for who they are while approving only those things that are beneficial. When we do this, we show God's glory, His essence. Because this is what God does for us. He accepted us while we were sinners. He loved us before we loved Him.

Sometimes the truth is painful. We may not like what we hear. Current reality is an acquired taste. But "favor" (grace) is not about pandering, telling people what they want to hear. That is self-serving. In giving grace (favor) to serve the best interest of others, we should be focused on both what is true and how to communicate truth in a way that elevates and benefits.

Ponder Today: Jesus dwelt among us in truth and grace. We are called to do likewise.

DECEMBER 8: A LIFESTYLE OF REASONABLENESS

"Rejoice in the Lord always; again I will say, rejoice. Let your reasonableness be known to everyone. The Lord is at hand; do not be anxious about anything, but in everything by prayer and supplication with thanksgiving let your requests be made known to God." – Philippians 4:4-6

Anxiety comes because we fear what might happen next. Because the Lord is at hand, we can rejoice. There is no need for anxiety. No matter what happens, the Lord is the Lord.

Paul wrote these words in the context of imploring two women he loved to be of one mind. To stop disputing. To come together in unity.

We often dispute because we are fearful. We seek control. We demand a particular outcome, and if someone is standing in our way, we oppose them.

When we step back and see a broader perspective, we see that the Lord has all things under control. So we can rejoice.

We can also petition God and leave it in His hands. God is available. It is a beautiful reality that the Lord is at hand.

In the midst of Job's suffering, he requests an audience. Moses enters the temple. Jesus sought solitude to pray.

When we take this perspective, it leads to a lifestyle of "reasonableness." We are not demanding. We don't need to quarrel. We can strive while holding results loosely. We can lay our fears at the feet of God, and know that our concerns will be well provided. For the Lord is at hand.

Ponder Today: We cannot demand peace for ourselves; we can only trust God to provide it.

DECEMBER 9: THE FOUNDATION OF INFLUENCE

"...be eager to keep the unity of the Spirit in the bond of peace." – Ephesians 4:3

When something goes awry, we tend to blame. We find a foe we can point at and touch with our hands rather than internalizing responsibility. We point our fingers at one another. Name and blame.

The results are tragic. The casualty of blame is often broken relationships and wrecked opportunity for happiness.

Healthy community is one of the greatest blessings in life, and it thrives when we hold to a common purpose. But unity doesn't occur without good leadership. The good news is that each of us can provide that leadership. It is a matter of choosing a true perspective and making good choices.

The foundation of leadership is taking responsibility for things we can control. We can't control others. So there is no real benefit to blame. What is within our control is taking action to seek the truth. Without truth, unity dumbs down to conformity, which requires submission to a tyrant. One of the primary weapons of a tyrant is blame.

When we name another person as our enemy, we misdirect our emotions, make imperfect choices, and leave potential on the table. There is a better way. We can take responsibility to discover the truth, and invite others to join in. Taking responsibility does not mean taking control. It means seeking what is true.

When we make the choice to lead we sow the seeds of peace and unity, and lay the foundation for the blessings that flow from participating in a vibrant community.

Ponder Today: Taking responsibility does not mean taking control. It means seeking what is true.

DECEMBER 10: SET FOR JOY

"...fixing our eyes on Jesus, the author and perfecter of faith, who for the joy set before Him endured the cross, despising the shame, and has sat down at the right hand of the throne of God."
– Hebrews 12:2

Joy is what allowed Jesus to endure the cross. His circumstances were overshadowed by the truth of what was to come. We can experience the same outcome when we exercise our gift of faith.

The joy Jesus looked forward to was the seat at the right hand of God. We are told Jesus received that honor because He obeyed, and did the will of His Father.

Joy is the product of joining awareness and truth by faith. Faith is the adhesive that links the two together. The Lord invites us to come and eat at his table. To listen to Him. To discover the truth and believe the truth. It is a meal set for joy.

Jesus' perspective of joy is an example for us to follow. We have the opportunity for the same joy by "fixing our eyes on Jesus" and following his example. When we follow the example of Jesus, we can experience a joy that transcends the emotion of circumstance. Not that it disregards emotion, Jesus grieved greatly as He went to the cross. But neither was He inhibited by His emotions.

The same perspective of faith is available to us, and with it a bottomless well of joy.

Ponder Today: Jesus' joy was rooted in faith that there would be no greater reward than doing the will of the Father.

This is the second in a 4-day series focused on Advent. The series will be spread throughout the 4 weeks of the Advent season, with one per week, ending on Christmas Day.

DECEMBER 11: DAY 2 - AN ADVENT ATTITUDE

"Have this attitude in yourselves which was also in Christ Jesus, who, although He existed in the form of God, did not regard equality with God a thing to be grasped, but emptied Himself, taking the form of a bond-servant, and being made in the likeness of men. Being found in appearance as a man, He humbled Himself by becoming obedient to the point of death, even death on a cross. For this reason also, God highly exalted Him, and bestowed on Him the name which is above every name." – Philippians 2:5-9

We all love Dickens' Christmas Carol. In part because it reminds us that Christmas is a season for remembering a proper attitude. An attitude of service toward others. Of charity and mercy. It is an annual opportunity to remember to "keep Christmas in our hearts" all year round.

This verse commands us to copy the attitude Jesus had when He left heaven to came to earth. We could call it the "advent attitude".

"Have this mind which was also in Christ Jesus" tells us to choose the same perspective Jesus chose when He emptied Himself of the riches of heaven to take on the poverty of earth. To set aside comfort for service. To set aside rights in order to serve and to love in the trenches.

He humbled Himself by taking on the form of human flesh. But this was not without aim. He "became obedient to the point of death" because of the joy set before Him. Because of His obedience, He gained the approval of His Father, who "highly exalted" Jesus, and elevated His human name above every name.

And God invites us to follow in Jesus' footsteps. Jesus has offered to share His throne to all believers who "overcome" as He overcame (Rev 3:21). To elevate the name of all who set aside self and walk in the humility of obedience.

Ponder Today: Jesus came in humility to serve and to empower us to serve. And to show us that this is the path to true riches.

DECEMBER 12: WISDOM BEGINS

"The beginning of wisdom is this: Get wisdom. Though it cost all you have, get understanding." – Proverbs 4:7

This verse makes an audacious claim. It says that wisdom is more valuable than our material possessions. That means it is the greatest of treasures. We are commanded to seek wisdom with all our available resources. To love and pursue it with all our might.

In the Bible, wisdom means choosing behavior that God deems to be in our true best interest. That means understanding and practicing the teachings of Scripture is the best use of our time. Listening to God and engaging with The Bible is foundational. But more important is the discipline of practicing what we learn all day long.

Only through listening to God can we gain wisdom. Too often, we settle for a photographed version of the truth. We catch glimpses (once a week or once a year or once a lifetime). But we don't "go there". We don't press in. We don't listen for more. We don't make a decision to pay the price of discovery.

Wisdom begins when we do make that decision. When we do decide to actively obey the truths we discover. Photographs are nice. But there is more out there. Let's not settle. Let's fight for understanding. Listen to God. Commit to the discipline of exercising what we learn in everyday life. The promise is that the reward will be worth more than all the material possessions we could ever dream of accumulating.

Ponder Today: The beginning of wisdom is decision-making. We need to choose a perspective that nothing else is as valuable.

DECEMBER 13: INTERNAL JUSTICE

"For the word of God is living and powerful, and sharper than any two-edged sword, piercing even to the division of soul and spirit, and of joints and marrow, and is a discerner of the thoughts and intents of the heart." – Hebrews 4:12

God promises he will bring all things to account, including every deep and hidden thing. There will be no thought, deed or motive that will not be brought into full transparency.

When we perceive a wrong done to us, our initial instinct is to seek justice. To judge, then to make right. When we desire this we are seeking something good. Jesus installed justice in our souls.

We are, however, much less inclined to judge ourselves similarly. When we see and react to injustice, it is worth asking ourselves whether our reaction is informing us of some deep injustice within our own soul. Perhaps something buried deep, between soul and spirit. Something Jesus can see, but we cannot.

Since all things will be brought to light, it follows that it is to our great benefit to root out darkness now, in this life. To set aside weights and encumbrances that lurk just beneath our consciousness. To clear away the muck that poisons our souls.

Rather than succumbing to our first instinct to criticize, let's first look for specks in our own eyes. Let's remember that God is God and we are not. Conviction is the Spirit's job. When we put on God's robe and sit in His judgment seat, we are out of order.

When we see injustice, let's ask God to open our eyes to peer into our own hearts, and let His cleansing light clear out the dark places, while we are still on this side of glory.

Ponder Today: The battle for justice begins within.

DECEMBER 14: THE TOP BRANCHES

"For am I now seeking the favor of men, or of God? Or am I striving to please men? If I were still trying to please men, I would not be a bond-servant of Christ." – Galatians 1:10

We have a tendency to reach for the lowest hanging fruit. Whatever is easiest, serves us the quickest, or gratifies instantaneously. Shortcuts. Ease. Comfort. Familiarity.

This isn't all bad. We have a limited amount of energy, so following patterns often makes sense.

But this tendency can also get in our way. When God's way does not appear easy, we can find ourselves looking elsewhere. Following another path we can understand or one that seems more comfortable. We can forget that Christ is our comfort, a comfort that surpasses understanding.

Our hearts long to serve Jesus and receive the full and rich benefits of relationship with him. No matter the difficulty, following Jesus is always the best way. The journey is complex, but that creates the opportunity to know God by faith. It is in knowing God by faith that our greatest fulfillment lies.

The temptation is strong to serve people and their opinion of us. It seems a low hanging fruit. But the favor of man ebbs and flows. It changes like a tide, brushed away by the rushing wind. The fruit withers and fades just as quickly as it blooms.

But the favor of God is eternal. It seeps from this life into the next. Our striving pays immense benefits. Listening to God, seeking humility and truth, is worthwhile in a quest for the highest branches and the eternal fruit.

Ponder Today: Are you reaching for the lowest hanging fruit at the expense of God's great desires?

DECEMBER 15: CROUCH OR CONFESS

"If you do well, will not your countenance be lifted up? And if you do not do well, sin is crouching at the door; and its desire is for you, but you must master it." – Genesis 4:7

When we make a mistake, there is often a quick and aggressive attempt to cover it up. To hide. It is what Adam and Eve did in the garden. And ever since, humans have been trying to duck our imperfection. We do not have to teach our children how to rationalize their faults. This "skill" is built in.

Rationalizing, defending, and blaming breeds anger. But responding well strengthens our character, feeds our joy and enables our peace.

When we do not do well, it is urgent that we turn it around. Because sin is crouching at the door. This verse says that it desires us. The notion here is that sin desires control over us. And when we do not do well, and decline to turn from bad choices, we end up doing sin's bidding. It demands and we obey. This can throw us into a vicious cycle of temptation, disobedience, and shame.

But, at the same time, each time we mess up creates a new opportunity. An opportunity to do well with the next choice. Make the right next step. We cannot eliminate our former choice. We can either allow the next choice to fall into the trap of the crouching sin or we can step into the countenance of better decisions.

By adopting this perspective, we can avoid being entrapped in a downward spiral of dysfunction, while admitting our human imperfections. We can accept God's gracious invitation to do well.

Ponder Today: There is nothing like the feeling of doing well, the inherent truth of right action, thinking, and perspective. It is its own reward.

DECEMBER 16: A PATH TO PROSPERITY

"Therefore, Your Majesty, be pleased to accept my advice: Renounce your sins by doing what is right, and your wickedness by being kind to the oppressed. It may be that then your prosperity will continue." – Daniel 4:27

Whether we say it outright or not, we often think of religion as an oppression; a list of rules we are not allowed to do. A buzz-kill. We think of God solely as a Judge looking to sentence us for crimes rendered.

The truth is God wants the best for us. His guidelines are not to inhibit our freedoms but enhance them. He knows what works, He knows what is best. After all, He designed the system. And He wants to lead us toward what is best for us. He wants to lead us toward prosperity.

Daniel proves his value to the King by interpreting his dreams. He makes known the path to prosperity.

One of the hangups (for us as well as Daniel's king) is we too often equate the concept of prosperity with our material or worldly successes. We measure what is good by how we feel and what we can accumulate.

The real prosperity of the gospel is in who we are. Character is worth more than gold. It is the great prize of life, to become who God has created us to be. To break through the fake world and discover the truth. God does not care so much about our bank accounts and social media followers. This is not prosperity in his eyes.

Prosperity is found in the intimacy we develop with God Himself. The riches of His kingdom are the fruits of the spirit. Renouncing sin is not about "doing what we are supposed to" just for the sake of obedience. It is about trusting in God's version of prosperity and participating in the riches of the Kingdom of God.

Ponder Today: The real prosperity of the gospel is in who God is and who we are in response.

DECEMBER 17: MIRRORED FAITH

"Here is a trustworthy statement: For if we died with Him, we will also live with Him; If we endure, we will also reign with Him; If we deny Him, He also will deny us; If we are faithless, He remains faithful, for He cannot deny Himself." – 2 Timothy 2:11-13

Truth is an acquired taste. Paul's words to his top disciple Timothy are hard to hear. Which might be why he prefaces this bit of poetry with the phrase "here is a trustworthy statement".

The theme of this passage is that our faithfulness allows us to participate in The Kingdom of God. To "reign with Him". If we deny God by refusing this opportunity, He will allow that choice. But we will suffer the consequence; we won't reign. We still belong to God as His children. If we lack faith, God remains faithful to us. If He rejected us, He would be denying Himself, because when we believe we are placed into His body through the blood of Jesus.

So what does that mean, to "reign" in His kingdom? Jesus told us His kingdom is not of this world. So at least to some extent this likely refers to rewards for faithfulness in the New Earth that is to come. But even though Jesus' kingdom is not of this world, He still invites us to live as citizens of His kingdom in this life by walking in faith. Just as He did.

Jesus had desires, He didn't want to suffer, but His desire to follow the ways of His father as a faithful servant trumped all. Jesus has been granted the power to reign. But instead of taking physical occupancy of His throne on earth, He is waiting. He is giving each of us the opportunity to walk in His footsteps. to make the same kinds of faithful choices. To make disciples, as He made disciples. This is Paul's charge to Timothy in what will be his last written words prior to being martyred by Nero.

Paul wants Timothy to follow his example. That is why he writes this poem, to challenge Timothy to make the choice to serve God's will, even in difficulty. The challenging opportunity of The Kingdom of Heaven is to trust God in all circumstances - suffering and triumph. To believe and know that every circumstance is an opportunity to choose to be faithful, and in doing so to win the greatest blessings of life.

The book of Timothy tells us our own self-interest is served by living in faithfulness. To make choices that align us with God's own faithfulness. He will traverse any circumstance or season to be with us. Our own choices are the only thing that will keep us from Him. And our choices are one of the few things we have authority to steward.

Ponder Today: What is the heart and the motivation behind your choices for today?

This is the third in a 4-day series focused on Advent. The series will be spread throughout the 4 weeks of the Advent season, with one per week, ending on Christmas Day.

DECEMBER 18: DAY 3 - THE ADVENT OF GIVING

"Each of you must bring a gift in proportion to the way the Lord your God has blessed you." – Deuteronomy 16:17

Throughout The United Kingdom, Canada, and elsewhere in the world, one of the staples of the holiday season is Boxing Day, the day right after Christmas. It has devolved into a day about sports and shopping deals. But the origins of Boxing Day are about giving.

We look forward to Christmas and the presents under the tree. Often we are focused on the ones with our names on it. We head into Christmas looking to experience the blessings and the hope of the holiday season, including the gifts for ourselves.

This verse in Deuteronomy reminds us of the cyclical nature of giving/receiving. These words are written in regards to another holiday - The Feast of Tabernacles. Life is about being a blessing as well as receiving blessings. It is about giving "in proportion to the way the Lord" has blessed us. Not more, not less. In proportion.

We are meant to work with one another in this mutual relationship - where we give to one another according to what has been given to us. Our treasures are not to be hoarded, but shared. The sharing is to be according to what we have, not what we wished we had.

This was the original design for Boxing Day. People filled boxes with goods to give to the poor. Or to share with others. The day after Christmas was giving day.

If the holiday season becomes all about what we can get, what we can consume, we are missing much of its opportunity. And missing much of what life is all about, much of what God calls us to. We ought to rejoice in the opportunity to receive as well as the opportunity to give.

Tis' the season for sharing; not just our goods but our attention and affection. Each of us has different talents and opportunities. All of us are invited to use our opportunities as unto the Lord. To spread the name of Christ, the spirit of Christmas, by sharing what has been given to us with others.

Ponder Today: What do you have to give this holiday season?

DECEMBER 19: ALL INTENTIONALITY

"For this very reason, make every effort to add to your faith goodness; and to goodness, knowledge; and to knowledge, self-control; and to self-control, perseverance; and to perseverance, godliness; and to godliness, mutual affection; and to mutual affection, love. For if you possess these qualities in increasing measure, they will keep you from being ineffective and unproductive in your knowledge of our Lord Jesus Christ."
– 2 Peter 1:5-8

In this verse we are called to grow in knowledge, trust, and relational intimacy with Jesus Christ. Doing so builds a foundation to effectively steward our career, our money, and our relationships. All to positively affect the world around us.

It takes a lot of intentional living to be in fellowship with the Divine. There are no shortcuts, no easy path. We have to avoid the quicksand of apathy and the flaming arrows of the evil one. It requires daily faith and discipline in the "small things". It requires us to steward our emotions, our ability, and our capacity to endure.

Without discipline, this verse tells us, our knowledge of the Lord Jesus Christ can be "ineffective and unproductive." Unproductive in every way. Unproductive for our own fulfillment. Ineffective for our capacity to bless others. In other words, poor stewardship leads to a poor quality of living.

The strivings, effort, and work of a disciplined life are completely in our best interest. For being effective and productive in the knowledge of Jesus lays the foundation for our brief time on this earth.

Ponder Today: Each day we have this basic decision that will shape the perspective catalyzing our choices: "Will I take the necessary actions to be effective in the Kingdom of our Lord Jesus Christ today?"

DECEMBER 20: SWEET AROMA

"But thanks be to God, who always leads us in triumph in Christ, and manifests through us the sweet aroma of the knowledge of Him in every place. For we are a fragrance of Christ to God among those who are being saved and among those who are perishing" – 2 Corinthians 2:14-15

When we listen to God and follow Him in faithful obedience, it does not always lead to the superficial and worldly riches we so often desire. But it does lead to an amazing sort of victory, the truest kind. The riches of the Kingdom.

Faithfulness covers us like an aroma, a fragrance pleasing to the Lord. And as we walk through our lives, people start to notice. The smell is invisible to the eye. But it can grab your attention and send you contemplating the source.

As we walk through this life, smelling of the aroma of God, we join the beauty of nature and diversity of human life. We become a fragrant garden, the nasal manifestation of the body of Christ.

Our superficial and short-sighted view of success is the result of our obsession with what we can see and touch. We are focused on what we can do rather than who we are.

The aroma of Christ is wafting through all of our circumstances. In every person. In every place. The true victory of living comes as we tune our nose to smell him and to radiate the fragrance of His Kingdom.

Ponder Today: What supernatural smell are you emitting?

DECEMBER 21: BORED

"In everything give thanks; for this is God's will for you in Christ Jesus." – 1 Thessalonians 5:18

As impossible as it seems, Scripture invites us to give thanks in everything. That includes the everyday routines we often take for granted.

In the seasons of sameness, we have the opportunity to choose thankfulness. It is in thanksgiving we discover the opportunities we have to grow, to create, and to adventure. By choosing to be thankful, we gain contentment. We avoid depending on circumstances for happiness. That is to say, we avoid having circumstances reign over us.

We are often bored when in a season of routine. But boredom is an attitude not a circumstance. When we feel bored, it is likely an important signal that we are choosing a wrong perspective.

Boredom means "I want more stimulation from my surroundings." A fundamental choice we make is whether to be bored or to be grateful. We can choose to see boredom as a signal that we are failing to fully see all God is and all He is doing in the world. This will then trigger action that will eliminate the boredom. We can create the stimulation we crave, by seeing (through the eyes of faith) the amazing opportunities God grants us to be faithful in our routines.

As with any circumstance, sameness and routine should be viewed as fertile fields of opportunity.

We can pray for the Lord to open our eyes, to see things for which we can be thankful. Life on the plains is ripe with glory. Truth, after all, motivates and moves us more than anything else.

Ponder Today: Pray for the truth in all circumstances and see your life transformed by thankfulness.

DECEMBER 22: FAMILY STYLE

"I do not hide your righteousness in my heart; I speak of your faithfulness and your saving help. I do not conceal your love and your faithfulness from the great assembly." – Psalm 40:10

When we think of God as a Cosmic Vending Machine, we think of him sitting and waiting to supply our wants when we want them. If we don't feel like going to the machine, we stay away, hardly noticing it. When we want something, we rush to it, hungrily grab what it spits out, and continue on our way.

One byproduct of this approach is that we actually see God as someone we control. We want, we get, we "eat." Amazingly, God still chooses to bless us when our thinking is amiss. He is a Good Father.

But this isn't optimal. We can do better. A more fulfilling opportunity awaits.

God's blessings are served family style. We are called to share, to testify, to declare the goodness of God. Tell our stories, our parables, our experiences. It is the fuel for the body of Christ.

We are not just consumers in the Kingdom of God. We are participants, co-heirs. When we share, we are much more likely to see God as He truly is. As God, not Santa.

It takes courage to share what God is doing. The stories we choose to tell open us up to ridicule and rejection. We'd rather just digest them internally for what they can do for us. To share them with others is a whole new level of faithful living.

God's blessings are served family-style. The choices God has given us to steward are for the benefit of both us and the communities to which we belong. The glory of Christ shines within us.

Ponder Today: The Kingdom of God is a team sport.

DECEMBER 23: SELF-GOVERNANCE

"And since they did not see fit to acknowledge God, God gave them up to a debased mind to do what ought not to be done. They were filled with all manner of unrighteousness, evil, covetousness, malice." – Romans 1:28-29

Self-governance is a fruit of the Spirit. It means we curb our selfishness and choose to love our neighbor as ourselves. When we are self-governing, God is our King. We serve God as our ruler by stewarding our own life and participating in the complex system of the body of Christ.

The alternative is tyranny. At a personal level, the tyrant is our flesh.

Romans 1 gives a sobering warning. If we insist on pursuing our lusts, God will relent, and "give us over" to the flesh. To be ruled by the tyrant. If we still persist, we are "given over" to a "debased mind" - we are no longer able to govern ourselves - we can't even think straight.

Sin leads to addiction, then to loss of perspective. So why does sin still seem so attractive?

We are drawn to what appears to be the easy road, the comfortable path. We are drawn to be like the rest of the world. We are drawn to the tyrant. We want a quick fix, an easy out, a simple solution. Like all things superficial, the tyrant of the flesh offers ease and understanding and control.

Self-governance is harder. Like love, it is complex and humbling. Hard to wrap our heads around or hold in our hands. It leads us to "acknowledge God" rather than lean on our own power and understanding.

To be self-governing we must choose to trust God over self as well as choosing to submit to the Spirit rather than the flesh.

Ponder Today: Acknowledging God in all things brings an abundance of life, and a major part of that abundance is self-governance.

DECEMBER 24: WITH GOD

"'Truly I say to you, it is hard for a rich man to enter the kingdom of heaven. Again I say to you, it is easier for a camel to go through the eye of a needle, than for a rich man to enter the kingdom of God.' When the disciples heard this, they were very astonished and said, 'Then who can be saved?' And looking at them, Jesus said to them, 'With people this is impossible, but with God all things are possible.'" – Matthew 19:23-26

When we think of God doing impossible things, we often think of Him overcoming painful challenges. But there are other things that threaten us; other ways in which we need supernatural rescue.

Mountaintop experiences can be particularly challenging. It is on the mountaintops the illusions of self-dependence are most easily believed. It is easier to think we control circumstances and that circumstances can make us happy.

The superior way to perceive the mountaintops is to see them as opportunities to grow in faith. To see the mountain simply as an additional opportunity for stewardship. A greater responsibility to use our influence to advance God's kingdom. Jesus told his disciples it was virtually impossible to live on the mountaintop of riches and serve God's kingdom at the same time. When His disciples expressed dismay, Jesus answered that "With God, all things are possible."

That is where we want to be when the seasons of life take us to the mountaintops. "With God." When we lean on God even when circumstances scream that it is unnecessary, then everything becomes possible. The riches that could be a stumbling block now become a resource.

The danger of the mountaintops is when we try to go there without God. Or when God beckons us into the plains and the valleys for His purposes and we refuse to go. The true mountain is God's presence, which travels with us through every terrain of life.

Ponder Today: All the richness and joy in life only happen when are with God.

This is the fourth and final devotional in a 4-day series on Advent:

DECEMBER 25: DAY 4 - THE ADVENT OF THE KINGDOM

"For a child will be born to us, a son will be given to us; And the government will rest on His shoulders; And His name will be called Wonderful Counselor, Mighty God, Eternal Father, Prince of Peace." – Isaiah 9:6

One of the most interesting inclusions in this list of the names of Jesus is the phrase "the government will rest on His shoulders".

This is a very specific claim that Jesus came to set all things right. It is one bookend for the life of Jesus. His earthly adventure begins in a humble shepherd's cave. Its counterpart is found at the end of his journey on Earth when He leaves the disciples with The Great Commission, which begins with the assertion: "All authority has been given to Me in heaven and on earth..."

The disciples understandably asked Jesus if He was going to use all that power and authority to accomplish what they were expecting the Messiah of Israel to do all along. In Acts 1:6 they inquired "Is it at this time You are restoring the kingdom to Israel?" Jesus' reply is incredible. He says that it is not for them to know when that prophecy will be fulfilled. It will happen when it happens.

Then Jesus tells the disciples to go wait for power - the indwelling Holy Spirit, who He sent as our Helper.

The Kingdom of God is not of this world. Our job is to exercise Jesus' authority by living and speaking in a manner that encourages others to obey His commands. To serve, to love, to speak truth with grace, seeking the best for others.

Jesus' advent was the beginning. The end is yet to come. In the meanwhile, Jesus has delegated to us His power and authority to serve. The fullest expression of the Christmas spirit is to pursue the true perspective of His Kingdom - on earth as it is in heaven. As Scrooge pledged to "honor Christmas in my heart, and try to keep it all the year," so can we take the Christmas season as an opportunity to reflect on the incredible opportunity and responsibility Jesus has delegated to us.

Ponder Today: Jesus did not come to establish a kingdom to dominate this world but to confirm a Kingdom that transcends all worlds

The following is a 6-day series on The Book of Ecclesiastes:

DECEMBER 26: DAY 1 - VAPOR

"'Vanity of vanities,' says the Preacher, 'Vanity of vanities! All is vanity.' What advantage does man have in all his work which he does under the sun? A generation goes and a generation comes, But the earth remains forever." – Ecclesiastes 1:2-4

Solomon begins the Book of Ecclesiastes with an enigmatic statement about life on this planet. He says it is "vanity", some translations choose the word "meaningless". The Hebrew word is hebel and is best translated as "vaporous".

Solomon's point is not that there is no purpose to life, but that we cannot fully understand the purpose of life. It is vaporous, like a puff of air or a wisp of smoke. We try to grab it and it slips around our fingers and into the air.

We all have a compulsion to understand. It is part of being human. To pursue knowledge and understanding. But there is a place where our capacity ends and trust begins. Faith is the true foundation for human knowledge.

It can be frustrating when our compulsion to understand is not being satisfied. We cannot control (or even foresee) how things will work out. There is so much we don't comprehend, so much we cannot do. And often our reaction is to do nothing. To freeze. But the better path is to embrace a biblical perspective, which is rooted in trusting God.

The Book of Ecclesiastes is a book that shows us the potential of that perspective. It encourages us toward self-awareness and embracing the reality of life on earth. Life on earth is a mystery, a vapor. We don't know all the whys and whats and whens. Solomon will argue that this is by design. The point of life is not to feed our compulsion to understand but to guide us into worship of its Creator, and enjoying our lives within God's design. Adopting a true perspective about the nature of our world and the limitations of our self is the first step.

Ponder Today: Will the mysteries of life guide you toward worship or into despair?

DECEMBER 27: DAY 2 - THE TEMPORAL

"There is a time for everything, and a season for every activity under the heavens... He has made everything beautiful in its time. He has also set eternity in the human heart; yet no one can fathom what God has done from beginning to end." – Ecclesiastes 3:1,11

One of the main themes of Ecclesiastes is the reality of Time. Our world is limited by its temporal nature. We cannot know what comes next or even rightly remember much of what has past. With the result that our present is often confused.

But scripture lets us know that there is beauty in every moment of time. God has made it so. Every minute is an opportunity to know and worship God. Every moment is a once-in-an-existence chance to know God by faith.

One of the challenges for us is that God has "set eternity in the human heart". This means we have a faint idea of forever, an inkling of eternity. But it is too big for us to comprehend. We cannot fathom beginning to end and everything in between.

So we feel pulled between two worlds. We know eternity in our hearts, but we live in a moment. We are bound by Time. We confuse the temporal for the eternal. We tend to act as though material possessions will last forever, when we know deep down they are passing. We can behave as though fame will endure, but our hearts tell us otherwise.

The bridge for this tension is to adopt a true perspective rooted in faith. A perspective that humanity has an incredible opportunity on this earth; the chance to do something the angels cannot - live a life of faith. Put our trust in an Eternity we cannot fully grasp or understand.

We live in Time. And the beauty of each moment of Time is the hint of eternity it alludes to. Each moment has its own glory. Making the most out of our time, no more and no less, is a significant part of living under a true perspective.

Ponder Today: The reality of time plays tricks on our perspective. The eternal truth is that every moment is an opportunity to worship.

DECEMBER 28: DAY 3 - CONSIDERING CIRCUMSTANCES

"In the day of prosperity be happy, but in the day of adversity consider— God has made the one as well as the other. So that man will not discover anything that will be after him."
– Ecclesiastes 7:14

Our lives are just the prologue of a cosmic journey. And it is just one journey among a symphony of billions, in concert with a creation that declares the glory of God.

The goal of life is not to smooth out circumstances, but to see how we might fully participate in the great song of the cosmos. The praise of Heaven. The worship of the King.

It is important to enjoy prosperity. But This verse makes it clear that not all circumstances will be pleasant. Yet they are all part of the journey.

It is not easy to adopt the perspective that God is benevolent toward us when circumstances are hard. "Why would a loving God not want me to be comfortable?" Solomon waxes eloquent about the vaporous nature of human existence. We can't understand it all. But when we trust God, and adopt the perspective He invites us to take, it makes a lot more sense. When times are bad, it is particularly important to worship. To believe that God has our best interest at heart.

Let's not get stuck in trying to eliminate adversity. Adversity is a temporal thing that is inviting us into an eternal thing. Worship. Trust. Knowing God.

And this life is our one and only opportunity to know God by faith. Our vaporous existence on this planet is providing a cosmic blessing that we can only begin to understand. Let's exercise faith to embrace our tremendous opportunity, and embrace life's challenges while enjoying its blessings.

Ponder Today: God is kind and good even when we are in fear and chaos.

DECEMBER 29: DAY 4 - BE GLAD

"So I commend the enjoyment of life, because there is nothing better for a person under the sun than to eat and drink and be glad. Then joy will accompany them in their toil all the days of the life God has given them under the sun." – Ecclesiastes 8:15

In the second chapter of Ecclesiastes, Solomon tries all manner of pleasures and achievements to feed his compulsion to understand, to be satisfied with the mystery of the world. And he concludes they are all vaporous.

After eight chapters, he recommends that we enjoy life. What has changed? Nothing. Solomon has simply discovered that a proper perspective brings color to an otherwise colorless world. Faith makes meaningless things meaningful. It invites us into the deeper reality of what is happening in the world. Food is not the idol we would try to make it; it is not the source of eternal meaning. But it is a gift, an opportunity for a glimpse of the goodness of God.

We often think that piety and proper perspective are antithetical to joy and satisfaction. That we have to live sad and somber to be "spiritual" (the very reputation Ecclesiastes mistakenly has). God exhorts us in the opposite direction. This verse says we ought to enjoy life. It's just that the things the world offers as enjoyment don't deliver. True joy is not found through chasing particular circumstances. True joy is rooted in a perspective that sees things as they are. Even simple things like eating and drinking are causes for celebration.

Adopting a true perspective is what is best for us. It is what unlocks true peace and joy. It turns out that the "little" things are actually the big things.

God wants what is best for us. He wants what truly brings us the peace and joy we desire. He is not going to approve of our immature and incorrect ways of trying to gain joy and peace. He is going to call us into truth and reality. For that is where the real treasure of joy is to be found.

Ponder Today: The enigma of existence is not an adversary to joy. It is the background for it.

DECEMBER 30: DAY 5 - OUR DUTY

"Now all has been heard; here is the conclusion of the matter: Fear God and keep his commandments, for this is the duty of all mankind." – Ecclesiastes 12:13

The result of all Solomon has to say in Ecclesiastes is this: obey God. Listen to him. This is the purpose of mankind. Time and gladness and uncertainty are all contexts to invite us to intimacy with God.

It takes a great deal of respect to fear someone in the way Solomon suggests here. Our compulsion to understand is never going to go away. It is transcendent. No matter how much progress we make, we will never be fully satisfied with the answers to our questions and the scope of our comprehension. How humbling to approach The One who does have the answers. How terrifying. What are the answers He has decided on and why? What part will I play in His plans? What will I do if He hides His approval from me because of my destructive behavior?

Even when a child knows they are wrong, they fear the consequences of their parent. Like Adam and Eve, we are ashamed.

But the point of our limitations is not to shame us but to exalt God. And by doing so, exalting who we are in His Image. It is scary how much the whole thing depends on Him, how little control we have. How much His voice beckons us to obedience, to belonging. How much we need Him.

But this is the reality of the world. This is the truth. Life is an intricate design to invite us into relationship with God.

Ponder Today: Time and gladness and uncertainty are all contexts to invite us to intimacy with God.

DECEMBER 31: DAY 6 - DAY OF DAYS

"I thought to myself, 'God will judge both the righteous and the wicked; for there is an appropriate time for every activity, and there is a time of judgment for every deed.'" – Ecclesiastes 3:17

Solomon recognized that all we do, all the decisions we make and the actions we take, are leading to the most important day of our current lives. The day of days. Judgment Day.

Judgement Day is the culminating day when God will give meaning to everything we did in this life. "There is a time of judgement for every deed." Paul encourages us to self-examine, but exhorts us to "judge nothing before the time" because God is the one who will judge. Not us.

"God will judge" means that God will decide. He will decide the purpose of all. His perspective will give meaning to all we have experienced. That ought to give us extra enthusiasm to seek His perspective now, by faith, that we might pursue a well-lived life.

As Solomon worked to discover what is true about this world and how best to interact with it, his seeking led to one unavoidable truth: he did not understand it all. He could not. He was a finite being with a heart to seek infinite truth.

This left Solomon with two choices: Try to control his circumstances and recreate purpose in his own image. Or, accept God as the arbiter or truth and do all he can to trust, serve, and submit to God's purpose.

In doing the latter, Solomon shifts his time horizon. He knows by faith he will find meaning on Judgment Day. There is a time and purpose for all things, but we won't necessarily discover them until much later.

When we tell our hearts to choose the perspective Solomon recommends, obedience to God and His commands makes perfect sense. Solomon tells us that when we engage with the uncertainties of this life through faith, it leads to wisdom, enjoyment, and gratitude. But by faith it extends to an even greater horizon.

Ponder Today: God is the Judge. In the end, it is His perspective that matters and, therefore, it is His perspective we should seek.

This concludes our 6-day series on The Book of Ecclesiastes.

Made in the USA
Middletown, DE
22 September 2021

47871873R00215